# LIVING WITH DRINK

## Women Who Live with Problem Drinkers

# LIVING WITH DRINK

## Women Who Live with Problem Drinkers

Richard Velleman, Alex Copello and Jenny Maslin

Longman
London and New York

Addison Wesley Longman Limited
Edinburgh Gate
Harlow
Essex   CM20 2JE
United Kingdom
*and Associated Companies throughout the world*

*Published in the United States of America
by Addison Wesley Longman, New York*

First published 1998

ISBN   0 582 29887 3

**British Library Cataloguing-in-Publication Data**

A catalogue record for this book is available from the British Library

**Library of Congress Cataloging-in-Publication Data**

Living with drink : women who live with problem drinkers / [edited by]
Richard Velleman, Alex Copello, and Jenny Maslin.
     p.   cm.
Includes bibliographical references and index.
ISBN 0–582–29887–3 (pbk.)
1. Alcoholics' spouses—Biography.   2. Alcoholics' spouses—
Psychology.   3. Codependency.   4. Alcoholics—Family relationships.
I. Velleman, Richard.   II. Copello, Alex, 1957–   .   III. Maslin,
Jenny, 1961–   .
HV5132.L56   1998
362.292′3′0922—dc21                                              98–20267
                                                                                        CIP

Set by 35 in 10/12pt Palatino

Printed in Malaysia, PA

## Dedication

For the six women whose stories are the foundation of this book.

For 'Ruth': one of our participants, who died of cancer before she was able to see this project through to fruition.

For Gill: thanks as always for all your help and support.
RV

For my parents Juanita and Jorge: with love and gratitude.
AC

For David and Paulette: with thanks for your love and support.
JM

# Contents

# Notes on contributors

**Alex Copello** is a consultant clinical psychologist, Head of the Psychology Addiction Speciality with Northern Birmingham Mental Health Trust and a lecturer in addiction at the School of Psychology, University of Birmingham. He is a practising clinician as well as the lead professional for the Addiction Research and Development Programme for the Trust. In addition he is one of the investigators in a national study evaluating alcohol treatments. His research and practice interests include the impact of addiction upon families, the evaluation of services for alcohol and drug users both in primary care and specialist settings and the use of qualitative research methods. He has extensive experience of training.

**Barbara Cottman** is a psychiatrist and psychoanalytical psychotherapist. She trained at the Tavistock Clinic and has worked for more than 20 years as a psychotherapist in the NHS. She is currently in post as a consultant with the Bath Mental Health Care Trust where she contributes to the teaching and the development of psychotherapy services. She is also a training therapist for the Severnside Institute of Psychotherapy in Bristol.

**Liz Cutland** has been a counsellor in the addiction field since 1975. Currently, she works at Farm Place, a residential treatment centre in Surrey. There she is involved in the treatment of alcoholics, their partners and children. She has had two books published, *Kick Heroin* and *Freedom from the Bottle*.

**David Fryer** is Reader in Psychology at the University of Stirling, Scotland, where he coordinates an undergraduate course in Community Psychology and carries out research into mental health consequences of unemployment. He is a member of the European Network of Community Psychology and book review editor of the *Journal of Community and Applied Social Psychology*. He is a Fellow of the British Psychological Society and a former C. S. Myers

Lecturer who has published widely and given invited presentations on his research at Universities in Europe, Australia and New Zealand. He is guest editor of a special issue of the *Journal of Community and Applied Social Psychology* focusing upon community psychological perspectives on Recession, which is due to be published in 1998.

**Jenny Maslin** is currently researching into the development of services for people with combined substance use and serious mental health difficulties, and she has recently been researching into heavy drinking in the community. Her research interests centre on psychosocial aspects of problem drinking and drug use, with a particular focus on family and life-stage factors. She has worked as a researcher on a project examining the coping methods of families living with a drink or drug problem and has been with the Alcohol, Drugs and the Family Research Group since November 1993. She is currently completing her ESRC-funded PhD.

**Jim Orford** is a clinical psychologist by training, currently heading a research group at the School of Psychology, University of Birmingham, who are carrying out a number of studies on drinking and drug taking and related problems. Since carrying out his PhD work at the Institute of Psychiatry, London, the effects of excessive drinking in the family has been a special interest of his. In collaboration with colleagues at the University of Bath, the Institute of Psychiatry in Mexico City, and at the Living with Alcohol Programme of the Northern Territory, Australia, he has been carrying out a large, cross-cultural study of the ways in which family members cope with drinking problems. His many books and articles on drinking, drugs and the family include: *Alcohol and the Family* (with Judith Harwin, 1982), *Excessive Appetites: A Psychological View of Addictions* (1985), and *Risk and Resilience: Children of Problem Drinking Parents Grown Up* (with Richard Velleman, 1998).

**Jane Ussher** is a senior lecturer in psychology and director of the Women's Health Research Unit, at University College London. She also works part time as a clinical psychologist in the NHS. Her books include *The Psychology of the Female Body* (1989), *Women's Madness: Misogyny or Mental Illness?* (1991), *Fantasies of Femininity: Reframing the Boundaries of Sex* (1997) and *Body talk: The Material and Discursive Regulation of Sexuality, Madness and Reproduction* (1997).

**Richard Velleman** is Director of Research and Development, Head of the Addictions Service, and a consultant clinical psychologist with the Bath Mental Health Care Trust, and a senior lecturer in psychology at the University of Bath. His research and practice interests centre on the families of problem drinkers and drug users, the use of volunteer counsellors in the substance abuse fields, the development of counselling practice, and the evaluation of services for people with alcohol and drug problems. He was a member of the Alcohol Concern Executive from its formation in 1983 until 1991, and spearheaded the creation of the current Volunteer Alcohol Counsellors Training Scheme. His last book, *Counselling for Alcohol Problems* (Sage), was published in the autumn of 1992, and his next (on the children of problem drinkers) will be published in 1998.

**Arlene Vetere** works both as a lecturer in family psychology at Reading University and for the NHS as a chartered clinical psychologist. She is a family therapist, registered with the United Kingdom Council for Psychotherapy, and currently works therapeutically with families where violence is of concern. She has established a couples and family therapy service in the Reading Community Alcohol Service. She has recently completed three years as Chairperson of the UK Association for Family Therapy.

# Preface

In writing this book we hope to increase understanding of the experiences of women living with problem drinking men. Clearly it is also the case that there are men living with problem drinking women. However, the focus here is on women in this situation, as they are currently the largest group to face these difficulties, and have lacked attention for such a long time.

The editors and a number of colleagues have been researching the experiences of family members of problem drinkers and drug users for a number of years (Orford *et al.*, 1992; Orford *et al.*, 1998a, b, c; Velleman, 1993; Velleman and Orford, 1990, 1993a, 1993b; Velleman *et al.*, 1993). However, in doing so, some of us felt that by aggregating the experiences of many individuals, we were in danger of losing sight of what the overall experience was for any one of the hundreds of people we had interviewed. Moreover, because we were focusing on certain issues, such as the range of experiences, how people coped, whether or not they were supported by others, and so on, we felt that there was a danger we might be missing some important components of their individual experience.

Our solution was to collect some extremely detailed 'life stories' from six women who were living with or had lived with a problem drinker, reflecting techniques of qualitative research which are discussed in Chapter 2. Chapters 3 to 8 present the stories of the six women, including:

- accounts of their background and early years;
- how they met their partners and something about these partners' backgrounds;
- the development of their family lives; and
- the extent and impact of the drinking throughout this period, including when it became problematic.

We particularly wanted to hear from these women how they understood their own lives, because we recognised that none of them had planned to end up in a relationship with a serious problem drinker, and yet somehow this had happened. We were interested, then, in asking the women to reflect on this situation; to try to examine the question of how, looking back, they could understand what decisions had been taken and why they had been taken.

Following these six life stories, proponents of six different theoretical and practical persuasions, who have all conducted significant work in their fields, were asked to offer us their interpretations of the women's experiences: these are presented in Chapters 9 to 14. These perspectives reflect the broad range of current thinking in the area and include a codependency perspective, a psychodynamic perspective, a family systems perspective, a coping perspective, a feminist perspective and a community psychological perspective. We asked all the authors to provide three sections to their commentaries:

- to outline their perspective;
- to examine the six biographies and see how the ideas and understandings developed from their perspective could be illustrated and brought to life by using material from the biographies; and
- from their perspective, to suggest how change might have been achieved in the lives of the biographees.

We also asked everyone to use non-technical language, as far as possible, bearing in mind the wide readership that we are aiming for.

The biographies are an intensely personal expression for the women involved; because of this, we asked whether they would like to comment on the different interpretations. Chapter 15 reports the thoughts and feelings of two of the women. In fact, we would have liked to have continued this recursive process, and have had all the six commentators read each other's chapters and to revise their own accordingly; and for all of the commentators to have read the responses of the biographees, and to have responded in turn. Unfortunately, time and publisher's deadlines meant of course that a line had to be drawn somewhere, and the process stopped after only two rounds of comments (the six chapters of commentaries on the biographies, and the response to those from two of the biographees).

The final chapter in the book summarises and reflects on all of the biographies, the commentaries and the responses, from the perspectives of the editors.

No book is the work of the authors/editors alone, and this one is no exception. This work was conducted as part of a wider network of people who form the 'Alcohol, Drugs and the Family Research Group', and we have been well supported by our fellow members. In particular we would like to acknowledge and thank Julian Bath, Jill Davies and Liz Howells who, along with two of the editors (RV and AC), conducted the original biographical interviews; and we want to thank Jim Orford for the inspired idea of commissioning commentaries from a number of different perspectives. Most of all, however, we are grateful to the six women who told us of their often painful experiences, in the hope that their stories would help others in the future.

Finally, the biographies contained in this book contain very real experiences. "We must learn to connect biographies and lived experiences" as Denzin reminds us, for "there is no way to stuff a real-live person between the two covers of a text" (1989, pp. 82–83). We have provided the biographies and the commentaries: we hope that the readers decide that we have provided material which retains some of the richness of lived experiences.

Richard Velleman, Alex Copello, Jenny Maslin
December 1997

# Introduction

# CHAPTER 1

# Living with a problem drinker

*Jenny Maslin, Richard Velleman and Alex Copello*

The stories of six women deeply affected by living with problem drinking men form the foundation of this book: Ruth, whose partner's drinking became problematic after the birth of their second child; Lisa, 25 years old, with four young children and married to a problem drinker in prison for assaulting her; Dawn, whose husband had recently stopped drinking after being diagnosed with a brain tumour; Sylvia, the ex-wife of a problem drinker, divorced after many years of his extreme violence; Emily, having a year's trial separation from her problem drinking husband, while trying to deal with her own health problems; and finally, May, whose first husband had a drink problem for the best part of their 25-year marriage, and whose second husband's drinking and violence had resulted in her being seriously injured.

This book has been written for the benefit of anyone who is interested in understanding more about the experiences of women living with a problem drinking partner. Current research suggests that over half a million women in the UK live with alcohol dependent men (figures extrapolated from Meltzer *et al.*, 1995). The USA figures suggest that up to 8 million women have experienced serious drinking problems in the context of the family (figures extrapolated from the Alcohol Research Group, National Alcohol Survey, 1995). Traditionally, it is the drinker who has been the focus of attention, and the women who live with them have been comparatively neglected. This book reflects the authors' attempts to address this imbalance.

## The effects of heavy drinking on female partners

The majority of problem drinking men are far removed from the stereotype of a homeless, unkempt and isolated drinker. Drinking problems are frequently unnoticed by those outside (and sometimes within) the family, often because of the non-problem drinking partner's struggle to maintain an appearance of normality for the family. The effort and strain of doing

3

this is graphically described in the biographies contained in this book. Excessive drinking precipitates varying degrees of changes in the physical and emotional states of the individual drinker, and although not all experiences may be as extreme as some of those described in this book, the consequences for the partner without a drinking problem can still be significant.

There is often a common sequence of events within families where a partner's drinking becomes problematic. Initially there may be instances of drunken behaviour, perhaps becoming drunker than anyone else at a family social occasion and spoiling an otherwise happy event, which are noticed but excused as isolated incidents. As the frequency and type of problem behaviours start to increase, it becomes more difficult to explain them away. Velleman (1993) summarises a range of problems experienced by families living with a problem drinker, which can appear whatever the extent and pattern of the drinking problem. They include the disruptive effects on family rituals and routines; altered roles within the family to accommodate the drinker's reduced participation; communication difficulties; effects on the family's social life and finances; and the unpleasant, sometimes violent, behaviour of the drinker.

Partners without a drinking problem become more concerned and more uncertain about what is actually going on. Frequently they look for underlying reasons as to why drinking has increased: perhaps difficulties at work, or an inability to talk about concerns. The drinking problem demands increasing amounts of time, attention and emotional energy. As the drinker becomes more and more unpredictable, the family have to face the problem. They have to find ways of coping with it and often take on more of the drinker's responsibilities in the process of doing so. The biographies in this book are full of examples of attempts to cope: trying to keep partners busy so they cannot drink, hiding alcohol, trying to protect the drinker from any upset. For non-problem drinking partners with children, there is the very real dilemma of where to focus their attention: on the drinker or the children.

Clearly the pressure on the partner without a drinking problem is enormous and depression and anxiety are commonly reported. The embarrassment that women in this situation so often feel can lead them to become increasingly isolated from social support in their extended family and community. This is illustrated by Ruth, one of the women whose story is told in the book, who said her partner was fine when he was sober, but she could not stand it when he was drunk: 'he quite often became very maudlin, very self-pitying; or he would be very jolly and hearty . . . inappropriately so'. Ruth described putting up barriers with her friends because it was difficult to talk about her relationship, and not wanting to bring people home because she felt embarrassed about her partner's drinking and resultant behaviour. Often it seems that the more frequent and intense the problems, the less likely women are to talk about them. A woman living with a problem drinker might feel that seeking outside help for the problem would be disloyal to her partner and an admission of failure within the family unit. The traditional position of women as nurturers within the family may induce feelings of inadequacy when family functioning is threatened by heavy drinking.

## Theoretical perspectives

Reading the stories of the six women in this book, it seems clear that their early hopes and expectations of relationships and family life were very different from the situations they later found themselves in. Yet early work in this area suggested that women often choose heavy drinkers as partners to meet unconscious needs of their own (e.g. Whalen, 1953), and this has been termed the 'disturbed personality hypothesis'. Implicit in these formulations was the idea that it suited women to be in this situation, because it removed attention from their own inadequacies. Furthermore, it was suggested that women would lose out in some way if their partner stopped drinking and, to compensate for this loss, they would develop severe psychological problems, such as depression or anxiety. This has been termed the 'decompensation hypothesis' (e.g. Futterman, 1953).

The pathologising of female partners of problem drinkers is also reflected in the concept of 'codependency'. The codependency movement is an off-shoot of Alcoholics Anonymous and incorporates their 12-step philosophy. From this perspective, partners of problem drinkers are seen as suffering from a disease. In spite of the enormous amount of literature discussing codependency, there seems little consensus on the definition of the term (Hands and Dear, 1994). However, its impact on the field has been enormous and has been especially important in giving much needed attention to those living with problem drinkers. In this book, Liz Cutland discusses the biographies from the codependency perspective.

Nace (1987) cites several studies that refute the idea of a 'disturbed personality' and also discusses methodological flaws in the work on 'decompensation'. Later work points to the same diversity of personality styles in women who live with problem drinkers, as there are in all women. The symptomatology shown by women when their partners cease drinking is more logically explained by considering the stress that they endure. As drinking careers are often characterised by bouts of relative stability (Maslin *et al.*, 1998), an enormous amount of uncertainty will remain even after partners appear to have stopped drinking. Concerns about whether this will really be the last time, whether it is safe to stop using the strategies that have helped the family survive for so long, and so on, will understandably be present. Ruth talked of finding it difficult to go back to feeling the way she had about her partner, particularly because of some of the things he had said: "although I know it's the drinking . . . you can't erase them when they're said". In addition, it is often the drinker who receives all the praise at this time and little or no attention is given to the women for enduring such hardship and keeping the family together.

5

The acknowledgement of stresses resulting from living with a problem drinker was first proposed by Jackson (1954). She noted a common process through which female partners move, from the initial appearance of a drinking problem through to its resolution. Jackson concluded that the symptomatology shown by women in this situation was a reaction to the continued stresses that they experience as they progress through this process. In this book, Jim Orford discusses the biographies from a coping perspective, which acknowledges the work of Jackson in its history.

Since the 1970s, in addition to work focusing on the effects of families living with a problem drinker, other research has looked at the behaviour of the drinker within the context of the family. Steinglass *et al.* (1987, p. 9), writing from such a perspective, suggests that the excessive use of alcohol "is a condition that has the capacity to become a central organising principle around which family life is structured". Drinking functions as an integral part of the family system, maintaining rigidly established patterns of behaviour. Arlene Vetere contributes here from a family systems perspective.

There now exists a range of explanations for why women end up living with a problem drinker. These range from the individual, reflected in the contribution from Barbara Cottman writing from a psychodynamic perspective, to the sociological. Jane Ussher writes here from a feminist perspective and at the broadest level David Fryer discusses the issues from a community/sociocultural/political perspective. Although this book does not claim to include all ideas relevant to the subject, the perspectives incorporated have been chosen to reflect the broad range of current theory in this area.

# Why do women stay in this situation?

The biographies in this book reflect the limited options for women living with the trauma of excessive drinking. Women who leave their partners usually do so only after many years of frustrated attempts to help and support the problem drinker. Why women stay in this situation is more easily understood when we consider the natural path of a drinking career. These paths are seldom fluid, rather they are more typically characterised by changes in frequency and quantity of alcohol consumption (Maslin *et al.*, 1998). For partners without a drinking problem, this may mean periods of relative stability, when the drinking and associated behaviours diminish. The men they first knew may momentarily reappear. Sylvia described the uncertainty of these periods of change as alternating between feeling despair and feeling in a fool's paradise: "it's so baffling, you see . . . [he] goes back to normal and you always think he's given up drinking . . . then it would be better and it always took me by surprise the day he started drinking again". Holmila (1988) has suggested that control of a husband's drinking is a normal part of a wife's role. This activity is seen as caring work and there are strong ideological forces that bind women into the task of paying attention to another person's behaviour and attempting to direct it.

Reading the women's stories and the descriptions of the intense difficulties they faced in living with problem drinkers, it seems hard to understand how the women's feelings for their partners remained so strong. Yet they often do. When May talked of meeting her first husband she described him as striking, charming, kind, considerate, with interesting friends and sharing a common interest in their work. She talked of being "very much in love" with him, and in spite of everything that happened during their 25-year relationship she still talked of loving her husband even after they had separated. Lisa, whose friends could not understand why she put up with her husband's violent behaviour, was emphatic that she loved him and did not want to throw away what they had together. Finally, Dawn described feeling very angry with her husband, but did not want to leave him, as he was a different person when sober and she really cared for him.

As well as hope and strength of feeling, there are many other more obvious barriers to relationship breakdown. Economic issues are frequently mentioned, as in the case of Dawn, who described looking through the newspapers and wondering whether she would be able to find a job that would pay enough money for her to live on her own. With little outside support, it would be easy to believe, as Sylvia believed her husband when he told her, that she would never manage on her own. Concerns about the effects on children and what would be the best for them are also common. Leading lives which at times may become chaotic and demanding, women rarely have the time or space to think objectively about the long term.

Many women talk of having to endure their situation because of the commitment they have made to the relationship. Emily described this when she said "this is a cross you have to bear, you've made your bed and you have to lie in it". She also talked of the difficulty of contemplating a change in her relationship, because in spite of everything that happened she felt security from being in the role of a married woman and the idea of becoming a single person was devastating for her. Other women described their fears of being alone and less frequently concede that this would be a better option. Women living with a problem drinker so often feel trapped, and in so many ways: physically, economically and emotionally. One major contributor to this sense of entrapment must surely be a severe lack of facilities and support for women contemplating changing their situation.

## What support do women receive?

The women in these biographies frequently describe their attempts to get help, and often they are looking primarily for help for their partners. There is a strong sense of isolation as they struggle to provide support for their drinking partners, and try to encourage them to take or continue with the help offered to them. Both the women themselves and the available services tend consistently to see the problem drinker as the priority, and the needs of the non-problem drinking partner are often only an afterthought.

Yet women in this situation clearly have needs of their own. They need time and space to express their feelings and discuss the difficulties they face with someone who is non-judgemental, understanding, sensitive, responsive, and does not condemn them for the choices they make. In addition they may need information about what is actually happening to their partner, where their partner could go for treatment, and help in gaining access to services. They need advice about possible ways of dealing with drinking behaviour and the ongoing difficulties associated with it. Counselling for partners of problem drinkers, who do not themselves have drinking problems, should be available at whatever stage they choose to take it.

It is only relatively recently that professional support has been offered individually to women who live with problem drinkers. The type of support available is reviewed by O'Farrell (1993). Most often, group support is available when drinking partners are receiving some form of treatment, for example, concurrent groups, which are mostly for non-problem drinking partners and run concurrently with groups for their problem drinking partners, or couples groups, which consist of several couples per group. Couple or family therapy can also be available, whereby each couple or family are seen together. Relatives' groups, such as the self-help group Al-Anon, based on the principles of Alcoholics Anonymous, are open to relatives of problem drinkers either in or out of treatment. Finally, it is now possible to find individual counselling, open to relatives of problem drinkers not currently in treatment and sometimes called 'unilateral family therapy'. Individual counselling comes in two strands. In some instances, the emphasis is on working with family members in order to help the problem drinking member of the family with his or her drinking problem (e.g. Meyers *et al.*, 1996). In other instances, the emphasis is specifically on the needs of affected family members as people who are themselves under stress and at risk for health problems (e.g. Howells, 1997; Copello *et al.*, 1998; Templeton *et al.*, 1998; Yates, 1988).

Before presenting the six biographies (in Chapters 3 to 8), the next chapter briefly examines the use of biographies as a method of furthering our understanding of people's lives.

# CHAPTER 2

# Qualitative methods and biographies

*Richard Velleman, Alex Copello and Jenny Maslin*

Qualitative methods are frequently juxtaposed and contrasted with quantitative ones. Quantitative methods are about counting, frequencies, probabilities and so forth. There are many contexts where quantitative methods are extremely useful. If you want to know how likely you are to pass your driving test with one versus another school of motoring, or if you want to know whether people live longer following one form of cancer treatment versus another, then quantitative methods can be extremely helpful. Qualitative methods are concerned with interpretation and meaning, as opposed to counting. If you want to know why people still share injecting equipment, despite the publicity related to the risk of HIV infection; or understand the issue examined in this book, the depth of experience felt by individuals living with someone with serious drinking problems, then qualitative methods may well constitute the best approach. Although there are many exponents of one or other of these main types of method who believe that their type of method is 'the correct one', we believe (alongside many other researchers) that such extreme views are not helpful. Our position is that both sorts of method are invaluable, in different ways, at different times, and for different purposes.

It is certainly the case that both types of method have been used in human societies for many thousands of years. More recently, however, much of science and social science has tended to reify controlled, objective and quantitative methods, and be less welcoming of more qualitative approaches, and for a time psychology was in the vanguard of championing quantitative approaches at the expense of qualitative ones.

Gradually, over the years psychology has accepted less 'rigorous', 'scientific' data as admissible and even valid, be they based on objective but uncontrolled methods (e.g. ethology) or on more subjective but controlled methods (e.g. certain standardised tests and techniques), and indeed the use of such a database has always been championed by a small number of leading theoreticians and researchers in psychology (Freud, 1933; Murray,

1938; White, 1952, 1966, 1975). Furthermore, there has been for some time now a growing move in psychology, away from some of the simplistic assumptions which have underpinned the field, where psychology was seen as (or at least sought to emulate) a branch of the pure or 'natural' sciences, and which implied a need for rigid experimentation in order to arrive at proven psychological facts or laws. In the intervening century, the natural sciences have themselves moved away from this position, realising both the relativity of discovered facts or laws and the impossibility of either proving or disproving hypotheses. Psychology also has begun to move on, developing new fields of interest, and both new techniques of data gathering and new methods of analysis (e.g. Reason and Rowan, 1983; Kratochwill and Levin, 1992). Clearly, there is still a need for good experimentation in psychology, for careful control over the variables and conditions in a laboratory (or even naturalistic) setting. Yet it has become increasingly apparent that psychology needs to widen its base and accept as valid, information which previously was considered to be too unscientific. This is now happening more and more and, for example, self-reports are currently widely accepted as an admissible form of information (albeit with faults and idiosyncrasies as with any other method).

There are a huge number of qualitative methods, including ethnography, participant and non-participant observation, focus groups, collecting and analysing visual data, using case studies, analysing conversations, action research, and so on. This book is concerned with the use of biographies, and hence the remainder of this chapter will concentrate on biographical methods.

## The use of biographies

Numerous writers have been arguing over the last 20 years that researchers need to take more account of individuals' reports about their lives, and that they should accept biographical accounts as a form of scientific evidence (e.g. Bannister, 1975; Denzin, 1989; Hamel et al., 1993; Smith, 1994), and even more writers actually use biographical or autobiographical data as valid information (e.g. Helling, 1976; Lindzey, 1980; White, 1981; Levinson, 1981; Howe, 1982; Runyan, 1988; Elms, 1994). Furthermore, this move matches one apparent over the same time period in many other fields, such as history and social policy, where researchers are widening their database from an exclusive reliance on documentary evidence to allow for oral traditions, oral history, biography and autobiography to play a part (e.g. Vansina, 1961; Thompson, 1978; Ridley et al., 1979; Bertaux, 1981; Johnson et al., 1982; Job, 1983; Hooper, 1992; Stanley, 1992; Marcus, 1994; Hatch and Wisniewski, 1995).

A growing number of scholars have become excited by the possibilities of biographies (or life histories, as they are termed in some publications). The excellent collection edited by Bertaux (1981) contains a host of fascinating essays on life stories, including material from Poland, where autobiographical material is very well respected. In fact, Bertaux's book describes public competitions being organised in Poland from 1921 onwards, which collected hundreds of topical autobiographies at a time. These were then analysed, allowing for the better description and understanding of the formation and transformation of major groups in society, such as peasants and workers. Another excellent collection (edited by Hatch and Wisniewski, 1995) examines a wide range of issues, and the concluding chapter by the editors reflects many of the interesting questions and conclusions which arose for the editors of this present book, some of which will be examined later in this chapter: the understanding of the personal nature of the research process when conducting biographical interviews, the focus on the individual, the practical orientation of this work, the emphasis on subjectivity, and so on.

Denzin (1989) defines the biographical method as "the studied use and collection of life documents . . . (including) autobiographies, biographies, diaries, letters, obituaries, life histories, life stories, personal experience stories, oral history, and personal histories" (p. 7). In fact, he goes on to list 26 forms and varieties of the biographical method (Table 2.1, pp. 47–8). What is it that links them all, and makes them such a valuable source of material for our purposes? For us, they are exciting because:

- They are about real people with real lives.
- They are historical: they describe a family and a personal history.
- They describe individuals within their context: their current and past lives, their gender and class structures, and their housings, schools, and jobs.
- They are based around objective life events, which act as key markers around which other events can be anchored.
- They are ostensibly truthful: they are not purporting to be works of fiction (although there are issues here as to how honest and truthful we should expect them to be).
- They are not conglomerations of many people's answers to questions, grouped to allow comparisons across these individuals but with each answer removed from the context of the person's life. Instead they are rich documents, attempting to encapsulate important truths about these individuals, as they see their own lives.

## How reliable and valid are biographical memories?

One major issue which arises in biographical research is the reliability and validity[1] of these biographies. There are two sorts of answer to these questions about reliability and validity.

The first states that historical information is only relevant in that it informs individuals' current lives, and their current views about themselves as the people they are. Hence, the issue here is not the truthfulness, reliability or validity of what people tell us about their histories. Instead these accounts act as windows into their understanding of their own pasts. Whether what they tell us happened actually did happen or not is unimportant: what is important is that they believe that these things happened, and that they attribute some of their current lives (both positive and negative elements) to these past events. So we cannot understand who they are now, and how they understand themselves as people now, without hearing their accounts of their journey to 'now'.

The second sort of answer takes a more quantitative approach to this qualitative area, and examines evidence from experimental studies to see whether or not people's memories are reliable and valid. In fact, considerable evidence does exist to suggest that long-term memory is both valid and reliable, and there are many studies which show this (some relevant ones are listed in the footnote below[2]). In terms of *reliability*, in the main these studies show that:

- individuals can recall events from their childhood,
- they can recall the emotions that were associated with these events, and
- they can do this reliably (although it is true that the more memory is stimulated, the more memories emerge).

This finding that individuals can reliably recall personal experiences has been replicated many times and all these studies show that recall is not dependent on either the age of the memory or its pleasantness.

To give only one example from many available, a researcher named Waldfogel, in 1948, asked a group of over 100 students to write down all the experiences they could recollect from their first eight years of life. He gave them over one hour to do this, and then got the students to rate each experience on a scale ranging from very pleasant to very unpleasant, and to indicate their emotional reaction at the time of the original event. Without warning, he then repeated the whole procedure 40 days later. He found that the students gave substantially the same answers, except for the fact that almost half as many new experiences were reported in addition to those reported before.

The issue of *validity* is less easy to assess, but it is clear from many studies using a variety of validity measures – recall of individuals' names, memory for photographs, recall of natural disasters, dates of marriage and births of children – that it is possible to get accurate recall of information over a very long period. There is also evidence that material in memory becomes increasingly resistant to disruption over time.

Again to give but one example, a researcher named Job interviewed 204 elderly people aged 80 or over, in one suburb of Brisbane, Australia, about their life histories. The author reports that "it was soon evident that those respondents who volunteered verifiable information were surprisingly accurate in the details they provided, though it was, of course, always presented from a personal viewpoint" (Job, 1983, p. 371). Job gives several examples of the recall of natural disasters, severe economic conditions, the Boer War, the names of ships which brought them to Australia, and so on, all of which proved verifiable from records and press reports.

The conclusion that biographical memories can be both reliable and valid, however, is not clear cut. Various of the studies do not confirm so clearly that valid memories can be recalled, and most studies show a very large degree of forgetting of facts and other verifiable information.

There are many ways of trying to understand better why this happens. One of these was suggested by two psychologists, Ross and Sicoly, in 1979. These authors approached the issue from the perspective of attribution theory, an influential theory in psychology. They argued that there is evidence that individuals' memories are not accurate, and that this lack of accuracy may occur not because of deliberate deceit or simple forgetting, but because in individuals' memories, their own behaviour is both more obvious and more important to them than is other people's – that is, they have an 'egocentric bias'. Ross and Sicoly suggested that this bias could operate within any or all of four psychological processes.

1. People may selectively perceive, think about, and store in memory more of their own contributions than others.
2. People may selectively retrieve more of their own contributions than others.
3. People may have access to different informational bases than others – individuals who participate in a joint event will have greater access to their own internal states, thoughts, and strategies than will observers.
4. People may be motivated to be more egocentric in that doing so might enhance a person's sense of self-esteem or personal efficacy.

One can, of course, argue with the methodologies used in the studies which produce negative findings. In one study, for example (Messé et al., 1981), the researchers used as their measure the percentage of agreement between married spouses, and yet it is known that two informants who both offer their own perspective on events do often disagree: this does not necessarily imply that both reports are invalid, only that one is. Similarly, a study of maternal retrospection (Yarrow et al., 1964) used an interview procedure to check on information, initially provided largely by questionnaires many years previously and for purposes which may have encouraged the parents to be less than honest, as the authors freely admit:

it may be that the mothers wanted to get their children admitted to the nursery school and therefore were hesitant to admit using certain techniques which they may have felt were not in vogue or acceptable to the school administrators. It is also possible that, now the child has turned out well, there is no need to be defensive about their child rearing techniques and they are freer to admit less "acceptable" techniques. (Yarrow *et al.*, 1964, p. 216)

The problem, of course, is that it is equally possible to argue with the results of the other studies which showed good long-term recall.

Perhaps the most important point which needs to be made about these long-term memory studies concerns the *salience* of the stimuli to be recalled. Why should a person recall information accurately many years later? An obvious answer is because the information was (or still is) important to the individual. For example, if one of the authors of this chapter (Richard Velleman) places himself in Messé *et al.*'s paradigm, he finds that he cannot accurately recall the details of his brother's birthday, or his own, eight years ago – these events are simply not sufficiently important to him to be worth storing or recalling. Yet he can recall important events very well: his brother and himself would have a good measure of agreement on the details of his father's or his mother's funeral (18 and 10 years ago respectively) and so on. Similarly, salience plays an important part in the recollection of child care and development, to take Yarrow *et al.*'s paradigm. If a mother breast-feeds for 24 hours immediately after the birth and then goes onto a bottle, this may not be very salient 20 years later; but if she did it for nine months, had problems of latching on, infection, cracked nipples, and so on, then she is likely to recall it forever. These ideas on salience receive some support from studies of the saliency of life events in which it is found that events which are salient to the individual are recalled more consistently and more validly.

Further support for the concept of saliency comes from the experimental psychological literature on memory and emotion, in which a number of investigators (Robinson, 1980; Turner and Barlow, 1951) have concluded that 'intensity of affect is more systematically important in memory retrieval than is pleasantness . . . or time lapsed' (Robinson, 1980, p. 156). These researchers have also argued that intensity of feeling both at the time of the event and at the time of recall is conducive to effective recall. The importance of salience is also supported by the work of Robbins (1963) who shows that highly salient and important items such as birth-weight, when the 2 a.m. feeding ceased, and whether breast-feeding was regularly used, are all recalled far more accurately than relatively less important items such as the specific week in which bladder training began.

Having said that salience is an important dimension in accurate recall, it must also be true that subsequent events may make people want to recall prior events differently. For example, with the change of ethos in child-rearing, with breast feeding being highly approved of now, it is possible that mothers who did not breast-feed might now feel sufficiently regretful about that to convince themselves that they had indeed done so. (It should be noted that the example of breast-feeding given above is used in order to demonstrate the point. In fact, as Robbins (1963) has shown, misreporting whether or not breast-feeding occurred is extremely rare.)

## Conclusions

It seems then, that one of two conclusions can be drawn.

There is the relatively naive conclusion, which says that although results are equivocal, there is abundant evidence which implies that high levels of reliability and validity in long-term memories are to be found, and that these levels can be considerably improved upon if the information which is requested is salient or relevant in some way.

Secondly, there is the more complex conclusion, which says that equivocal results are to be expected. It is well known and accepted that 'reality' is a social and psychological construction. Clearly, no one remembers anything exactly – all perception, never mind memory, is a reconstruction of the external world into an internal perception – and therefore all memory will be a reconstruction based on numerous factors. Amongst these will be:

- a person's current feelings about the past generally and the to-be-recalled event(s) particularly (asking someone to suspend their current feelings is of only limited utility),
- their recall of their past feelings,
- their relationship with the interviewer,
- their degree of motivation and effort.

Hence, this conclusion would argue that as all experience is interpreted, all recollection of past experience must go through a double set of interpretations – the first when the original experience took place, the second when the memory is then reconstructed. Clearly, then, perception of the present and recollection of the past are never going to be 'exact sciences'.

Furthermore, the issue also arises as to whether it even matters if an individual's recollection is 'correct' or not. It can be argued that if people recall something, what is important is how they recall it, its emotional impact on them and importance to them, and the effect the memory has on them now, rather than the issue of whether what they now recall did or did not actually happen. This argument queries whether there is any 'truth' or 'objectivity' other than individual and subjective perceptions of an event, and argues that researchers and theorists should not be side-tracked now into worrying about the truth of a recollection but should instead concentrate on its current value to the individual. A position somewhat similar to this is taken by Miller and Jang (1977) in their study of the adult children of problem drinkers, who argue:

the potentially negative consequences of memory lapses or retrospective falsification are diminished because, for the study's purposes, the memories and impressions a subject retains of his childhood experience and family ambience are at least as important as the precise reality. To the extent that a particular recollection or impression seems real to the subject (irrespective of actual inaccuracy or distortion), it influences his attitudes and behaviour. (p. 25)

## *Further issues in biographical research*

There are many other issues which arise in this type of research. As suggested above, there are a number of debates within the group of international researchers who are interested in using biographies to throw light on the complexities of the human condition. Issues related to many of these arose in the preparation of this book. We briefly discuss some of these below, using as headings some suggested by Hatch and Wisniewski (1995) in their chapter referred to above.

### *The understanding of the personal nature of the research process when conducting biographical interviews*

The conducting of the biographical interviews summarised in the following six chapters was a very personal experience. This was the case both for those of us who acted as interviewer, and for the participants. As one of them (May) states in Chapter 15:

You know, I found doing the tapes distressing. I'm talking about going back to 1959. I'm talking about a very violent second husband, 1990, and I still don't go shopping on my own in case he finds me. I find writing all this [i.e. her commentary on Chapters 9 to 14] exhausting but I feel I must.

Biographical interviews are not like participating in or conducting other research, or at least they are a more intense version. Other research might use a questionnaire, to be completed in writing; or might use an interview schedule designed to take (say) one hour to complete. In biographical research one conducts a series of long interviews with each individual, during which one asks individuals to reveal intensely personal, and often intensely painful, experiences and memories. The two participants, interviewer and interviewee, have to work together to come to an agreed understanding of the life history that is being revealed. Biographical research is amongst the most collaborative of research endeavours. As an extension of this collaboration, we invited the biographees to give their views on the six commentaries, and the responses of the two who were able to do so are contained in Chapter 15.

## The researcher–participant relationship, and the issue of 'voice'

Related to the last point, there is the issue of whether the biographies successfully capture the voice of the individual whose life story is being portrayed. The interviews were conducted in the collaborative way described above, but they then underwent a number of other processes:

1. Most of the interviews were initially tape recorded (or highly detailed notes were taken throughout).
2. The interviewer then wrote the interview up as a long report.
3. These long reports were then rewritten by one of the editors (a) to ensure that they were comparable, and (b) to reduce them to the 6,000 words each that were available for this book.
4. Finally, each interview was edited to ensure the participants' anonymity.

The question this raises then is whose voice is coming over? Clearly everything possible was done to try to ensure that what is read in this book is faithful to the original,[3] but given that what is included and excluded is a subjective decision, it seems highly likely that biases will have crept in. It certainly must be the case that what is present in this book, long though each story is in publishers' terms, is a far cry from those intimate collaborative interviews where one individual revealed her life story to another.

## Balancing individual stories with social-historical contexts

There is a tension implicit in presenting individual biographies in isolation from a description of the context in which these lives have been lived. Clearly, by presenting biographies at all we are including a multitude of background facts and contextual settings; yet these lives have been lived as small parts of a far wider historical, cultural and social context. To what extent is what they have told us a series of stories about individuals, as opposed to these tales being a statement of something profound about the nature of the relationships that women have with men who have drinking problems? We hope that simply by raising this issue, and by including as two of the six commentaries, perspectives which take this wider context as their central backdrop (feminism and community psychology), we are addressing the need to achieve this balance.

## The practical orientation of this work

Biographies are real to readers. By presenting research in this way, we can make the findings of research (which otherwise might be accessed only by other researchers) accessible to a far wider readership. But why might we want to do this? There are a number of reasons:

1.  We know that there are many people in similar situations to those which our participants describe. We want to show them that alternatives exist, that they are not alone, that others have shared these experiences, and that some solutions are possible.
2.  We want to bridge the gap between theory and practicality, between academe and the wider audience. We want to take not only the lives of our participants, but also the theoretical perspectives of our commentators, and expose them to a wider readership.
3.  We want to provide a book that has practical implications. The biographies in this book are only the proverbial 'tip of the iceberg'. We are interested in the practical implications of these stories, and of the suggestions and understandings provided by our six commentators. We are looking for changes in policy and practice as to how family members of those with drinking problems are dealt with.

### *The non-linear life, the non-coherent self*

The final issue relates to the fact that these women's lives are not linear, they are not ordered and organised. People do not plan out their lives logically, nor do they always do the logical thing when confronted with stark choices. People's lives are complex, and so are their senses of self. People do the things they do for all sorts of reasons. This is why we have asked commentators from many different perspectives to examine these biographies, to see how they can understand and explain these non-linear lives and selves.

## Conclusions

It is clear that the emerging area of biographical (or life story) research is full of discussion and contradiction. The usefulness of a method lies in its application, however, and it is only after examining the biographies and the commentaries on them in this book that the reader can decide whether or not a biographical approach provides added value to the study of the field of the experiences of the families of problem drinkers.

## Notes

1.  *Reliability* in this context means that the information which someone provides in answer to a question at one point in time is the same as they provide at another – that people's stories match up over time. *Validity* in this context means that the information provided is 'true' – that it does represent what actually occurred. The two are different, in that people could give the same answer each time they were asked (i.e. their answers were reliable) but on checking one could find that in fact these reliable answers did not match up to the truth of the situation (i.e. their answers were not valid).

2. Bahrick *et al.*, 1975; Jenkins *et al.*, 1979; Job, 1983; Messé *et al.*, 1981; Ridley *et al.*, 1979; Robins *et al.*, 1985; Waldfogel, 1948; Yarrow *et al.*, 1964, 1970. The research of Job and Waldfogel is described in the main text.

Bahrick *et al.* (1975) tested 392 people on their memories of the names and faces of classmates selected from school photographs. The interval between high school graduation and memory testing ranged from two weeks to 57 years, with 192 individuals having an interval of more than seven years. The graduating class sizes ranged from 90 to at least 650. These researchers found that identification of faces, and matching of names and faces, remained approximately 90% correct for at least 15 years after graduation, even for members of very large classes, and that a free recall of names of classmates only fell below 34% of classmates after 25 years, and never fell below 19.5% even after 57 years.

Jenkins *et al.* (1979) gave two identical sets of questionnaires nine months apart to 382 men. The questionnaires assessed life events which had occurred during the six months immediately preceding the first administration. There was substantial agreement (ranging between 66% and 54%) between the questionnaires, although different types of event were forgotten in different proportions: reports of events relating to respondents' children, housing, deaths/losses and legal problems were all relatively stable, whereas reports of events relating to the work situation or to financial difficulties were far less stable.

Messé *et al.* (1981) interviewed 12 sets of married couples who had all been married for at least 10 years. Each member of the couple was independently asked to recall details of joint celebrations and holidays (such as birthdays, wedding anniversaries, trips taken together) conducted one, two, five and eight years previously. They found that individuals could recall a good deal about the previous year's events and that there was a quite good level of agreement between the spouses for these events, but that there was a large drop in the amount recalled and in the agreement between spouses as to these events as soon as events more than one year previously were considered. Furthermore, there was a continued decrement in memory (but not in agreement) as the interview-recall period increased, but this was minor compared to the dramatic decrement between pre- and post- 12 months.

Ridley *et al.* (1979) interviewed 50 American women aged 66 to 76 who were or had been married in order to collect retrospective fertility histories. On re-interview three weeks later they found almost all of these women highly reliably able to recall the details (including such 'hard' data as dates) of a wide variety of items such as year and month of marriage, of first and second birth, and of death of husband, if such eventualities had occurred.

Robins *et al.* (1985) examined the agreement between sets of close-in-age siblings for reports of their early home environments. They recruited samples from two sources, one where one of the siblings was diagnosed as alcoholic or depressed, one where both siblings were free of psychiatric disorder. They found no evidence that "either patient status or psychiatric disorder itself affected the number of childhood environmental variables accurately recalled" (p. 35), but they did show that agreement rates depended on the type of information. When the presence or absence of verifiable facts was examined, the rate of agreement was 82%; when the respondents were asked to quantify how often these factual events had occurred, the proportion of significant agreements dropped to 66%; and when questions were asked that involved value judgements or inferences about feelings, this dropped again to between 54 and 57%. As the authors argue, however, this is not surprising since "agreeing on inferences about feelings and value judgements requires not only similar recall of events from childhood but similar interpretations of those events and similar reassessment of them in adult life" (p. 37).

Yarrow *et al.* (1964, 1970) examined the reliability of maternal retrospection. They examined the degree of concordance between information – observations, tests, ratings and reports – gathered in the past about a child and its family, and information gathered from retrospective interviews with a sample of 224 mothers. They found that there were significant (although weak) correlations between the two on over 90% of the measures.

3.  The initial report that was written following each interview was shared with the interviewee, and any errors or suggestions for changes were incorporated. Each report was then made into a shortened version for this book, and each of these was checked back with the original interviewer, to see if any substantial information had been omitted, and to check that the spirit of the biography was still present. Finally, after the interviews had been made anonymous, the chapters were checked with both the interviewer, and the interviewee where this was possible (contact had been lost with one, and a second had died).

*Biographies*

# CHAPTER 3

# Ruth: The impact of children

Ruth was 47 when interviewed and her partner was 40. They had two sons, aged 11 and 13. Ruth was working as a secretary but would have enjoyed a more challenging job. Her relationship with her partner, James, had been through good and bad patches and this was greatly affected by his drinking. When his drinking was not so problematic they got on a lot better. When they first got together she felt that she had found someone she wanted to settle down with. More recently she had begun to feel, "Well, we're together now but I can't quite foresee us being together in, say, 20 years time".

## Ruth's background and early years

Ruth remembered her childhood as being happy. She lived with her parents and her two older sisters. Her parents got on reasonably well and were still together at the time of the interview. Ruth dimly remembered her maternal grandmother, who died when Ruth was about five years old, as "a bit frightening". She remembered her paternal grandmother quite well and said she was an important person in her life when she was growing up. This grandmother was quite austere (although not to Ruth) and also very religious.

Ruth and her family lived in a "nicish area of a very large city . . . we were comfortably off. We had a large house with a huge garden and it was very nice. We went to a nice school . . . I got on very well at school and I worked very hard and I got on well academically, and I had lots of friends". However, Ruth did not particularly like the school, finding it a bit "staid".

One thing that stuck out in Ruth's mind about her childhood was being shy and not very self-confident, unlike her sisters. She described her eldest sister as extrovertly conventional and her other sister as extrovertly unconventional: "a complete anarchist really!" Ruth felt that she was in-between the two of them and would have been more unconventional if she had not been so shy.

She did not participate much in extracurricular activities at school, but she did have a lot of friends and played music so "I wasn't a complete recluse". Her shyness was most apparent with people of other age groups or from other environments. Ruth's mother always wanted her to be more forthcoming but Ruth resisted being forced into talking about her thoughts and feelings. Her mother felt uncomfortable if her daughters were saying or doing things that would set them apart from other people because she did not want them to embarrass her. At the same time she wanted her children to be different, so there was a narrow line to tread.

Ruth remembered constant arguments between one of her sisters and her parents which she described as "a sort of fairly typical rebellious youth against parenthood". Her sister "was anorexic" and Ruth felt this was largely to do with past relationships but also partly a rejection of her family background. Everyone was very distressed but this all happened at a time when Ruth did not see a lot of her sister and consequently, although they were close, Ruth's memories of this time were not very clear. Her mother felt terribly guilty, did not understand what was going on and could not bear the thought that there was some kind of mental instability in the family.

Ruth was introduced to alcohol at home. She did not remember alcohol being a rite of passage into adulthood but just something she grew into. No one in the family ever had a problem with alcohol or drugs. Although her father probably drinks more than the recommended weekly limits, Ruth never felt that he drank more than he could cope with or that it was a problem.

She was and is very fond of her father and felt that he was very fond of her. They would spend time working in the garden together and she always felt at ease with him and enjoyed his company, although they did not talk to each other in great depth. She talked more with her mother and they were very close. Although they had rifts from time to time, on the whole, they had a good relationship. This started off as a mother–daughter relationship but became more like that of two sisters, particularly when Ruth was the only one left at home.

Ruth did not recall her father showing much emotion and thought that he could be quite morose sometimes. She felt that her mother took the initiative in their relationship. She remembered her mother being quite unhappy for a while, perhaps unhappy with her father and dissatisfied with their relationship. She had often said that he was insensitive and unimaginative and only cared about his job. Ruth thought her mother's unhappiness was also partly related to her children growing up and moving away. However, her mother did get involved in outside interests, some of which her father participated in as well. Ruth felt her parents did not communicate very well, although she did not feel this when she was younger and never felt insecure because of their relationship. She saw her parents as two individuals rather than a couple, with her father very caught up with his work and her mother very caught up with her children.

Her parents might argue about every six months "over something trivial that, you know, flared up, and then everything would come out". The arguments would last about half-an-hour, followed by an "atmosphere" for 24 hours and then things would slide back to normal. Overall, Ruth felt that she had a reasonably good supportive family background. They would talk and negotiate or sometimes things would start out as an argument but then everyone would come to terms with the situation.

Ruth met up with her sisters once or twice a year and always at Christmas. Her elder sister married when Ruth was still living at home and Ruth never got on with this sister's husband. She always felt that he was in some way judging her and because of this she gradually lost touch with her sister.

Her other sister married, had a daughter and then separated from her husband after about seven years. She married again and had two more children. Ruth felt that since they both had children and had moved a fair distance from each other they lost regular contact with each other. Ruth said that she sometimes envied her sister: "I always wished I was more like her, I suppose". She would have liked to see more of this sister and thought perhaps she was just allowing the physical difficulties "to let the relationship sort of drift into a bit of disuse".

Ruth was about 16 or 17 years old when she had her first sexual relationship, although she had boyfriends prior to this. He was several years older than Ruth and married. The relationship lasted about nine months. He was very good-looking, drove a fast car and Ruth was "completely bowled over by him", but "by its very nature, it couldn't have lasted". Her parents disliked her boyfriend and her mother broke up the relationship by sending Ruth abroad for the summer. Ruth enjoyed this time away, after she got over parting, and did not resume the relationship when she returned.

She went to university but did not think she got as much out of it academically as she could have done, although she had a good time. In some ways she felt pushed too far too soon and university "got a bit boring in the end". Her parents were pleased she had gone to university although she did not think they would have been bothered if she had decided not to; "they were mostly concerned with us being happy".

At university Ruth was still shy and sometimes found it difficult to meet men although "once I sort of clicked with somebody, that was fine". She spent a year with one boyfriend who she found a bit "soulless" and not really the right person for her. During her final year, Ruth met someone she was "very, very, particularly fond of, and I think I could perhaps have had a successful long-term relationship with him". However, he was not interested in a physical relationship and so they separated. Ending this relationship had been upsetting "because I began to feel that I either had a good sexual relationship or that I had a good non-sexual relationship, but that I wasn't going to have both".

After university, Ruth did a secretarial course and then worked as an editorial assistant, changing jobs when she wanted something more challenging. At this time Ruth was enjoying living in London and had many friends. She was happy, feeling satisfied and fulfilled with work, stable where she was living and more self-confident. These had become important things for Ruth and she no longer felt that having a boyfriend was the most important thing, and everything else secondary.

She began a relationship with someone whom she eventually lived with for about five years. Neither of them wanted to marry or have children and Ruth said: "it was one of those relationships that started off with me . . . making all the running, and ended up . . . with the roles reversed". She acknowledged this was a theme that had been present in other relationships and said "I think I've always thought that I'm not really very good at long-term relationships". She felt perhaps she chose people that she did not find intimidating and a consequence of this was that she got bored. (However, she did not believe this to be the case with her current partner; although she was not intimidated, she did not think she would get bored with him.)

It took Ruth a long time to finish this five-year relationship: "I just find it incredibly difficult to break patterns of living with someone. I find it very liberating when I've done it, but I find it difficult to do". Subsequently Ruth had a few relationships, including a relationship with another married man which she said "seemed very important at the time but it was totally doomed". The next important person in her life was her current partner.

## Meeting and getting to know her partner

Ruth met James when she was in her early thirties, at an evening class where she was learning French. "I thought I'd found somebody that . . . well, I had as far as I was aware then, I had found somebody that I wanted to settle down with and have children with . . . which I think coincided with a point in my life where I realised that if I didn't have children then, then that was it (age-wise)". Ruth had been considering going to live in France (where her parents now lived) for a while, but after meeting James, "suddenly I wanted to stay in England".

She described James as intelligent, sensitive, interesting and he "seemed to have all the things that I wanted, in one person". They got on well, and laughed at and liked doing similar things. In addition they both enjoyed, and had similar attitudes towards, drinking.

James had not talked to her much about his childhood. His father had a long-standing drink problem, which Ruth knew about because his mother talked to her about it. James had one older sister who died in a horrific car crash and just a year later his father also died. This left him forced to be together with his mother in a way they were not used to, and they did not get on well. Ruth thought his mother knew there was a problem with his drinking before he and Ruth met, and she may have blamed her husband for this (in that they used to go to the pub together). When James's mother first met Ruth, she said "I shan't blame you if you leave him, I would have done if I could have done, only I couldn't because of the children". For about five years before he died James's father was confined to the house with illness and his mother said, "those were the best years of my marriage" because her husband could not go out and drink. Until about a year ago, James's mother was the only other person who knew about his drinking, but Ruth did not feel close enough to her to talk about it.

Ruth described James's mother as very overweight and having an eating problem. After her husband and daughter died, she became very religious and Ruth and James found this difficult to take. She had always maintained that she loved her son desperately, but Ruth did not believe that anyone who loved her child could be so unfeeling, hostile and critical towards him. James would hardly talk to his mother and although Ruth tried to get them talking last time she visited, "it just didn't work . . . they just both closed up".

When Ruth and James first met, he was married, but Ruth did not consider him as a married man: "I'm not quite sure why now, but I think their relationship was not very – it was deteriorating. And they hadn't children, or anything". Ruth felt he would have left his wife even it he had not met her. They did not move in together immediately after he and his wife separated, because of Ruth's uncertainty about her feelings for him. She knew they were different from feelings she had in previous relationships but she was concerned they might not endure.

James was very keen for them to have an intense relationship. He told Ruth, "It's really nice being with you, you're just like me, only you're a woman". They had a very exciting sexual relationship, but Ruth said, "I wasn't confident in myself being able to have a successful relationship over a long time . . . I didn't want to let him down, basically". She was worried she would make the wrong decision and this would hurt both of them. Ruth felt this had been a difficult period for James, but eventually she decided she wanted to commit herself. Her expectations were that they would "go on caring for each other . . . that we would develop as parents and as a family, and that we would go on enjoying the same things, and do things together".

At this time going out to pubs and drinking was part of Ruth and James's social scene, but Ruth did not remember his drinking being problematic. After living together for about six months they decided to try for a baby and were "ecstatic" when she became pregnant. She left her job and in retrospect felt she got pregnant because she wanted to leave her job. This had either been because she did not want to delay having children or because the job was quite stressful. Whilst breast-feeding her first child Ruth drank much less and it was at this time that James began home brewing, partly because they were short of money. Ruth said, "That the home brewing was certainly one of the things that led to the heavy drinking". They moved to another part of the country and everything was wonderful until after their second child was born. Ruth had her second child sooner than planned and did not work again until this child was at nursery full time.

## Problems in their relationship

Ruth's second child did not sleep well and their first child was jealous. Ruth was incredibly tired and this interfered with their sex life and "that's where it all started to go wrong really". Her GP was not particularly supportive and she became very desperate and sometimes felt she could not cope. James started to become jealous about her past boyfriends because he said that she had not gone off sex with them, whereas she had with him. This seemed senseless to Ruth because they were together with the children and she said "at first, I just thought it was funny". She could have understood if he felt she did not love him, but she did not think that was the issue. Ruth felt he did not really understand what she was going through and this was the time they started drifting apart. It was also the time that his drinking started to become a problem.

He started to get jealous about the children, although Ruth felt his resentment was towards her because they appeared more important to her than he did. Ruth said "I don't want you to think that he was insensitive about what was going on. I just think he didn't know what to do". The days were difficult to get through. Ruth described a scenario of him coming home "at about half past six, and I'd be in tears, and then two hours later, the kids maybe would be in bed, and then I'd go to bed myself . . . he'd stay up, and do his DIY, and brew some beer, and drink a bit. And then stagger off to bed and get up the next morning, and go to work and come back and I'd be in tears". Ruth said this "set up a pattern", one that was still going on, of "two ships sailing away from each other". Occasionally they would go out together but "we would sit there staring at each other . . . because you get out of the habit of that kind of going out, and of communicating . . . And I didn't feel that I had anything to offer, because I wasn't an interesting person any more. I was just a mother".

## Ruth's partner's drinking becomes more problematic

Around this time, Ruth thought James's life started to become "more lonesome, more drink orientated". This, combined with a lot of drinking functions at work and a heavy drinking boss, meant that his drinking increased. Sometimes after a business function he would carry on drinking with a small group of people and not come home until the early hours of the morning, often without his briefcase. He was fine when sober but Ruth could not stand it when he was drunk. She said, "he quite often became very maudlin, very self-pitying; or he would be very jolly and hearty . . . inappropriately so. I found him embarrassing as well, when we had people to dinner". Ruth put up barriers with her friends because it was very difficult to talk about her relationship. She did not want to bring people home because of the drinking and his behaviour and also because their relationship "wasn't up to having a joint social life". But the main reason was that Ruth got fed up with feeling embarrassed.

As the children got older Ruth wanted to get back some independence. They moved home and James started a new job, which Ruth was involved with, and the children started school. She felt this would be a fresh start for them and there was a chance for them to build something again. She remembered saying they should both stop drinking so much because of the new job, and to some extent the drinking improved. Although Ruth felt better because she had more to do than look after the children, she also felt that James started to get jealous of this.

Moving meant they were financially more settled and Ruth really enjoyed this period in her life. James also got very involved in his job. Ruth said "he was a complete alcoholic . . . um workaholic, sorry a bit of a slip there, complete workaholic". Looking back, Ruth said it was a crazy time but they both really enjoyed it, "sex became a bit sort of contrived" because of the children, but Ruth felt their relationship was maturing.

They moved into a new house to give themselves some space from work, as they had previously been living in work accommodation. In spite of hoping that this would be another new start for them and trying to make things work, Ruth felt that she had begun rejecting James before they made this move: "I don't know what got in the way. Perhaps it was just that I'd had enough . . . I think my feelings just gradually died . . . I don't know what was cause and what was effect really". She found it difficult to go back to feeling the way she did about him particularly because of some of the things he had said: "although I know it's the drink . . . you can't erase them when they're said". He had told Ruth that he wanted to kill her and that the children wanted to kill her. He also blamed her for ruining their sex life and said that was the reason he drank. However, Ruth felt if he stopped drinking, she might start to see him as attractive again. She found it difficult to relate to him as though the drunken side did not exist even when he was sober.

The drinking went from bad to worse "with occasional bits where it got slightly better after a crisis". The most recent crisis was the previous Christmas, when James had broken down at work. After this he saw his GP who referred him to the local NHS alcohol treatment clinic. He had been referred to this clinic previously but said that he did not have time to attend the course. The doctor had replied, "Well I'm afraid you're not reduced to a low enough level yet. You've got a lot more drinking to do before you're going to be ready for this" and sent him away. Although Ruth thought that in a sense the doctor was right she found this really unhelpful. She did not think it was the best thing to tell James that "he had a lot more drinking to do", because that was exactly what he wanted to hear. He stopped drinking for a while but then started again and Ruth said "I think it was probably worse than ever".

This time, however, James said he would start the course. Ruth was not sure what had brought on the most recent crisis, although they had spent an abysmal Christmas together. She said "I just think he'd drunk so much that he realised that he couldn't go on really". He attended the course and stopped drinking "not all the time, but most of the time" and Ruth said "things seemed to be OK and we sort of started up our relationship again but I began to get sort of bad vibes about it all". She thought he was quite selective about what he told her while he was attending the course, and sometimes she found things hard to take. For example, one day he came home from the alcohol clinic and said "Oh, they all think I'm too hard on myself. I must be much nicer to myself". In some ways Ruth resented all the sympathy going to James, "because he was lapping it all up and not really considering me". Ruth felt she was excluded and no one was listening to her. Although she was apprehensive and perhaps a bit cynical, she also felt hopeful because he had realised that he had to have help. Until then he had thought he could manage without help, and Ruth thought: "it must have been very difficult for him and I think he must have been feeling very apprehensive about doing it as well". She tried to be very supportive, asking him how he felt and reassuring him that she was with him.

James left some information for her that he had been given at the clinic, specifically for partners to read. Ruth read it and got the impression that wives were held responsible for a lot of their husbands' drink problems. She said "I didn't receive that very sympathetically, I must say". Ruth felt it was written by somebody who did not have much idea of what it was like having a partner who drank a lot. She felt the problems were fifty-fifty rather than "ninety-five to me, and five to [her partner]".

At the time of the interview James was drinking more at week-ends and mainly in secret. She thought this was because he was afraid of drinking too much at work and drank as a kind of reward for getting through the week. The drinking would then get out of hand and take up the whole weekend. Often he was "at the sort of in-between stage before he gets . . . noticeably drunk". This meant he got slightly more irritable, slightly more aggressive and shouted a bit more or he got a bit more emotional, more affectionate and more "everything's wonderful". Ruth reacted differently to James if she knew he had been drinking. For example, if she wanted to talk to him seriously about something she would wait until he was sober.

About half the time Ruth and James spent together was taken up with him "being the worse for wear with drink, either very overtly or in this more covert way". However, this varied and at times he was almost constantly drunk and at other times predominantly sober. Ruth felt they were in some kind of transition phase and she was not really sure what was happening with his drinking. She said "I'm not really sure where we're going now . . . I think he's trying very hard, when he's at home with the children, to stay sober". The previous summer he had looked after the children and it had been a disaster. He knew this himself but Ruth also told him because she found it difficult to resist. Sometimes he never got up all day and the children were getting their own lunch. Other times he would get up and start drinking and just collapse on the floor.

## How Ruth dealt with her partner's drinking

Ruth mainly dealt with the problem "by hiding it from everybody". Sometimes she would ring work for James and say he was ill; and she used to clear things up so others would not notice. She described it as "a sort of conspiracy of silence" in that nobody wanted openly to acknowledge his problem. After Ruth had covered up for him she would confront him and say, "You can't go on drinking like this. You've got to stop for your own good. You'll lose your job". He would agree and say he would stop but then he did not.

At one stage Ruth threw away all the home brew. She said: "Looking back I was very naive. I sort of took one end of the problem and thought that that was the problem". Since then all alcohol was bought and James mainly drank beer, cider and wine but not spirits.

James used to tell her it was all her fault and if only she did not put the children first, or if their sexual relationship was as it used to be, or if she cared for him more, then he would stop drinking. Sometimes Ruth did try to change her behaviour towards him but she said "it never lasted really", and she thought they were both responsible for this. They talked at great length about why he was drinking and about their relationship. There would be short-term positive changes but then things went back to how they were. Over the previous few years they had talked less about it, Ruth just realising that it was no use: "Nothing I said made any difference, and I got tired of saying the same things". When James first started drinking again after treatment Ruth wondered "whether he was just drinking again, or whether he was attempting to control his drinking, and if so whether he was being successful or not". But she did not get clear answers from him and thought maybe he did not know himself.

She dealt with the frustration she felt by getting on with other things in her life. She became more independent, both with and without her children, and got involved with activities which were separate from James. Eventually she stopped covering up for him. Every now and again things would flare up and they would have a row but on the whole she avoided this and thought, "If you really want to talk to me about it you'll be sober and then we can have a proper discussion about it; but unless you're going to sober up then it's pointless me trying to talk to you". Ruth felt that getting angry with James had not been a constructive reaction as he would get angry with her and say "things which I don't particularly want to hear".

For a long time Ruth did not talk to other people about James's drinking. She said "I didn't feel I could", because it was unacceptable and other people would not know how to deal with it. She once talked to her mother who was staying with them when James got very drunk. Her mother thought it was just because of the time of year (New Year's Eve) and not an on-going problem: "I think she found it too hard to cope with then". Ruth went along with this because she did not want to give her mother a problem she could not accept. The previous year, however, Ruth and James had been on holiday with her parents and Ruth "quite enjoyed bits of it but it was blighted". His drinking was more explicit and her parents were particularly shocked about the way he behaved towards Ruth. He would say "what an unpleasant person I was . . . how all I was interested in was the children. I wasn't interested in him, and I was selfish, and things like that" in front of her parents. Her parents did not really get angry with him because they realised he had a problem. They wrote to him saying they wanted to help, but Ruth said it turned him against them. She thought he felt very guilty about it all. Her parents were sympathetic and Ruth felt their first loyalty would always be to her. She had always felt very loved by them and particularly so when they realised she had this problem to deal with. She was sure her sisters would also be supportive if she had more contact with them.

Ruth had very little support and understanding from professionals. She said, "It's been a big strain on me . . . it's an awful lot to carry . . . and it's an awful lot to keep secret". She was talking more to other people about James's drinking once they had noticed it for themselves. Until they did, however, she would not say anything "because it's something which is rather shame-ful and embarrassing and needs to be kept quiet". Some of her work col-leagues knew about her situation and Ruth found them helpful, sympathetic and supportive. If anything, she thought they took her side too much. She felt there were also disadvantages to this kind of support: "sometimes people's support can be rather strongly advice-giving". One of the friends Ruth talked to was also a counsellor and she had helped Ruth clarify some of her feelings. This friend had listened, asked questions and been very understanding without being judgemental or shocked.

The strain of coping with James had affected Ruth emotionally and she talked of "this sort of great sadness a lot of the time, which has sort of been there all the time". She also felt very alone, isolated, angry at times, impo-tent, helpless, hopeless and guilty, as if she was "responsible for the whole mess". This feeling of responsibility stemmed from her uncertainty about being able to maintain a long-term committed relationship in the first place.

## How Ruth has been affected by her partner's drinking

Ruth had been deeply affected by the deceit and did not feel they could have an open and trusting relationship while James continued to lie about his drinking. On a day-to-day basis they were communicating, but on a deeper level Ruth said, "I'm sure there's a lot there, but there's nothing happening". She was not sure whether she wanted to put the effort into keeping the relationship going without knowing how it would eventually work out. She was also uncertain if the real issue was the drinking: "it's so difficult to separate it out – the drinking from so many other negative things I might have about the relationship". She felt James's priorities were his drinking, his job, and then his family with her more important to him than the children. Her priority was family first with the children more important to her than James. Six months ago she had felt more hopeful that they could make a new start but then began to feel, "How many times can you go through the hopeful stage, thinking that it's all going to work out . . . and then a few weeks later you realise that it's not working?"

Ruth had not had any other relationships since she had been with James and probably would not have done even if she had met someone she was interested in, because of the children. She had felt a strong sense of responsibility since having her children and thought they were largely the reason she had stayed with James. She imagined if she ever left she would take the children with her and she worried about how he would cope without them. She could not see herself getting him to leave the house, she did not know how "either legally or physically or morally" she would be able to do so. She felt that if she left, this would be a sign of her taking action and control, but asking him to leave would be forcing him into action and losing her control.

She worried that there were effects on the children that she could not see. She described her eldest child as being quite introspective, self-reliant and not at all demonstrative. She was most concerned about this child and felt he was very aware of his father's drinking and had lost a lot of respect for him because of it. Ruth was not sure exactly what her eldest child thought and felt about it, although he had said he would not drink himself. She did not think he would talk to her about it because she had tried without success to find out if things were worrying him on a more general level. When James's drinking did get talked about it was "more to do with the particular situation at that moment . . . how we're going to handle it, or what we need to do". Ruth got the impression from things her child had said, that he partly blamed her because she chose his father. She thought he coped by keeping out of the way.

Ruth described her other child as much more extrovert, more open with his feelings and his thoughts and more empathetic. His way of coping with his father's drinking seemed to be by making a joke of it, although he did feel embarrassed about it and had sometimes said, "I don't want my friend to come because Daddy might be funny".

Ruth felt very guilty about much of what had happened and that if she had loved James more or better then he would not have needed to drink. On the other hand she also felt a lot of resentment about his behaviour and that there were other ways he could have coped with her being tired and the children being demanding. Ruth found these two sets of feelings very confusing.

## Ruth's understanding of her situation

Ruth said, "I think it has to do with my making a decision to go into a relationship and have children, without perhaps realising that the children weren't a substitute for the relationship, or something like that. That the relationship ... had to have carried on as the strongest thing. A sort of expanding to encompass the children rather than the children replacing it. So that in the process I sort of pushed him out. And that because he had a tendency to have recourse to drink when things got stressful or weren't going the right way for him, he used this as a substitute for, for our relationship really".

She felt she had a tendency to pack up and move on without expanding to incorporate existing things in her next life. An example of this was with friends, partly because she was "lazy about keeping up contacts", but also partly because she felt it was not "appropriate to sort of drag friends along with you somehow". Her past experience was always finishing something and then moving on to the next thing and she felt that if she and James were to carry on together this was a pattern she should change. Ruth was not sure why she developed this pattern in the first place: "Maybe I didn't like the person I was, so I wanted to get away from her ... I don't think I've ever looked at it like that before ... but thinking about it now, it does appear to be a pattern, for me, which might also explain the bit about how I got into this position I'm in with him".

Ruth had come to terms with the lack of self-confidence she felt when she was younger: "Maybe it's just being in the world long enough to realise that you've got this far so you can't be that useless at things". Over the years she had given herself less priority than she used to and this might have been because of having children. She found it difficult to adjust to motherhood (the loss of status and identity and not feeling in control), but she managed, and the result was putting her needs second and becoming more responsible than she had been before. She became very good at maintaining a fairly even keel, for herself as well as her children, even though she might not have been feeling too good. She did not feel she had been desperately unhappy all the time but neither had she been terribly happy either: "It was a kind of in-between state of just taking each day and getting on with it, and perhaps feeling no great elation and no great despair".

# CHAPTER 4

# Lisa: The young family

Lisa was 25 years old when interviewed, and married to Kevin who had a drink problem and was also 25. They had been together for eight years and had four children under eight years of age. Lisa's husband, Kevin, was in prison serving a sentence for assaulting Lisa, but was due to be released shortly when he would be returning to live with Lisa and the children.

## Lisa's childhood and early years

When Lisa was 10 months old her parents left her with her paternal grandmother for about 10 months. She did not know why her parents left her or where they went but her mother was only 18 years old at the time. Her parents returned when Lisa was about a year and a half old and took her to live with them in a caravan. Both her parents were working and they never married. Lisa started going to school at the age of four and she remembered that her father was rarely around at this time. He often disappeared for whole weekends after being paid on a Friday afternoon. Her paternal grandmother would bring groceries for Lisa's mother during this time to help her "make ends meet", as Lisa's father left her mother very short of money.

The family moved when Lisa was six years old and she liked the new school she went to. At this time her mother would regularly get "dolled up" and go out with her friends to the pub and leave Lisa to look after her younger brothers. Sometimes there would be a babysitter and Lisa would go out, mainly around to her friends' houses for tea. When there was no babysitter she sometimes took her elder brother out with her in order to look after him. Once, in her frustration at him not being able to keep up, she left him outside. Later on that evening she went out and found him but was resentful at having to be responsible for him. Lisa hated having to look after her brothers and felt that this was her mother's responsibility and not hers. Sometimes when there was a babysitter for the evening Lisa's father would decide to stay in. The babysitter was 14 years old and Lisa felt that her father "liked" this girl.

Lisa's mother did not know where Lisa was half the time as Lisa was always out, often until nine o'clock in the evening, mainly because she did not like the atmosphere at home. The house had no electricity and there was rarely food in the cupboards. Lisa wore her mother's socks and shoes because she had none of her own.

When Lisa was about seven her father was sent to prison for five years for theft. Lisa was only taken to visit him once and she remembered going there on the train and staying overnight in a hostel. Her mother got a boyfriend and he moved in shortly after her father went to prison. Lisa's father also used to see other women before he went to prison. Lisa thought her mother's boyfriend was horrible as he used to beat up her mother and verbally abuse her after they had been drinking. She would often hear her mother crying and felt that her mother protected her from her boyfriend, as she would send Lisa to her room when he began to shout or threaten violence.

Eventually Lisa's mother finished with this boyfriend and began seeing a friend of his (who she later married). Lisa's mother was admitted to a psychiatric hospital soon after she began this relationship and Lisa and her brothers went into temporary care (although Lisa went to a different foster home to the two boys). Lisa's mother was discharged after a couple of months and all three children returned home. They only stayed for a couple of weeks as Lisa's mother was unable to cope with them and she asked Social Services to intervene. She could not trust herself with her children as she believed she might throw them down the stairs. Lisa admired her mother for doing this, as she felt her mother was doing what was best for her children and said she never felt resentful about it.

Lisa and her brothers went into permanent foster care and although her brothers were fostered together, Lisa went to a different set of foster parents. She was seven years old at the time and happier with her foster parents than with her mother, as she was given smart clothes and good food. Lisa only saw her mother once in the next few years, on her eighth birthday when she came to the foster home with a present for her. Lisa did not see her father, although she would occasionally receive letters from him while he was in prison.

Lisa stayed with these foster parents for three months and was then moved to another foster couple. She lived there for another three months before being moved again, as the male foster parent was physically very ill and unable to cope. She then went to live with a foster couple who she hated. When Lisa wet the bed the foster mother would rub the sheets in her face in front of Lisa's friends. On another occasion the family's pet rabbit died and Lisa was served rabbit for dinner that evening. Lisa still liked school at this stage and also made friends with her foster parents' 17-year-old daughter, who was very friendly towards her. The foster parents had an adopted son whom Lisa did not get on with and who tried to get her into trouble. He was treated as if he was their own child, whereas Lisa felt they were just doing a job for the Social Services in having her there. Her foster parents tried in vain to keep Lisa in the house but she would escape and go around to a school friend's house.

When Lisa was nine years old her foster parents telephoned the Social Services and asked for her to be taken back into their care. She felt they simply did not like her. Lisa went to an assessment centre, where children normally stay for six weeks before moving to a foster family, but ended up staying there for six months (she also returned here on six different occasions in the future). She then moved to a children's home where she stayed for a year and was happy. She subsequently went to another set of foster parents with whom she stayed for six months. She was then moved to another children's home where she stayed for about three years, the longest period of time that she stayed anywhere during her childhood.

When Lisa was nearly 13 years old she started running away from this children's home with her room-mate who was 16, just for "something to do". Sometimes they would stay away for up to four days. The manager of the home became tired of this behaviour, and arranged for Lisa to be returned to the assessment centre. Later Lisa went to another children's home where she met her future husband.

Lisa used to sniff glue when she was about 13 because everyone else was doing it. She sniffed "anything going" for about two years although she was eventually caught and threatened with removal from the children's home. The only other drug she tried was cannabis on one of the occasions when she and her friend had run away from the care home. They had ended up in a flat with some men who were taking cocaine, which Lisa refused, although she did smoke some cannabis from a pipe.

## Lisa and her husband get together

Lisa's husband, Kevin, had been taken into care at the age of nine, along with his four brothers and sisters, because his parents were having marriage problems. He was ill-treated while living with a foster family and was placed back in a children's home. When he was 14 he went back to his parents and was arrested for the first time on his fifteenth birthday. Kevin had some friends round for his birthday and everyone got drunk with alcohol that his mother had bought. His father, who had been drinking at a club, came back and began to spoil the party. In the turmoil Kevin's mother called the police. When they arrived Kevin became abusive and his mother let the police arrest him. He still hated his mother for 'getting him arrested'. After this, he began to play truant from school and was eventually taken back into care.

Lisa met Kevin when she was 16 and became friends with him soon after she arrived at the children's home where he was living. He found out that two other boys who lived there were interested in Lisa so he asked her out himself. He was obviously embarrassed when he did this and she said "no" because at this time she just wanted to be friends. He was not put off and wrote a letter to her asking her again if she would go out with him. This time Lisa said "yes" although she was not really that interested in him and was worried about getting a bad reputation at the children's home, as she had not been there very long.

She had not had a serious boyfriend before but felt she and Kevin had a lot in common, as they had both been in care for a long time and had been through similar experiences. A few months after starting their relationship Lisa became pregnant. They kept the pregnancy a secret from the manager of the children's home as otherwise Lisa knew that they would be separated. They had no doubts at all about keeping the baby because within the few months they had known each other they had become very close. Living in the same children's home meant they spent a lot of time together and after the pregnancy became common knowledge, they were allowed to spend even more time together. However, they were told that they had to leave the home in one month's time. Lisa moved into lodgings for a couple of months and then into a council flat.

## Drinking and violence

Kevin had started drinking before he went to the children's home. Lisa, who did not start drinking until she was 16 years old, used to drink with him at the home. She would buy two litre bottles of cider from the corner shop, as she was the only one who looked old enough to be served. Lisa would hide the empty bottles at the top of her wardrobe and get Kevin to take them out in a bin-liner when there were too many. They only got caught with alcohol once and after a chase around the garden of the children's home, it was confiscated. Kevin had never used illicit drugs extensively, although after they moved in together he would occasionally buy an eighth of cannabis. He had also experimented once or twice with amphetamines.

They both drank cider on a regular basis at the children's home until Kevin was arrested during an organised sit-in at the children's home. Lisa had become involved with a care organisation and helped organise the protest. The police were called and Lisa, who was then pregnant, was pushed up against a wall by a member of staff. Kevin became very angry and "went for" the manager of the children's home. He was arrested after the ensuing scuffle and taken to a remand centre and then to a probation hostel. On his release several months later, he moved into the flat that Lisa had moved into after leaving the children's home.

Their first child was born when Lisa was aged 17. Kevin was not drinking much when he first moved into the flat because he had a job, although he would sometimes drink all day on a Saturday. He began drinking cans of lager but eventually found that large quantities had very little effect other than on his bladder. He then started drinking cider and found he got drunk extremely quickly. He did not drink on Sunday as he had to go to work on the Monday morning. They sometimes went to the pub with their son and had a few drinks in the beer-garden, although most of the time Kevin would drink cans of cider at home.

At this stage, Kevin would occasionally drink large quantities of alcohol, "go mad" and destroy things in the house. Afterwards he claimed not to remember what he had done and never expressed any remorse. Lisa got upset that they had to keep replacing broken items of furniture. He also became physically violent towards Lisa at around this time. The first time he was violent Lisa responded by hitting him with a baby chair and locking herself in the bathroom. Because he was of slight build, Lisa was able to stand up to him if she needed to. Over the ensuing months Lisa became used to her husband being violent towards her after he had been drinking. Occasionally she would hit him back although most of the time she was resigned to accepting the violence. The attacks often occurred for no apparent reason and Lisa would "just put up with it". After a drink Lisa felt happy and liked to have a laugh and a joke. However, this was impossible with Kevin as he usually thought that she was "having a dig" at him and took everything personally.

He was not violent while sober and had never been violent towards their children, although occasionally they witnessed his violence towards Lisa. The children did not see anything unusual about his drinking as they had grown up with it. In later years, however, the older children developed a negative attitude towards the police as a result of seeing their father arrested on numerous occasions. They would call the police "pigs" and ask Lisa why they were always so horrible to him. They also played "arresting games" imitating what they had seen happening to their father.

Kevin had been in trouble with the police before Lisa met him and on the day they began seeing each other he was starting a community service order for assaulting a policeman. He did not get into any trouble with the police during the time they lived in their first flat, and to Lisa's knowledge had never been arrested when sober. When Lisa was eight months pregnant with their second child they moved to another town and Kevin began to get into violent confrontations with the police on a regular basis.

About five months after the birth of their second child, Kevin started drinking at home and then going out and becoming aggressive with policemen on the street. Lisa felt that his problems with the police originated from when he was first arrested on his 15th birthday. He was also verbally abusive to Lisa and would become violent if she was abusive in return. Sometimes he would go out to "cool off" so he did not take his frustration out on her. Inevitably he would then get into a confrontation with the police.

After he had been in trouble a few times, Kevin became well known to the police and Lisa felt that they picked on him because of his temper. She felt that living in a small but lively town amplified the problem as there were a lot of police around at night and Kevin soon came to their attention. About 18 months after they had moved Lisa was in hospital preparing to give birth to her third child, when Kevin was arrested and his arm was broken whilst he was detained at the police station. After being released from the police station he went straight to hospital where his arm was put in plaster. However, because it had not been a clean break, he was told he would eventually need an operation to free a nerve and pin the bones together. His arm was in plaster for two years and he was unable to work over this period. He once cut the plaster off so he could do some work but after a few weeks he began to experience further trouble with his arm. His attempt to sue the police for breaking his arm was unsuccessful.

About a month after this incident Kevin was drinking every day and although he would make sure there was enough money for provisions for the children, he inevitably spent what was left on drink. He continued to hit Lisa even with his arm in plaster and this left graze marks on her body. Eventually he had the operation to replace a bone in his arm. This whole episode left him feeling even more resentful and bitter towards the police.

A few years later Kevin was arrested again even though there were several witnesses to the fact that he had done nothing wrong. The family were in their garden one afternoon when a police van pulled up at the gate and a policeman got out and began questioning him. Another policeman jumped over the gate and held him up against a wall before handcuffing him, throwing him in the van and taking him to the police station. Kevin was kicked and punched in the police van and came out with bruises and red marks on his back. During the arrest one of the children was knocked over by a policeman and Lisa made a complaint against the officer. Because the witnesses would not go to court, Kevin was charged with assaulting a policeman and fined. Again their attempt to prosecute the police was unsuccessful.

They got married shortly before Lisa gave birth to their second child. Kevin proposed to Lisa but she could not really see that getting married was necessary, as it seemed to her that they were married already in everything but name. She joked with him that getting married would be "a hassle, in case I want to leave you" and he told her that he wanted to marry for tax reasons. Although Lisa was not that keen on getting married (the children had already taken his surname so there seemed little point), she agreed. Lisa thought Kevin may have wanted to marry because he feared she might run off and leave him. If they were married, on the other hand, she would be stuck with him. However, Lisa said that if she wanted to leave Kevin she would do so and being married would not make any difference.

They had always been a fairly insular couple, happy with their own company. They had another child, so there was a lot to do around the house, leaving little time for them to socialise. From time to time friends came to their house although this was not a regular occurrence. Kevin had always been happy drinking at home and would rarely go out drinking with anyone other than his father.

Kevin's father had a major problem with alcohol, and sometimes he came to their house with a bottle of whisky. Lisa felt that Kevin's problem may well have been inherited from his father. When Kevin had his arm in plaster and could not work, his father came to the house every lunch time and would drink a few cups of cider with him before going back to work. When he was younger Kevin had not been close to his father, as he felt that his father favoured his older brother. As he got older they became closer and began drinking together. His father started a relationship with a woman who lived across the road from them. They would visit Lisa and her husband at the weekend with a lot of cans and bottles of drink. Kevin was fairly happy when his father was there though Lisa felt he encouraged Kevin to drink by bringing so much alcohol every time he visited. Occasionally they went to his father's house and they would also take a fair quantity of alcohol with them.

## How Lisa deals with the situation

Friends of Lisa's doubted whether Kevin really did not remember his violent outbursts when he smashed up their furniture. However, Lisa believed it was quite possible that he had complete blackouts considering the amount of cider he drank. She protected the children from realising what their father had done by telling them that she had knocked things over or broken them. Whenever she tried to talk to Kevin about his drinking or violence he remained silent or acted bored and sometimes she did not even know if he was listening to her. Eventually she gave up trying to talk the problems over with him.

She never minded Kevin drinking as long as it was not to excess but he always drank until the money ran out or the shops closed. She never contemplated trying to hide or pour the drink away. In fact, he tended to hide his own alcohol thinking that Lisa would drink it if he fell asleep or went out. He got very angry if Lisa tried to have any of his drink. She occasionally bought alcohol for herself which Kevin would drink if she left it around. She did "moan" at him about his drinking and on one occasion this motivated him to pour the remains of a Christmas drinks hamper down the sink. He was not happy when he realised what he had done and this incident did not motivate him to change his drinking behaviour.

Lisa felt that she could not make Kevin stop drinking and the only way he would change was if he wanted to do so himself. Her friends could not understand why she did not get rid of him, and told her that she should not have to put up with his behaviour. Lisa, however, said then (and still says now) that she loves Kevin and does not want to throw away what they have together.

She did once leave Kevin after the situation became intolerable. He was very drunk one day and Lisa was fed up with him being verbally abusive, insulting and continually talking nonsense when he had been drinking. She pretended to go into town but in fact took her children to a women's refuge where they all spent the night. When Kevin eventually sobered up he became very worried and telephoned the police. The police found out where Lisa was and informed him that she was all right. Lisa had left him so she could think things over, but she had no idea what to do in the long term. She found the women's refuge disturbing and returned home the next day. Kevin then begged her to stay, saying he would change his behaviour and things would be different from then on. For the first few days he did drink less and was not abusive or violent. However, within a matter of weeks things returned to the way they had been before she left.

About a year and a half after this, Lisa pressed charges against Kevin for assaulting her. He hit her and the neighbours called the police because they were worried for Lisa's safety. The police took photographs of the bruising on her body and persuaded her to press charges. A court injunction was placed on Kevin which prevented him from going anywhere near the street in which they lived. Lisa dropped the court case after breaking the injunction on the day it was issued by allowing him back into the house. She appeared in court to say why she no longer wanted to press charges against Kevin and that she was prepared to give him another chance. Lisa felt she had to accept Kevin the way he was as she could not change him.

Kevin worked in various jobs over the years but was unable or unwilling to keep them for any length of time. His longest period of employment was for eleven months. Lisa also began work after the birth of her second child to gain experience before starting a college course. During the time they were both working Lisa and Kevin had more money than ever before, even though they had to employ a child-minder and pay for taxis to get to work. Kevin only drank on his day off and rarely to excess as he had to work the next day. Lisa saw this as the most stable period they had spent together because Kevin was not drinking excessively. Unfortunately, he lost this job after a dispute with his supervisor who wanted him to work a full shift with only one 15-minute break. Lisa felt he had really enjoyed this job and began drinking more heavily after losing it. She felt that he drank from boredom when not working. He liked to work but often found it difficult to get jobs because of his criminal record.

Lisa had to stop working when she became pregnant with her third child, as her job involved a certain amount of lifting. She was forced to postpone going to college because of the baby (although she had not ruled this out for the future). A couple of years later both Lisa and Kevin applied for a college course and Lisa was accepted. Kevin was also accepted initially, but then received a letter saying there had been a mistake and the acceptance letter he received should have been sent to someone else. Lisa was going to turn down her place as she felt Kevin had been poorly treated, but she had become pregnant with her fourth child at this time and so would not have been able to start the course anyway.

More recently Lisa worked in a factory but had to stop as she could not rely on Kevin getting the children to school. He would be unable to get up after drinking the previous night and Lisa used to get a friend to go to the house at five in the morning to wake him up.

## Kevin attempts to stop drinking

Eventually Kevin wanted to do something about his drinking. He had started to drink most days at eleven in the morning and would rarely eat anything at all during the day. He did not eat because that meant parting with his bottle for 10 minutes and he was afraid it would disappear. Lisa felt he had known his drinking was problematic for a while but did not have the right attitude to be able to stop. He had always felt that he could stop when he wanted to without any outside help.

With the backing of his social worker Kevin attended Alcoholics Anonymous and went to an alcohol advisory service, though neither of these proved successful. He then saw a psychiatrist who said that his problem was only habitual and was therefore not a major problem. Lisa saw this reasoning as stupid. It meant that the doctor was not willing to get him into a detoxification unit which Kevin saw as the only possible solution to his problem. He had been offered a place at a rehabilitation centre but turned it down because he wanted a full detoxification followed by rehabilitation. Lisa thought this might be because he did not trust himself and would be happier with a doctor or nurses on the premises 24 hours a day, while he detoxified.

A few months after deciding he wanted to do something about his drinking Kevin was admitted to hospital after vomiting blood due to a stomach ulcer. On leaving hospital he became very worried about health problems related to drinking and was admitted to a detoxification unit of his own volition, with the help of his social worker. He was due to spend two weeks there followed by 12-week rehabilitation. He realised that his drinking was causing problems for both himself and his family and that he needed outside help to stop. However, he left the detoxification unit after 10 days, and subsequently relapsed. He had not been happy there because there was very little to do and he was "going mad" with boredom, especially at the weekend. In addition, many of the other clients had come straight from prison or the courts and did not have the motivation to stop using alcohol that Kevin felt he had. Drugs and drink were freely available on the wards and many of the others behaved in a destructive way, for example one person would blow drink fumes into Kevin's face. His social worker told him that if he wanted to return in the future or go to a different centre then she would try to arrange it. He was due to be admitted to a different detoxification unit but this did not happen because of his conviction.

Ultimately, Lisa felt it was not up to her to persuade Kevin to give up drinking, although she felt that he does want to give up totally, rather than just reduce his consumption.

# CHAPTER 5

# Dawn: Still together after many years

When Dawn was interviewed she was 49 and her husband had not been drinking for six months, since being diagnosed as having a brain tumour. He was told that he could be treated with medication so long as he did not drink and this would mean a chance of improvement.

## Dawn's background and early years

Dawn described her parents as being quiet and said that she got on well with them. She was the middle daughter of three girls. Her parents were very religious and involved with the church. Her mother, who did not work, was from a farming background and was the youngest of eight children, all the others being male. Her father, who worked as a motor mechanic, had two brothers and a sister and his mother came from a family of 13.

According to Dawn her mother was quite strict. Her father worked very hard and she did not see a lot of him. He would leave home early in the morning and return late at night and he also worked on Saturdays. Her paternal grandmother lived behind the garage where her father worked and Dawn had fond memories of going to her grandmother's house and spending most of her days there during her school holidays. Dawn described no drinking problems in her family; her parents drank rarely and were non-smokers.

Dawn remembered a happy childhood with lots of camping and caravaning holidays. Because of the nature of her father's job they had a car (something fairly unusual in those days), which allowed them to travel a lot and go out as a family. Dawn described the relationship between her parents as good. She said that her father was a bit stubborn and found it difficult not working after his retirement, as he was someone who liked being busy.

At the age of 10 Dawn spent some time in hospital and this interfered with her studies. She failed her 11+ and went to a secondary modern school. At 15 years of age she began a pre-nursing course, followed by her 'O' levels. She was a good mixer and got on well at school. She enjoyed her nursing training apart from going into theatre and she particularly enjoyed the patient contact. Her training lasted four years altogether. She left home at 18 when she went to live in a nurses' home. She still lived in the same town so she maintained contact with her own family.

## Meeting and marrying her husband

Dawn met her future husband, Martin, at a church youth group. She was 17 years old and he was 18 and they lived around the corner from each other. They were both part of a very close-knit church group and used to carry out lots of activities together. Dawn said that some of the qualities she found attractive in him were that he was very active, good-looking, kind and considerate.

During his childhood, Martin's family moved several times to different parts of the country and he spent a lot of time with his aunt. His father was very strict and had very fixed ideas, and Martin was in awe of him. His mother had a drink problem: she would work during the day and drink in the evenings. Dawn described her mother-in-law as "a nice person" and said that it was when she was about 20 that she began to notice her drinking heavily. Dawn's in-laws would go out as a couple to have a drink but she did not make anything of this.

Martin did not get on very well in his final year at school and had to retake his exams on three occasions. After school he worked as a packer and subsequently joined the Civil Service. During the early part of their relationship Dawn used to go to his house a lot and they would spend time in coffee shops with other members of the church group.

Before her relationship with Martin, Dawn had a couple of boyfriends and Martin had a number of girlfriends. They became engaged when Dawn was 21 years old and married when she was 23. Dawn had finished her training two years prior to the wedding and had worked for one year as a staff nurse and one year as a senior staff nurse. They were saving money to buy a house and they waited until they had enough to buy a property before they got married. They bought a semidetached house and Dawn started a part-time job as Martin did not want her to work full-time. At that time he was doing a desk job.

After marrying, Dawn and Martin visited their parents quite regularly. Martin's mother got rather jealous if they were visiting Dawn's parents and they slowly started to cut down their visits. Dawn's husband and father did not get on too well and their first confrontation had been over the wedding when Martin wanted a formal "do", which they eventually had.

Dawn's mother-in-law did not like to visit them, but she used to like them visiting her. Martin and his mother liked to tease each other and swore at each other a lot. His mother died from a cerebral haemorrhage at age 50 soon after they got married. Martin felt very guilty because prior to her death his mother had asked him to visit and he had refused. Dawn's father-in-law took his wife's death badly, he lost weight, became very depressed and stopped looking after himself. Dawn thought that he might have been feeling guilty as well.

Martin tried to help his father but his father continued to isolate himself. The summer after his mother died they went on holiday with his father. Dawn and Martin had planned to have children and it was after this holiday that Dawn realised she was expecting her first child.

She gave up work after having taken maternity leave following the birth of their daughter. At this time everything was fine at home. Martin had changed departments at work and was having some difficulties there which "got him down a bit". He had a recurrence of some gastric symptoms and his doctor prescribed Librium for him. Dawn stated that he was not drinking at this time; he hardly drank at all.

Martin had a report at work which was not very good and a change of job was suggested. At that time their daughter was six months old and he was transferred to another part of the country. He started to commute to work, staying away during the week. They subsequently put a deposit on a house and four months before this house was ready for them to move into, Dawn went to stay with her sister. Dawn, Martin and their daughter then moved into their own house. Martin had stopped taking his prescribed medication when he changed his job.

At that time, Dawn said, life was normal. Two-and-a-half years after their first child was born they had a second daughter. Dawn did not work between the births of her children. Their third child, a boy, was born when Dawn was about 30. Around this time the eldest child was starting school and Dawn had to be very organised to run the home. She had no real support and had to cope on her own. However, she did make some friends in the area and got a little support from neighbours. Her children used to play with the neighbours' children.

## Dawn's husband's gambling and drinking

Around the time that their second child was born Dawn found out that Martin was gambling. He was betting heavily on horses, started to get into financial difficulties, and their house had to be remortgaged. Dawn became aware that he was gambling because her signature was required to remortgage the house, and because of their obvious financial problems. She never found out exactly how much he spent and it was difficult to say how long it went on for, but she was certain that the gambling stopped about five years after they married.

Martin decided to take a job which involved a lot of travelling, with him therefore receiving paid travel expenses. He thought this would enable him to make more money in order to repay his debts. The way Dawn responded to his gambling was by talking to him about it. He agreed that it was a nonsense and the whole issue made Dawn feel angry and resentful.

Around the time his gambling stopped, Martin became friends with someone who lived locally and started going to the pub with him late in the evening. Dawn thought that it was at this point that Martin started to drink on a regular basis. According to Dawn, Martin and his friend did not drink excessively and they would always go for a late drink and be back home by closing time.

About two years after the birth of her third child Dawn said she began to feel like "a cabbage". She became bored at home and felt she wanted to use her skills to do some kind of work. She went to work at a playgroup and one of her neighbours babysat for her while she did a course related to her job. She helped out at the school where her youngest child had started when he was four, and this gave her the opportunity to use her skills.

After about 12 years of marriage, the family moved to a different part of the country because of Martin's job. At that time Martin stopped going to the pub and started making home-brew. Initially this was a joint activity with Dawn and they used to pick fruit together to make the wine.

The following year they moved again so as to be nearer Martin's workplace as he did not wish to travel any more. Dawn had already started working as a nurse again before they moved and she continued afterwards, working mainly weekends and evenings. She was beginning to enjoy being back at work. The move enabled Martin to stop travelling but he would still occasionally spend a night away. At this time he was not going to the pub but drinking his home-brew at weekends and with meals. Dawn did not see his drinking as problematic.

About a year later Martin's aunt died and he was very upset and started to drink whisky on his return from work. Dawn remembered feeling that at this time his drinking was very much tied to his emotions. Several months later his other aunt died and this also affected him enormously. Dawn tried to talk to him about it and suggested that he needed help to cope with his grief. Martin, however, tended to play his feelings down. At that stage he was drinking most days and developed diabetes. He had great difficulty coming to terms with his illness and felt very resentful about it. Dawn felt that his resentment was quite severe. Because of his diabetes he did not drink beer or wine but continued to drink spirits, and Dawn still did not see his drinking as problematic. She saw it more as a reaction to his emotional grief and the resentment he felt in relation to his diabetes. He started drinking about half a bottle of whisky per day and Dawn left him to it because she was working.

The following year Dawn's father-in-law died from a stroke. Martin was away in another part of the country at the time and Dawn had to locate him to let him know. Following his father's death, Martin began to drink more heavily although, as far as Dawn knew, he was still only drinking after getting home from work. At this time he would fall asleep downstairs after Dawn had gone to bed.

She used to worry a lot, particularly when Martin passed out. She did not know whether this was the effect of the alcohol or if it was due to his diabetes. Dawn tried to cope by ensuring that he ate regularly, and initially by attempting to control his drinking. She also tried to keep him busy, thinking that if he was, then he would not drink so much. In retrospect, Dawn felt these strategies did not work and sometimes led to arguments. He could become verbally aggressive and abusive. If he fell asleep she tried not to wake him until the shops were closed so he could not get more alcohol. She would not lend him money and initially poured drink down the sink. He would hide drink and Dawn would try to find it so she could get rid of it, but looking back, she felt this strategy did not work either.

## The problems continue

Prior to the death of her father-in-law, Dawn had injured her knee and was also found to have an ovarian cyst. While she was in hospital Martin was charged with his first drink-driving offence. Dawn had spent the week away and her father-in-law died when she returned. During the time she was experiencing health problems and went into hospital, Martin was no support to her whatsoever. He was getting drunk and trying to cope with his own problems but Dawn felt resentful and let him know of her feelings. It was also around this time that she discovered Martin was having an affair, when she found some photographs he had failed to conceal.

The affair was over by the time Dawn found out about it. She had been suspicious that something was going on, particularly on one occasion when Martin was going on a course on a Sunday. She drove him to the station and remembered wondering where he was going. She knew the woman Martin had his affair with; she had been to their house for a Christmas drink. The affair lasted six months and was finished by the woman involved.

The children were feeling hostile towards their father, and they would not bring their friends home because they felt embarrassed by him. At about this time, when Dawn was feeling very unsupported and fed up with the situation and had found out about his affair, Martin agreed to go for some treatment under pressure from her. She suggested visiting their GP and was prepared to pay for private treatment. Following an in-patient detoxification, he joined a six-week day programme for people with alcohol-related problems. Dawn was relieved that this gave her some respite from Martin being at home.

She used to think a lot about separating from Martin and she remembered looking through the papers wondering whether she would be able to find a job that would pay enough money for her to live on her own. She had also been taking time off work sick as a result of all these pressures.

In the same year that Martin went for treatment, Dawn's father died of a heart attack. Dawn felt very unsupported during this period. Her father had been ill for three weeks while Dawn was off sick and she spent a lot of time with both her parents prior to her father's death. She had very deep talks with her father and felt that he had been preparing himself and was ready to die. These talks she had with her father helped her in coming to terms with his death in the absence of support from her own husband.

She had not told her parents about Martin's drinking, but later told her mother. Her mother came to stay while he was in treatment and they both went to visit him together. Dawn never spoke to her father about Martin's drinking problem.

## Dawn gets some help

Martin had tried Alcoholics Anonymous in the past and it was through his contact with the organisation that Dawn found out about Al-Anon. She started attending meetings and found them very helpful. She experienced a great sense of relief through her contact with Al-Anon and found it encouraging to talk to others who really knew what she was going through. Dawn said she realised "you weren't as crazy as you thought you were". She started to make sense of some of her own behaviour, like crying or screaming, through sharing with other people who had similar experiences. Dawn said it was a shock to learn how much it had affected her. She felt that the telephone links through Al-Anon were crucial and she started developing coping strategies like taking herself away from the situation, walking away and trying to release her tension. She realised that she was blaming Martin for everything that went wrong.

Another form of behaviour Dawn had found unusual on her part was lying on the floor and stamping out of sheer frustration. She changed her outlook on the situation and realised that reasoning or attempting to reason with Martin was a waste of time. If she tried to have an in-depth conversation with him, he would subsequently not remember anything about it. Life became easier when she understood that drinking was his choice. She also "realised my life had become a bit of a mess" and that before joining Al-Anon she had lost all her confidence outside work situations.

She had a responsible job and felt she managed to "switch off" while at work because she "had to". She was given a challenging new position at work which she felt was an opportunity to do something constructive. Because of this she started to get very involved in her work, sometimes staying late, although this was partly to avoid the situation at home. Dawn said that she never hid her difficulties from people at work or lied about the problems she was facing at home.

## *Martin starts drinking again*

Martin remained abstinent for five months and then started drinking again secretly. Dawn could smell alcohol on him but she did not confront him or try to control his drinking. She did not argue or discuss the issue.

Thinking back, she felt Martin was not ready for treatment and had gone just to please her. While he was attending the unit they had a few sessions as a couple with a community psychiatric nurse and these were mainly focused on their sexual difficulties. Dawn found the sessions helpful and they also had some sessions as a family. Dawn felt she was happy to forgive, but Martin was opting out. She also felt that the family sessions were very helpful because they gave the children the opportunity to speak to their father about how they felt. Some of the feelings expressed were due to the frustration about his drinking, the feeling that he was not doing things that other fathers did, and the feeling that he was causing disruption to their daughter's studies. All these problems recurred when he started drinking again. The children then adopted Dawn's approach and tried Al-Ateen but they did not like it. Martin could not see the point of family meetings but Dawn felt she benefited from understanding the difficulties the children were having. This helped her cope better with the situation and also to cope better with them. Through the family meetings they tried to have communication sessions at home.

After Martin started drinking again he alternated between very short periods of abstinence and periods of heavy drinking. Although he went back and forth to AA, he never again had contact with any services and if he went through a period of detoxification he would do it on his own.

During this time Dawn felt that she wanted to do something for herself and decided to learn to drive. The following year at Christmas, her mother had a heart attack, collapsed on the way to Dawn's home and died. Although her mother had previously had a heart attack she had recovered well and her death was unexpected. Dawn was devastated and found it hard to cope.

By now Martin had begun to drink at work. He was found asleep in the office and as a result of this was reprimanded and lost his security status. He would buy drink or go to the pub on his way home from work. He got into debt and did not sort out unpaid bills or take any responsibility at home. Dawn closed their joint bank account and just kept her own. Because of the debts they had to remortgage their house again, but although Dawn felt very angry with Martin, she did not want to leave him. When he was sober he was a different person and she really cared for him.

He would remain abstinent for periods of five or six weeks but never more than a couple of months. During these periods his health would improve. At other times Dawn remembered him drinking whisky while at the same time having milk and indigestion tablets to deal with the effects of the alcohol on his stomach. On occasions he would go into withdrawal fits and Dawn remembered one very bad time at about one o'clock in the morning, when he banged his head badly while in the bathroom and she had to call an ambulance. Another time he had a fit while out in town and ended up in casualty, and on another occasion went to casualty, having cut his hand by sweeping glasses off the table in anger. Dawn remembered times when the family would get on with their meals while he sat drinking heavily.

Particularly difficult times that she remembered were at Christmas, when the whole family routine fell apart. For example, by midnight service Martin would be totally drunk and every Christmas he would promise that the next one would be different. Family meal times were also affected, although not only by his drinking but also sometimes by Dawn's shift work. The children all had different reactions to their father's behaviour. Their son would argue a lot with his father, the eldest daughter was very submissive, and the youngest daughter would concentrate more on her studies.

Dawn used to pray a lot although at one point when things were really bad she became angry with God and stopped going to church. She also used to find herself planning what to do if Martin died. She felt that throughout the period of his drinking she found a lot of support in her own work and through her contact with Al-Anon and her friends.

## Dawn's husband becomes physically ill

Later, Martin started to have a different type of fit from the ones he had previously. Dawn "knew they were different" because during these there was no loss of consciousness and he experienced speech difficulties and weakness on his left side. She persuaded him to go to the doctor. He had an EEG which showed some abnormality, and then a CT scan which showed a brain tumour. Since that diagnosis he had stopped drinking and Dawn felt that his attitude had changed. He was more determined, more positive and wanted to remain abstinent. This was partly due to the doctor's advice that he could only be treated if he stopped drinking.

Dawn felt that Martin stopping drinking had been of definite benefit to the whole family. Their younger daughter, who was still living at home, was getting married in a few months time and was training for a career. This daughter, who is of a nervous/anxious disposition, felt she was perhaps the one most affected by the drinking and she worried about her father. Their son was at college and planned to go on to further study and their older daughter was married and doing further career training.

## Note

Since conducting this interview, sadly Martin has died. Dawn and her family have fond memories of the good times they all had together.

# CHAPTER 6

# Sylvia: Drinking and extreme violence

Sylvia was in her mid-fifties when interviewed, and the ex-wife of a problem drinker. They had divorced a few years previously after 16 years of marriage. They had two children, neither of whom regularly kept in touch with Sylvia on their own initiative. Sylvia feared she would lose touch with them if she did not keep up the contact herself.

## Sylvia's background and early years

Sylvia had a happy childhood but it was very sheltered: "too sheltered really". Her family were financially "quite comfortable" and they lived in a small village. Sylvia's mother (who had died a few years before the time of interview) was "very snobbish and fussy" and did not allow Sylvia and her younger sister to play with the local children.

At school Sylvia and her sister had "extras" like elocution lessons. The aim was that they should turn out well and "make brilliant marriages". Sylvia did not like school at the time, although looking back she had enjoyed it. She was not "all that popular" but did have one or two best friends. Academically, Sylvia was "not too bad". She started further education but left before her exams because her parents were running short of money.

Sylvia's father (who had died many years before interview) was a very devout Christian and lived for the church. Sylvia thought her mother felt he was "over the top". Her mother was also religious but Sylvia felt it was "all on the surface". If ever there was any trouble Sylvia's father would remind Sylvia and her sister that God would help them. When Sylvia was younger she "turned her nose up at that".

Later in Sylvia's life, as the troubles in her marriage grew worse, she could feel her father's presence close to her as though "he and all his forebears were all looking down from heaven feeling for me and encouraging me". Sylvia felt the presence of her father for over a year and a counsellor suggested that perhaps her father had unfinished business with Sylvia and had come to sort it out.

Her mother used to put her father down and he would withdraw. He wore a hearing aid which Sylvia thought he probably often turned off when her mother nagged him. Although her parents discussed and agreed things together, Sylvia felt it was probably her mother who initiated things, and her father agreed so as to keep the peace. He had been shell shocked in the war and as a result was retired early from work. Sylvia did not recall her father ever cuddling her. However, "since he has been so close to me, since his death, I can't wait to get to heaven to cuddle him".

Her mother "held everyone at arm's length". In spite of this Sylvia recalled missing her "very badly" when she was little and went to stay with her grandmother. Sylvia knew her mother was very proud of her because she had a good singing voice, and Sylvia felt closer to her mother than her father when younger. Sometimes when her mother was making sarcastic remarks about her father, Sylvia agreed with them. However, since he had died, Sylvia realised how wrong she was.

She recalled overhearing her parents quarrelling once during her childhood. Her mother was going to leave her father and she took off her wedding ring and threw it at him. Later her mother calmed down but Sylvia felt her mother was unhappy: she always had headaches and was overweight and run down. They moved house quite often and Sylvia thought this was because her mother felt that moving to a different place would improve her health.

Their mother used to hit Sylvia and her sister on the back of the legs with a split cane. Once, she and her sister had been playing, forgotten the time and were too late back to go to church. They got the cane and Sylvia remembered feeling how unfair it was. She described her mother as "a harsh disciplinarian" but "loving at the same time".

Her parents drank occasionally, but did not have any particular attitudes towards alcohol, although Sylvia suspected that if her mother had "been allowed to she'd have been an alcoholic". Sylvia felt her mother was frustrated but also felt she was doing "a disservice" saying these things about her, as there was no evidence for it. Sylvia remembered feeling how very selfish her mother was and always had been.

When Sylvia was a child she felt her parents, particularly her mother, favoured her younger sister and Sylvia felt resentful: "I think that coloured a lot of how I grew up". Sylvia said that it was a strong feeling "when you feel you're out of favour or unloved". She felt her sister was more attractive than her, "more colourful". Her sister was "a wow with the boys" and had poached Sylvia's boyfriends, which led to some rivalry between them. Recently, Sylvia had received a letter from her sister in which she said "I always looked up to you". Sylvia was surprised by this as she had not felt it to be the case.

As a young adult, Sylvia once got very upset with her mother "and I actually punched her; I raged at her and told her I hated her; I don't know what effect it had on her". Sylvia was quite surprised at herself and hoped she had not hurt her mother. Towards the end of her mother's life, Sylvia visited her in hospital, "and our eyes welled up in tears with love". Sylvia felt there was "a great bond; no matter how cruel you feel your mother has been to you".

Sylvia had a baby when she was in her early twenties. Although the father wanted to marry her "it meant going into a different culture and I was afraid, and my parents said they wouldn't speak to me again". Sylvia "fell from grace" with her mother at this time, although their relationship improved after the baby was adopted. Her father was also pleased when the baby was adopted and felt "proud" that Sylvia had organised it all herself. Sylvia then got married to someone else and her first husband had "something to do with" the baby getting adopted. Sylvia thinks that her feeling grateful for this may have led to their marriage. Her father was pleased when she married and Sylvia said "I seem to have been a bit of a people pleaser". The marriage ended after about a year, "he stopped paying attention to me and started looking at other women" and she reacted to this "quite the wrong way; I went and paid attention to another man; he caught me and divorced me". Sylvia felt they were both equally to blame for the relationship breaking down.

After the end of her first marriage, Sylvia had a "nervous breakdown". Her father was concerned for Sylvia's "soul", but her mother was "concerned with how things looked". In spite of this, Sylvia recalled her mother making her some dresses at this time which "fit me perfectly and I looked a proper sexpot when I had them on, and she wanted me to look attractive like that. It was strange when, before, she was so firm and strict. I think she was a mixed-up woman". This is something Sylvia and her sister had talked about and both agreed that their mother was probably unhappy and frustrated. Sylvia wondered if maybe her mother had "a bad menopause or something".

## Sylvia meets her second husband

Sylvia moved to a different city after her first marriage ended. About two years later, she met her second husband, Bill, at a social event and "he was holding a drink in his hand; it's only when I look back that I realise that when he took me out, or treated me, it was always in a drinking place, at a club, or he'd buy a bottle of champagne which was lovely at the time". She described him as "an ordinary, pleasant man". At the end of the evening he invited Sylvia for a meal and she recalled him being cross because they had to have water with their meal. Sylvia stayed the night with him but they did not sleep together. He put Sylvia in his bed and slept on the settee, "and that impressed me". She said he "seemed good; I liked him", he had a career, his own home, enough money and was fairly good-looking.

Bill had been married before and had children who Sylvia never met. Sylvia understood that his first wife had left him in "a great hurry in fright". He had told Sylvia something of this before they got married "but I took no notice", she said, "I suppose I was in love and I was quite different to her".

Sylvia thought Bill had been attracted to her because she was the opposite of his first wife. Sylvia was intelligent and well-spoken and maybe he thought "we'd have a good life together". Sylvia remembered telling him that she could not have children. She felt guilty about this and did not really know why she said it, since she had already had a child. Sylvia thought perhaps she felt she would not be "allowed" to have another child. She supposed he did love her, although if he had not "it wouldn't have mattered" because "I didn't fulfil his expectations and my promises".

Sylvia recalled that on their second date, Bill stayed the night at her flat and in the morning could not find his wallet. He "went on so much" that she felt perhaps he thought she had stolen it, so she left him in her flat to search for it when she went to work. He read Sylvia's diary and afterwards kept accusing her of different things based on what he had read. She felt that he was "inveigling his way into my life; trying to find out about me in underhand ways". But Sylvia "still accepted it; I don't know why". She was very unhappy after her first marriage and thought she was probably looking for another husband: "grabbing at straws really". She thought he had taken advantage of her vulnerability. They married about a year after meeting and her parents thought it was "a wonderful marriage". Sylvia said, "Maybe I was anxious to get married; I never felt happy about the thought of being alone for the rest of my life".

When Sylvia first met Bill, his mother was already dead. His father died later: "He was an alcoholic as well; he was very fond of drink and often used to smell of it". Bill used to complain about his father, saying, "he seems to be dying for a drink all the time". When first married, Sylvia used to drink quite a lot with Bill and get drunk, sometimes: "people seeing us may have thought I was the one with the problem".

At first, everything was "lovely" and they had started a family. It all started to go "bad" when Sylvia was pregnant with their younger child and Bill went to prison for a white collar crime. When he was in jail, Sylvia's father kept in touch with him, "being a devout Christian", and her mother "virtually ignored the fact" that he was in prison. When Sylvia was in hospital giving birth, she felt "awful" because she felt like an unmarried mother. She was advised by a nurse not to tell the other mothers that her husband was in prison, because they might react adversely.

## Violence and drinking

Some time after Bill's release from prison, the family went out on a day trip. When Sylvia went to their children because they had started to cry, she was shocked to hear Bill say, "I'd like to bash their heads against a rock". Although he was not violent towards the children, they were frightened of him and Sylvia felt sure it affected them.

Bill was working away from home a lot and they were very short of money. When the children were very young, he started being violent towards Sylvia, "very violent: he hit me lots of times". She "had to wear a cardigan or a jumper all the time [to hide] where he'd poked and prodded me". Sylvia recalled one night: "It was absolutely terrible; he started smashing everything in the bedroom and throwing it out; I was so frightened I went and stood in the children's bedroom; it went on for hours and hours, and then he started in the sitting room. I didn't know what to do; whether to get the children out" (they were asleep). Eventually she got into bed with their elder child.

The next morning, after Bill had gone to work, Sylvia took the children to her mother's. After a few days Bill went to get Sylvia and the children. He had replaced the things he broke, "but he never said sorry or explained what had happened". Sylvia said she went back because "for years and years I've felt I had to stay faithful to my marriage vows and it really bothered me. Maybe it was for the sake of the children. With hindsight it might have been better to have left him when they were very small".

It was some years after they married before Sylvia began to make a connection between Bill's violence and his drinking. She once gave him a bottle of spirits as a present and "it was the most dreadful [time] I can remember; he threw everything all around and rushed out of the house breaking the glass in the front door; the children were crying, he drove off, I didn't know what to do. Ten minutes later he came back; he didn't know what he was doing".

When the children were at primary school Bill was drinking up to a bottle of spirits every day. He drank at home and in secret, although when he was working he would also drink with his friends in the pub. Sylvia used to look for alcohol around the house "it obsessed me to a degree that I looked everywhere". But she never threw it away ('I'd never dare') and could not remember whether she used to tell him she had found it. Sylvia described alternating between feeling despair and feeling in a fool's paradise: "it's so baffling, you see. A person seems drunk and violent for a week and then goes back to normal and you always think he's given up drinking . . . then it would be better and it always took me by surprise the day he started drinking again. It was a fool's paradise".

Sylvia thought Bill felt she was paying too much attention to the children. Giving them all her attention was a way of coping for her. She wanted to make things secure for the children, but it also served to help her avoid the situation with Bill. She was concerned about how they were doing at school, helping them learn to read, making sure they were fed and clean and were learning good manners. Sylvia gave almost nothing to Bill because she had become afraid of him, she was "terrified, afraid to breathe even".

Sylvia described herself as "living in fear 24 hours a day" as Bill became increasingly violent. He would come into the kitchen "and make me stand to attention and look into his eyes; if I said anything out of place or defiant at all he'd hit me; I was frightened". Sylvia saw her GP frequently and at first he was not that concerned. He was a Christian who believed in the sanctity of marriage and all he really said to Sylvia was that she must have a lot of "grace" to put up with the marriage. Sylvia found this "a comfort" but on reflection thought his attitude possibly contributed to her staying with Bill.

She was determined to remain faithful to her marriage vows, particularly as she had not done so in her first marriage. She also felt she had to stay because of the children and because Bill told her so many times she would never manage on her own, she believed him. Sylvia also said another reason she stayed was because he was "a good love maker" although in the end "he was impotent and used to pee in the bed".

## *Sylvia gets some help*

Someone from Social Services once turned up on Sylvia's doorstep offering help and Sylvia thought perhaps a neighbour had contacted them, but she felt "I don't need any help". Although she "knew life was an absolute nightmare", at first she thought it was probably normal and then later that it was "fated".

She recalled an incident which had been a turning point in the way she reacted to Bill. One evening they were having supper after the children had gone to bed. He started shouting and reached over and punched her. He had punched her harder before but something in Sylvia "snapped". She felt she could have plunged a knife into him or picked up the chair she was sitting on and hit him over the head, over and over again until he was dead, "I could have killed him with no compunction whatsoever". Instead, she got up and ran into the kitchen and stood there shaking until she had regained enough control to go back into the dining room and clear the table. The next day she went to her GP who put her on tranquillisers ("I know his attitude was, silly woman what's she doing here?"). She said: "I knew something had happened in me; I knew I was capable of murder and this was a turning point in my life". She thought that what had stopped her killing him "was my religious faith; knowing it was only God who could take a life and this has stopped me committing suicide too". Sylvia used to imagine what it would be like if he died "and how happy I'd be and dancing on his coffin", but she had only once felt "like plunging the knife in . . . which shocked me and is why I shook and shook".

Sylvia eventually heard about Al-Anon through a friend. She "didn't know about alcoholism" until she started attending Al-Anon meetings and then it was "quite an eye-opener". Sylvia did not like the first meeting she went to, but having promised to go to a few, she continued. She felt disloyal talking about Bill and did not like "the horror stories of the others; it was too near the knuckle". She remembered thinking at the last meeting she had promised to go to, "good, I don't have to go again", but she did go again because she had found support there. She felt that only people who had been through it could really understand, and it was through Al-Anon that she realised the only person she had control over was herself.

Al-Anon "taught me little things", for example, when Bill was telling her off and making her stand to attention, she could look beyond him or at his ear rather than into his eyes. They suggested she kept her coat near the door so she could leave if she wanted to. The first time she did this it was "terrible" and Sylvia was afraid he was going to drag her back. This became a strategy which she often used, even if it was raining or cold, or she had no money. She would just stand in a local shop as she did not like to go "and land on neighbours". Sylvia felt no-one else knew what was going on, but in fact she discovered that all her neighbours did. Once Sylvia spoke about it, they were sympathetic and said that they had seen him shaking her, through the window.

When Sylvia visited her parents for support they would talk about her sister's marital troubles. Sylvia did not turn to her sister for support because she "disgusted me slightly". At just about the time when Sylvia's troubles were beginning, her sister came to stay and help her. Her sister told her she was having an affair and "went into graphic detail . . . it turned me off" and Sylvia wondered "what sort of morals has she got". This view of her sister prevented Sylvia from turning to her for help along with the fact she did not think her sister would be able to do anything.

## Sylvia leaves Bill

The more Bill drank the less Sylvia respected him. At the beginning of their relationship she "would have done anything for him" but by the end there was nothing really attractive about him. He had lost his looks and had a pompous arrogant way of talking: "I hated having the smallest conversation with him". She felt that everything he did was over the top. He would read *The Times* from cover to cover every day, drinking a huge cup of very strong black coffee. Sylvia said "they [alcoholics] can't be moderate in anything and that's what I thought every time I smelt the coffee".

She finally left Bill on "a Sunday afternoon; we had just had lunch and I still had my apron on; something blew up; he couldn't find a particular piece of paper and [he said] it was my fault. He stood over me shouting and poking. It was the last straw". Sylvia ran to her neighbours and he followed her shouting "don't come back". The police came and escorted Sylvia to the house so she could pack a few things. Bill was "very belligerent and stinking of drink" but Sylvia thought the police were surprised to see that the house was not smashed up, and there were no signs of a struggle. Sylvia asked the children, by then in their teens, if they wanted to go with her, but they did not. The police took her to a battered wives' hostel and Sylvia said, "I knew I'd come to the end".

A couple of days after Sylvia left home, she phoned to speak to the children. One of them was crying and asking her to please come home. Bill also came on the phone and was crying and pleading for Sylvia to return and promising that he would not drink again, but Sylvia did not believe him.

She saw a solicitor and got an injunction to stop Bill molesting her and moved back in with him and the children, although into a separate room. She was instructed by her solicitor not to cook or wash for anyone else in the family, but she did and recalled a meal time where no-one spoke to her unless to swear or spit at her. Sylvia felt Bill had "poisoned" their children's minds against her.

Sylvia and Bill went through a divorce and both applied for custody of the children. She described him as a "very clever, devious, manipulative man", and said he lied to the court, saying that Sylvia was a prostitute when he first met her and he got custody.

Sylvia got her own place to live and after a while her children seemed to accept the situation, and then "I did a foolish thing". She started a relationship with another man and her children saw her with him. Sylvia felt they did not understand and she wished she had not had this relationship. Her children would not speak to her if they saw her in the street. Some time later however, she saw her older child who was obviously "suffering" and looked "bedraggled and had no money". Sylvia offered him a home with her, which he accepted, until he moved away to take a job.

Sylvia had little support when she left Bill. Her parents were both dead and her other relatives were all surprised because Sylvia had never spoken about problems with him before. She felt people were "sympathetic but did not really understand". At the time of the divorce Sylvia wrote to all her and Bill's relatives saying that she had left him because she could not stand his drinking any more, and they all "took offence". However, some time after this, Sylvia became very ill from "grieving a lot" and went into hospital. Unexpectedly, Bill's relatives visited her there and subsequently wrote her a long letter saying they knew what Bill's mother had gone through with his father, hence expressing sympathy for Sylvia.

Her sister had never confided in Sylvia about her own violent first marriage. Sylvia knows her sister's ex-husband "liked a drink" and said "it's funny that both of us should have gone for violent, bad-tempered men when we were brought up in such a sheltered home with a gentle father". Sylvia and her sister were closer for a few years after she left Bill. However, since Sylvia was able to buy her own home, there had been "a long silence" from her sister. She had written but not telephoned or visited even though she came to Sylvia's home town quite often. Sylvia felt her sister might be a bit "jealous" because Sylvia had her own place and was independent.

## Sylvia's religion

When her children were young, Sylvia felt they should be going to Sunday School because she had gone. As a result, Sylvia herself began going to church again and became very interested in reading books about Christian lives. She read about someone who had suffered a lot of persecution and hardship in her life, and Sylvia felt similarities with her own situation. This woman prayed to God "quick little arrow prayers" at the times she was suffering and Sylvia adopted this strategy, for example, at times when Bill was hitting her. Sylvia said, "Sometimes you can know the angels are around you keeping you safe . . . after it's over you thank God for keeping you safe". She added, "It is not God who allows bad things to happen; it is either Satan or your own personality; God only wants good for you".

Bill was totally against religion. His first wife had been a dedicated evanglical Christian and "he lumped all religion in with her". When Sylvia started going to church, he felt she was becoming like his first wife. Sylvia felt that he often used religion as an excuse for violence and he accused her of having the children "brainwashed". She began going to church several times a week and after a while she felt she had grown in faith "almost beyond the church". She felt others who attended were just "Sunday social clubbers". Lately Sylvia had been going to church less, perhaps three times a week.

## Sylvia's concerns about her children

Both Sylvia's children, as toddlers, had been 'head-bangers', and Sylvia recalled being told that at a children's party they had been rocking "like you see disturbed children". She felt very "ashamed" when she heard this, thinking that it was her fault but not understanding why they were doing it. In retrospect she felt these were probably effects of their father's problem. Neither of the children did very well at school and they got into trouble, for example for shoplifting, as they grew up.

Recently Sylvia had told one of her children that her state of mind had not always been good when they were very young. This came as a surprise "so they didn't realise what was going on at home". Sylvia thought perhaps this had been a mistake, because it meant that when she left the children did not understand why she was going. In retrospect, Sylvia wished she had left Bill sooner and felt she could have made a decent life for them, but at the time felt it was impossible with two young children.

Sylvia was concerned that her children had grown away from her. She felt some of this would be natural (given their ages), but it had upset her more than if she was a happily married woman, because she worried about the effect their childhood had on them.

Her son had just been thrown out of his home by his girlfriend, and Sylvia thought this was because he had punched her. Sylvia said, "She's not a very good housekeeper; she doesn't cook" and she thought her son got fed up with having to cook when he came home from work. She hoped that they would not split up permanently and she hated the idea of losing touch. She felt perhaps her son had not told her the real reason why his girlfriend had thrown him out. If his girlfriend had done so because she thought he had become violent, Sylvia felt this was all right, but if (as her son said) he only pushed her, she thought his girlfriend had overreacted.

## How Sylvia felt

Bill told Sylvia that the cause of his drinking was her telling him she could not have children and then becoming pregnant, "so he reckons he was led up the garden path by me". However, Sylvia thought the reason was his addiction to alcohol, which was probably inherited. Both his father and grandfather had drink problems. She had sometimes thought Bill was "deliberately drinking . . . playing the devil . . . being devilish" and at other times she thought it was an illness, that once he had the first drink, he could not help going on and on. However, Sylvia felt she only thought that because she had been told this so many times. She could not understand why people take the first drink if they know this to be true. She thought maybe it is a psychological illness but was not sure. It was a long time before she could admit to herself that Bill had a problem and she used to think up reasons to defend his behaviour.

Although when Sylvia left Bill she felt she had lost everything, she also experienced a feeling of relief. She lost a lot of weight and people began telling her how "young and glamorous" she looked. Sylvia felt very pleased and thought "maybe there was a bit of a future for me after all". She had not worked for a long time and found the prospects of getting a job "not very easy". In spite of Bill telling her she would never manage on her own, Sylvia found she could and that she enjoyed her own company. She worried, though, about having no-one to look after her in the future.

Since meeting Bill, Sylvia felt she had changed because "I've been through the mill; I've brought up children . . . I suppose I've calmed down; I accept things more, I understand things more than I did; I have my faith which I didn't have . . . I'm more peaceful now, more accepting of life". Sylvia felt she was confident "maybe even overconfident" when she met Bill. However, during his drinking years, her self-confidence and self esteem "went to nil" and she did not feel they had come back yet. As an example, Sylvia said, "I sometimes wonder why people want to be friends with me".

Sylvia was still attending Al-Anon meetings because she felt it was a programme for life and not just to get you through the alcoholic times and "of course it's good to be able to help others who come". However, she had recently felt very upset at hearing so many horror stories there. She went to see a counsellor who advised her to stop attending, saying that part of her life was over and attending the meetings only raked up memories which unsettled her. Sylvia thought she probably would stop going to Al-Anon.

Sylvia had met someone and, after meeting up a few times, told him that she attended Al-Anon meetings. He was an ex-alcoholic and Sylvia found it strange that many people at Al-Anon go on to have a second relationship with a problem drinker. She read in a book from Al-Anon about "excited misery", that is, "an alcoholic has such a personality that he excites you, but you live in misery all the time. If you're used to this, anything else is boring". Although Sylvia could understand this idea, she did not feel this was true for her saying, "It's different if you've suffered violence". She was still seeing the same man and found that his past experience meant that he understood her.

Regarding her attitudes to marriage now, Sylvia said, "I think there is an ideal marriage which I wish I was able to have, where two people have grown older together; had their faith together". Sylvia agreed with the saying, "The couple that prays together stays together". She felt that "the best sort of marriage is where the husband and wife have God as their higher partner, and where they pray to him and welcome other people in their house". Sylvia had seen this sort of marriage but only in one or two couples and wished she had been able to emulate it. However, Sylvia did not feel she had been "strong-minded enough . . . to have a dream and follow it and not get swayed this way and that".

She would not give advice to anyone currently in the situation she had been in, because everyone is different. She said often the love women have for their husbands means they could not conceive of divorcing them.

Her hopes for the future were that she would be able to manage to her "dying day". Her main worry was that her money would not last. She thought perhaps she should marry again but could not be bothered to do all the necessary things to meet someone, "perhaps I should stir my stumps". Sylvia did not think a lot about the future: "I live from day to day'. She hoped her children would not go downhill like their father and said, 'I wish them all the best".

# CHAPTER 7

# Emily: Both partners in the couple have problems

Emily was in her early forties when interviewed, and married to a problem drinker. At the time of interview she and her husband, Paul, were having a year's trial separation and living apart.

## Emily's background and early years

Emily grew up surrounded by a large extended family. She lived with her parents and two younger siblings. All her grandparents lived close by. Her father was an only child and had been brought up by his mother and grand-mother. Emily felt she was very much like her paternal grandmother and described her as the most important person in her life. She was the first person, apart from her own parents, who made her feel special and loved. Emily thought that one of the reasons for this was that she was the first grandchild. She thought her brother and sister were jealous of her relation-ship with their grandmother.

When Emily got engaged to Paul, her grandmother told her she was mak-ing a terrible mistake in her choice of partner. Emily, however, doubted she would ever meet someone her grandmother would feel was right for her. In retrospect, Emily thought she had misjudged her grandmother who was being instinctive, as she had married a drinker and so had Emily's mother. Some years after Emily and Paul were married, and he had looked after Emily while she was in hospital, Emily's grandmother wrote to him telling him she had been mistaken in her opinion of him.

Emily's parents and maternal grandparents lived across the road from each other. Her own father shared a business with his father-in-law which was not successful. They constantly argued about techniques as his father-in-law was very traditional in his approach, whereas Emily's father had been to college and wanted to use more modern methods. Her father blamed his father-in-law for the business failing. However, it was also true that her father lacked the motivation to make the business work, knowing that his mother would bale him out if things went wrong. After the business ended Emily's father worked in a factory, in spite of the fact that there was money around in the family. He felt it was better than working for his father-in-law and it maintained his self-respect. Emily thought her father had been traumatised by going straight from school into the Services during the war, and never had a chance to do anything with his life afterwards.

Emily's father was a heavy drinker all of his life although he argued he was not an alcoholic as he could go a day without drinking. Emily was aware that her father had alcohol problems when she was very young because he used to become inebriated and unable to do anything every Christmas. He drank mainly at the pub and Emily described his drinking as 'an escape from responsibility to conviviality'.

In the past Emily had blamed her mother for making life at home so unpleasant that her father wanted to escape from the house, but changed her opinion as she grew older. She subsequently felt her mother condoned the drinking because it meant that she had a quiet life when her husband was out at the pub. Emily came to feel that her father's wartime experiences accounted for much of his attitude and behaviour, and her mother may have condoned some of his worst excesses because she was aware of his traumas during the war.

Her father had died from a heart attack a year before the interview. Emily's mother said that he had not really wanted to carry on living as he was tired and fed up. Since his death, Emily's mother would not hear a word against him. Her mother said she could only remember "the good side, the fun times". Emily, on the other hand, said she had "trouble remembering Dad in a good light" and could "only remember the awful side".

Emily's paternal grandmother left money in trust for Emily and her siblings. She felt this was because her grandmother thought Emily's father would otherwise drink the money away. Emily's mother was certain that money from her mother-in-law enabled her husband to drink, and she did not like giving money to Emily and her husband as she felt the pattern would repeat.

On the whole, Emily was happy as a child and enjoyed having her grandparents close by. From the age of 10 Emily had attended a smart boarding school and although she hated it, she had always known she would be going and accepted it. She felt, however, that she had missed out on part of her adolescence by being away. She was laughed at for the broad country accent she had picked up at primary school. Her parents always put on a good show when she and her siblings came home for the school holidays, with lots of outings and treats. This felt artificial to Emily and she thought her mother was covering up difficulties in her marriage and also that she felt quite guilty about sending the children away to school. When Emily was 14 she was asked to leave because she did not have high enough academic ability. Looking back, she knew this was an excuse made by the school in order to get out of a deal her grandmother had made over fees.

At the time, however, she did not understand why she was leaving nor why they gave her a party and a present. She remembered her mother showing her details of a new school in the summer holidays and a letter saying they would be delighted for Emily to start there in September. Emily felt surprised and asked, "Does this mean I am going to another school?" The situation was appalling and her mother was very upset about it, even though she had never liked Emily's old school. Emily chose to continue boarding at her new school as she felt it would be easier to study. She was again laughed at for her accent which had by now become very 'Sloaney'. Academically Emily did very well. She did not feel, however, that the reason for this was a burning ambition to prove others wrong about her abilities in the light of what had happened to her at her previous school.

Once Emily started college her mother was more open about how she felt, and Emily often found her in tears because of problems with Emily's father. Emily said that everyone in the village knew her father was a difficult man. He would become very verbally aggressive and Emily's mother spent a lot of time at her parents, escaping the household. In spite of this her mother was very formidable and could stand up to her father. Emily could not abide the awful way her father treated her mother, and she often used to "nag" him about his drinking, saying things like "Do you really need that?" As a devout Catholic, Emily's mother felt that marriage was for keeps and so she tolerated her husband's behaviour. Emily herself had always been a committed Catholic and went to church regularly. In spite of having problems with the Church and its dogma, she felt it was a great comfort.

Emily's mother was quite strict and keen that her children did well and had careers. However, Emily felt encouraged more than pressurised by this. She thought that if there had been effective contraception at the time her mother might not have had children and instead pursued a career herself. Emily's father and mother were quite affectionate but they were not a demonstrative family. Emily had more faith in the female members of the family. She felt her father was fickle with his affections and she 'wrote him off'. Emily never felt any pressure to be responsible for her siblings but she did feel resentful when they were allowed to do things she had not been.

When she was very young, Emily felt different from other children in the village where she lived because her family were relatively well off and had property. She did have one friend in the next village with whom she spent her school holidays, and they were still friends. She also had several very attractive friends during her youth who lived exciting glamorous lives which Emily always felt outside of. She was not sure why this happened, but felt it was possibly because her friends were the youngest in their families (unlike herself) and therefore had older brothers and sisters who encouraged their social life. Later, at school and college, Emily felt happiest as part of a group with several close friends, some of whom she was still in touch with. Emily had always been an independent person, which was something she had in common with her mother.

Emily's parents did not drink at home but they used to go to the pub as a family, where the children were allowed to have some alcohol "on the quiet". The landlord of the pub was a family friend and in some ways the pub was like a second home. Emily felt her parents' attitude was "we would like you to [have a drink] but the law doesn't allow it".

Emily said her sister liked gambling on fruit machines and drank quite a lot. Occasionally her sister would become nasty after drinking and make remarks about people on television. Emily said the remarks were "really offensive . . . racist and all the rest of it. But again we collude, don't we? We don't tell her to stop", although their mother would say, "Don't you think you've had enough?". Emily described her sister as being very shy and having no social life. She found it difficult to express emotion and Emily remembered her sister being miserable at school. She also suffered from a skin problem for which she would not get treatment and Emily felt perhaps she deliberately wanted to stay unattractive. Emily did not have the sort of relationship with her sister that would make it easy to talk to her about it.

Emily described her brother as having an easy-going personality and being very sociable, with numerous acquaintances but few close friends. He was not "into" relationships and only interested in having a good time. Emily felt she had little chance to get to know him when they were growing up as he went away to school when he was seven. She just remembered him as a lost little boy whom they used to take out of school for outings.

## Emily's relationships before meeting her husband

Before meeting her husband, Emily had two "serious boyfriends". She met her first serious boyfriend at college when there were just four women on her course. Emily felt she was lucky to have been so naive in this environment because it stopped people taking advantage of her. This was Emily's first love and she thought she fell in love with him because he fell in love with her. They had similar backgrounds and Emily said there was a spark between them.

They were very happy during their first year together and Emily got to know his family well. His mother thought Emily was "wonderful" and was delighted when they got engaged. Emily's own parents were horrified, saying they were far too young. However, as soon as they got engaged things started to go wrong. Initially they had behaved like 14-year olds, which Emily felt she had really needed. Her boyfriend also helped her get through her exams and without him she might not have passed. In the end she thought they just "grew up and out of each other". She also talked about her break-up with this boyfriend as a tragedy, because she had alienated many friends due to the intensity of the relationship. Emily had not had such an intense relationship since and still felt a slight twinge every time she saw him.

Her second serious relationship petered out at the end of college when they went their separate ways. Emily thought this was a shame because they had a lot in common. There was never any question of marriage because at the time this boyfriend considered himself to be a free thinker. He introduced Emily to soft drugs, which had no effect on her because she was not a smoker and did not inhale.

Emily had other casual relationships before she got involved with her future husband, but nothing serious. She had an unsatisfactory relationship with a colleague at work which started because they were both lonely. She also had an unsatisfactory affair with a driving instructor about whom she knew absolutely nothing, but did not care because she was getting free driving lessons. She was really using him and thinks he may have been married.

## Meeting and getting to know her husband

Emily met Paul when she was looking for somewhere to live and heard he was looking for two people to share a house with. They met up in a pub at lunch time to discuss sharing and Emily remembered thinking he was a "bit of a poser", as he arrived with his coat draped over his shoulders. At first Emily could not abide him because she found him "really smooth and too clever by half". However, the house was ideal and she moved in to share with him and another woman.

Emily used to go out to the pub in the evenings, particularly on a Friday night, and sometimes Paul would be part of the group she went out with. During the time they shared a house he had a girlfriend for a short time and Emily had boyfriends. One New Year he asked Emily to go to his parents with him and she thought this was partly to reciprocate for the times he had been to her parents. He kissed her when they were at a party and Emily realised she had quite enjoyed it. After returning from his parents, he asked Emily out for a meal and that was the start of their relationship. At this time Emily was quite lonely as she had not had any satisfactory relationships since leaving college, so she was beginning to feel she would like a steady boyfriend.

Two weeks after they went for a meal together, Paul asked her to marry him. He told her he had always fancied her. She thought he was attracted to her partly because she was slightly different and he liked her background. Emily also felt that he probably thought he would not meet anyone else like her. Because Emily was certain no one else would propose to her, she agreed to marry him. Her mother was very surprised as Emily had previously told her he was awful. He was different from Emily's other boyfriends, in that he was not so romantic but more pragmatic, although she said he could be romantic when he was in the mood. Emily felt comfortable with him, but there was not the same spark as there had been with her first serious boyfriend and, to a lesser extent, her second. Emily thought the spark was there for Paul, but her feelings for him were more slow burning and came on by surprise. She said she was attracted by the time and place and felt pleasantly surprised that he loved her. They got married a year later and had an enormous wedding, which they had both wanted. Emily enjoyed the wedding and felt it went far too quickly.

Paul's father was illegitimate and lived in an orphanage until the age of five when he was adopted by his mother, posing as his aunt. He worked very long hours, in his mother's business. Emily felt this absence led to the household being dominated by his mother and sister. Paul's mother fussed over him and he was always the centre of attention at home. In spite of the family business, they were not well off and had a male lodger to bring in extra money. Paul was very bright and won a scholarship to school although he did not go to university. He always felt like a misfit and Emily said he grew up feeling inferior.

Paul had always been a bit of a loner but Emily was quite accepting of this and felt they had a good relationship and communicated well. In hindsight, she thought her two other serious boyfriends were more suitable partners for her, as they were more sociable than her husband. Initially Emily and Paul would go out together but he became more and more anti-social and Emily went to many social occasions alone. At one point Paul was sent abroad by his employers and Emily's parents paid for her to go as well. Whilst Paul was working Emily went on a camping coach tour and enjoyed the best holiday she had ever had.

# Her husband's drinking and Emily's health problems

Both Emily and Paul drank heavily when they met. Emily was used to heavy drinking both from her father and from her student days, so it was not unusual. The first inkling that Paul's drinking was not purely social was when she discovered he liked drinking on his own. Emily was a heavy social drinker but Paul would binge occasionally. Emily could not remember getting drunk since she met Paul, although she had done occasionally as a student.

Emily and Paul worked for the same company. Emily did very well at work and was soon promoted, finding herself party to confidential information which she had to keep from her husband. She was "head-hunted" by another firm, and took the job because she thought it would make the situation easier. Soon after she started this job, financial problems within the company resulted in a lot of redundancies and Emily was left doing much more work. One day she became hysterical at work after being asked for some figures. She was sent home and Paul took her to their GP who gave her Valium. The Valium did not help Emily and she became very depressed and could not get out of bed. Eventually, after a psychiatrist visited her at home, she was admitted to hospital. Whilst in hospital she was given Largactil and spent weekdays on the ward and weekends at home. Her being in hospital was a nightmare for both Emily and Paul.

At first Emily's problems were attributed to an adverse reaction to the contraceptive pill. A psychiatrist told her she was depressed because being on the pill while married was against her Catholicism. It was suggested she would get better if she came off the pill and had a baby. However, Paul had never wanted children and Emily was feeling very confused because of the medication she was on. At the time she felt Paul not wanting a child did not bother her, but later she wondered if she had just not allowed herself to think about it.

Eventually Emily was diagnosed as having 'manic-depressive psychosis' and discharged from hospital with a prescription for Lithium. Paul was very supportive when she was in hospital, but would not let family or friends go and see her because he felt they would be horrified. Emily felt it was at this time he started drinking heavily. In fact, he subsequently told her that when she was in the psychiatric hospital he coped by drinking and would have left her if he had not done so. He also felt his career had suffered as he had taken a lot of time off work because of Emily's illness.

After Emily left hospital Paul found a job in another part of the country. He moved and began looking for a new house for them both. He found a house, but put in an offer without Emily seeing it, and they had to take out a bridging loan so that Emily could move as well. This was a very stressful time for Emily as she found the house depressing. It was very "hemmed in" with no view, and they had problems selling their old house. After a few years they moved to a new house in a nearby village where Emily has been very happy.

Emily got a temporary part-time job which she really enjoyed. When this job finished she started a new one where she had to work odd hours, which she did not enjoy. Paul felt she was becoming too stressed and she visited her GP. Emily was referred to a psychiatrist who prescribed more medication and after a couple of days she was persuaded to return to hospital, where she stayed for some weeks. When she came out she was prescribed Lithium again and also received a lot of aftercare. Emily felt that Paul was happy to have her in this situation.

Their sex life had never been very good and some years after they married, Paul said he would sleep much better if they slept apart. Emily thought he meant just for a little while but it became permanent. He could just about sleep in the same room as Emily but not in the same bed, as he did not want Emily even to cuddle him. She wondered if this was related to his childhood when his mother would tickle him as a punishment. She also thought things had started going wrong for them sexually when it was suggested that her depression would lift if she had a child. Emily did not miss the sex but she did miss the kisses and cuddles. They went to a sex therapist which did not help, as Paul would not practise the therapy outside the sessions and blamed the problem on Emily's illness. They also went to marriage guidance but her husband behaved in the same way.

Emily knew Paul was having difficulties at work because of his drinking, although he said that he needed alcohol to cope with the difficulties of work. For some time he had been coming home from work at lunchtime and having a drink. He would drink openly (about a bottle of gin and a bottle of vermouth every four days) but later became a secret drinker, which Emily found harder to cope with. His behaviour was quite bizarre: sometimes he would suddenly take off and not say where he was going or for how long.

Emily came off Lithium and began working as a consultant. She had been off medication for about a year when her father died suddenly and her mother was very ill for several months. At this time Paul's drinking and behaviour became even worse. Emily thought this might have been because he was upset, as he had been fond of her father. It might also have stirred feelings in him about his own father's death a few years previously, which he had not dealt with at the time.

The turning point was when Paul had a blackout in the car. This made Emily realise exactly what he was doing to himself and could do to other people because of his drinking. He was hospitalised and lost his driving licence. In hospital he was told the blackout was due to his drinking. Emily told him she did not want any more to do with him. She also told the doctor she would not have him home and that he must be discharged into treatment. Unfortunately there were no treatment facilities other than the local psychiatric hospital, which Emily knew from personal experience was unlikely to be conducive to her husband's recovery.

When Paul was discharged Emily told him to go to live with his mother. He said he was unable to go there because he could not drive, so Emily took him to the train station and he made his way from there. Emily, "more fool I", went and picked him up the following day and took him home. She did not know why she had made a stand and then given way. Maybe because at the time she had no support as her own mother was still very ill.

Having lost his job because of drinking, Paul started a course to learn some new skills. Emily used to get up at seven o'clock in the morning to get him to a bus so he could attend the course, and she felt he did not appreciate her doing this. After his exams he was still very tense and Emily felt it was around this time his drinking got really out of hand. About eight months later Emily broke down again and phoned the Samaritans in great distress because of Paul's behaviour, which was becoming increasingly abusive. He had always said that he disliked Emily's father's behaviour towards her mother when he had been drinking, but he himself had begun to behave in a similar way towards Emily. She became so wound up and distressed that she was unable to sleep and started to take Lithium again. This led to her leaving her husband to stay at her mother's house, although she said she "had to have a psychiatric crisis to allow myself to do so".

Whilst at her mother's, Emily spoke to Paul regularly on the phone. At one point he sounded really bad and Emily phoned the doctor, who sent a community psychiatric nurse to see him. A few weeks later he was admitted to the local psychiatric hospital for a detoxification, with the intention that he would go on to rehabilitation. A trial separation of at least a year was suggested, with a reassessment of their situation following his rehabilitation. Emily had previously been told by a psychiatrist that living with her husband was bad for her mental health and always would be.

During detoxification Paul was absolutely certain he wanted to go on to rehabilitation, but the staff said they could not arrange this straight away and so he went home. Social Services agreed to assist him with a place but they said that he should find it first and then ask for the funding. Paul said he was unable to go and look at places and never did anything about it. He has since gone off the idea. Emily was very angry about this situation and felt that if Paul's social worker had taken him to look at places then he would have gone into rehabilitation.

## How Emily felt about the relationship

Emily felt it was very tricky talking about how the medication she took might have affected her and Paul's relationship. When they first met she was competent, outgoing and dynamic. However, after her illness she became quieter and more accepting. She put up with behaviour that she would not have otherwise accepted because of the medication, which blunted her emotions. She did not feel she was very easy to live with when she came off the medication as she showed her anger more. She also felt cross that she had only been able to make a stand and break away from Paul by being ill.

During their trial separation Paul was living in the marital home and Emily with her mother. It upset Emily that he did not care about their house: "It doesn't have to be spotlessly clean, but it doesn't take much to put a few things away. It's made me realise how much I tidied around him". Their financial affairs were unsettled and Emily was still paying the mortgage. He received benefit which paid for his food and drink. Initially he had not received any benefit and they were living off what Emily's father had left her in his will. Their savings had run out and he had drunk away a lot of money. Emily's mother would bail them out in an emergency, although she did so reluctantly and they had to be desperate before she would do so. Her mother-in-law was no longer in a financial position to bail Paul out, although she had enough money for herself.

Emily felt that Paul had a strange attitude to the separation. He still telephoned her frequently and had just told her it would take longer to get his driving licence back than he initially imagined. He thought this would be bad news for Emily, but it was not because it meant she could continue having sole use of their car. Emily felt this was a sign of Paul's egocentricity in that bad news for him was bad news for everyone. She also felt he was assuming they would soon be back together and Emily would drive him around. She thought he considered the separation was just to give Emily space and not a real break. There was no evidence of a separation for Paul, because he was in the same house with the same things around him and even when Emily did live there, they had separate bedrooms and no physical contact at all. Emily felt she was losing out all the way whereas he had merely lost a bit of company for a while.

Emily felt Paul's drinking was masking an underlying depression. She wanted evidence that he had given up drinking before she could make decisions about the future. She did not know whether he was taking the Antabuse[1] he had been prescribed, and if so, she was worried about the effect on his health. She was also concerned that he had a vested interest in staying sick, as otherwise he would lose his benefits, and this was delaying him making the decision to give up drinking. He was telephoning Emily constantly to complain about his physical ailments and she felt he had got what he wanted – a hermit's existence with a bit of support when he needed it. Meanwhile, Emily was struggling while living with her mother, although overall she felt the situation was much better than it had been. In spite of being back on Lithium, Emily felt she was functioning a lot better without Paul. When they lived together she reacted to his drinking and abuse and this made things worse.

Emily's attitude to Paul's drinking had changed over time. She said that she was a hopeless judge of whether people had been drinking or not, but also felt that she used to block out or deny things because she did not want to know about them. She used to ignore his behaviour even when he was doing totally unacceptable things like urinating in the corner of the room. Even when she was not on Lithium Emily ignored this kind of behaviour because Paul denied it had happened. There would be a stain on the carpet and at the time he would be totally apologetic but the next morning he would refuse to talk about it, so Emily kept quiet.

When Paul went for detoxification Emily thought things would get better. Then he started drinking again almost straight away and went back for another detoxification. Emily was totally confused by this because all the literature she had read said that as soon as someone admitted they had a problem you were going to win. She was extremely disappointed and wondered what was the point of offering a four-week detoxification which does not work. They were also offered couple counselling, which was cut after two sessions, and Paul had art therapy which helped him but was also stopped. Emily wrote lots of letters to try and get more help but Paul did nothing. She felt the service was not empathic. No account was taken of the fact that she had previously been on the same psychiatric ward which Paul was placed on, and no-one wanted to know about the feelings this brought up for her. No one wanted to listen when she tried to discuss this and

Emily said that if she had not been on Lithium she might have made more of a fuss.

Emily felt the Church had largely influenced her to stay with Paul. She thought a combination of Lithium and guilt, induced by the Church, made her accepting of her situation: "This is a cross you have to bear; you've made your bed and you have to lie on it". Emily also felt that her pattern of responding to people who love her stemmed back to her relationship with her paternal grandmother. In spite of their difficulties, Emily felt her marriage to Paul and the knowledge of his love gave her a feeling of security. The security came from being in the role of a married woman; for example, it meant she could talk to other men with impunity. The idea of becoming a single person was devastating for Emily and so she found it difficult to contemplate a change in her relationship.

# *Note*

1. Antabuse is a drug used in the treatment of drinking problems which acts as a deterrent to further drinking by producing an adverse reaction when alcohol is consumed.

# CHAPTER 8

# May: "The wrong sort of man"

May was in her late fifties and living with one of her two children from her first marriage when she was interviewed. One of her children had a drink problem in the past but had stopped drinking several years before. Her first husband had a drink problem for the best part of their marriage. Within a month of marrying her second husband, Henry, she had to get a court order against him because of his violence. Whilst with Henry, May had a serious accident which left her "disabled and handicapped" and unable to continue with a career she very much enjoyed. She said "what makes it worse is that outwardly you look all right; inwardly you are in constant pain".

## May's background and early years

May described her father as "a bad tempered, evil man", with no social graces and "quite boorish". She said he was "emotionally dead" and incapable of getting concerned about anyone but himself. May did not remember him showing any sadness or regret when her mother died, although she added "to be fair to him, it might be to do with the war, when they didn't let their feelings show". She could only recall one occasion when he showed any sensitivity towards her as a child. She tried to "tolerate" her father, but did not enjoy "being in his presence".

As a child May lacked both material things and affection. She could not remember being hugged, kissed or the word 'love' being used. When the Second World War started May and her only sibling, a younger brother, went to live with May's paternal grandparents for six months, which she thought was "magic". She loved being away from her "dictatorial father" and not being screamed at and beaten by him. She did not recall ever being deliberately naughty, but was "always getting into trouble". She thought her father knew best and that it was just the way the world was. However, she also wondered if she should tell someone because her father really did hurt her. Her mother never intervened to prevent her father hitting her. May did not remember her father hitting her mother, although he was verbally abusive to her and May recalled her mother "cowering in a corner" and never answering back.

The family moved around a lot and May went to 10 different schools in five years, which was "unbelievably difficult". There had been no happy times for May at home and the only bright periods were visiting her grandparents once a year when she knew she would not be beaten for a while. Issues in the family were resolved by May's father making a decision and the rest of the family toeing the line. The attitude towards the children was "to be seen and not heard" and if they did speak they were told "not to be stupid".

May's mother was a tiny woman and "very timid". She died when May was in her late thirties and May "never got over it". They had been very close and May felt her mother died from the stress of living with her father. May had a recurring nightmare for many years about her mother leaving. She thought that her mother must have threatened her father that she would leave. Her mother was very concerned that May only associated with "people of our class". May was under enormous pressure to get to grammar school and this was "not a happy time" for her. She was expected to do well, but was also being beaten at home and could not tell anyone because she thought nobody would believe her.

May's parents were Quakers and the family often encountered suspicion from others because of this. May described herself as a "birthright Quaker" and said her upbringing "had its stamp". She did not practise her religion but occasionally went to the Meeting House. Her parents were anti-alcohol and would not have it in the house, and May said she was "not very with it" with respect to alcohol. She always thought her parents' attitude (that drink should be avoided because it caused all sorts of problems) was "narrow-minded", and she could not understand why they could not drink and enjoy life without it being out of control.

As children, May and her brother were very close. He was a fragile child and was not beaten as May was. As adults, May said, he "doesn't approve of me", although she did not know what he meant by this. He refused when May once turned to him for help, saying it was about time she "got herself together".

May's father hit her until she was with her first husband and even recently her children had told their grandfather not to treat her like a child. At the age of 14, May decided she was not going to be beaten and constantly harangued any more. She followed her own interests and did an apprenticeship, which meant working in another part of the country for a wealthy family. May was not used to this lifestyle and was "totally without any social graces". After a week, she was "relegated" to the kitchen where she ate with the staff for the rest of her time there; this was "a salutary experience". It was a lonely time for May, although the people who worked at the house were kind to her.

During her apprenticeship, May gained some qualifications through a correspondence course and was "over the moon" to be offered a place at university. She was surprised to find that she was "not thick or stupid" and that people enjoyed her company. May only had enough money to provide the basic essentials plus her keep. She lived with her grandmother for one summer and got a job but had to stop working when she became physically very ill. She could not stay at her grandmother's because she could not manage the stairs to get to the toilet. Her father refused to come and fetch her and eventually she went to stay with her boyfriend's family for the summer. In the autumn, still unwell, she returned to college. Every week she went to the city for treatment and would go without food that day because she could not afford it.

From the time she started secondary school May had boyfriends and this annoyed her parents. Her first sexual relationship was during her time as an apprentice, with a boy who was a year older than herself, and who was "charming and good looking". She was engaged to him for about two years but broke it off when she met someone else at university.

Her new boyfriend was "tall, bluff and gruff . . . charming . . . and down to earth" and they were engaged for seven years. He was more mature than other students on the course and a bit "anti-establishment". They were "very happy times" and they had "a very intense sexual relationship". May got a "real plum job" in another part of the country and they used to meet at weekends. As students they had both drunk heavily and May remembered he would be "absolutely sky high" when he came to visit her and "used to tank it up" on a Saturday evening. In spite of this, May described him as "extremely well balanced . . . reliable . . .a good shoulder to lean on". Their relationship developed slowly from friendship into a love affair, and she became engaged to him.

She had not found this boyfriend boring, but her next relationship proved to be even more intense: when she met her future first husband, they fell "desperately in love" and were "on cloud seven [sic] . . . it was absolutely magic". May loved her first husband from "first sight" until a couple of years after he left her, by which time she had met her second husband.

Just after May's first husband left her, her ex-fiancé (who she had been engaged to before meeting her first husband), contacted her "out of the blue" saying he had a feeling something terrible had happened. A few months later they met up and spent a few days together. She found they were "very much in unison" and she felt that she had made a terrible mistake not marrying him. She described him as "a wonderful person" and "the love of my life".

## May's first marriage

When May met her first husband, Chris, both of them were already engaged to other people. Four weeks later they had both broken off their engagements and got engaged to each other. Four weeks after that they were married. May thought Chris was attracted to her because "I wouldn't sleep with him . . . and just that chemistry". She had been a "challenge" to him because she was successful. May said "I would do it all over again; it was magic; it was really magic for us both", although "everyone said it wouldn't last". His mother was "dead against it", as she knew he had a severe drink problem.

May was attracted to Chris because "he was very tall, over six feet; very striking, he had a lovely head of hair; he was ex-public school, very charming, very well-bred with nice manners". They had a common link through their work and he had an interesting circle of friends. He was also "kind and considerate" and concerned about May and she said this was a new experience for her.

When May met Chris she was independent and "very self-reliant". She had been away from home for 10 years and developed her career which was her "main ambition". Although she wanted to marry and have a family, May saw herself as working throughout her life and was not keen on being at home, as the kitchen "was the last place" she wanted to be. When first married, they had little money and few belongings. Chris came into the marriage with lots of debts and May soon realised that his wages never came into the household.

During their early years together May and Chris shared hobbies, had an interesting social life and "lived it up". They visited family regularly: "A lot of time and energy was consumed in this way; we did give a lot to the family". May "never took a lot of notice of what he drank" and she "drank heavily too". Chris started drinking at the age of 14 when his parents divorced. This had been a traumatic experience for him. His father, who was a cruel man, won custody and his mother was never there for him. May felt he was basically "drowning his sorrows". When they were first together he might drink between four and six pints of beer in an evening ("everyone did") and then drive "and nobody thought anything of it". May never saw him drunk. She said: "the true alcoholic is so permanently tanked-up that their system seems to adjust to it and you never see them drunk . . . a sober drunk". May said this made it difficult for people to understand he had a drink problem because outwardly it was not apparent.

She was "very much in love" with Chris, but he began seeing other women, which May found "so hurtful and unbearable". She thought about leaving him and planned to get some further career qualifications before she did. May thought he must have realised her plan because she became pregnant with her first child and this pregnancy was unplanned. They moved into a house and May had to give up her job once she had the baby.

Chris had an affair with a friend of hers who became pregnant, and when May found out she was "horrified, I was so ashamed that he should have been so unfaithful". This was proof of his womanising that she could not ignore: "You cover up, lie, you do anything to hide what life is really like".

May felt she was being punished for thinking about leaving him so she did not think about doing it again. She felt "trapped" into staying because she had the children, no money and nowhere to go.

Around this time Chris was charged with a sexual offence. His solicitor's suggested defence was for May to say that she had refused to have sex with him and threatened to leave him, although neither of these things were true. She thought it would help him: "I was loyal beyond compare; I idolised him; it didn't matter what he did . . . it's incredible what you will do, looking back on it".

May began to feel she "couldn't cope with this man who did everything to hurt me". Chris was working but spent most of his day in the pub. In the evening he might set off for home, but not get there and go instead to a nearby city purportedly to meet customers, where he would carry on drinking, sometimes with other women. He would either phone May repeatedly through the night or not phone at all. She spent "the entire night waiting for him to come home" and when he did he would be "seething with hate" for her. On Sundays he would sleep all morning and go to the pub at lunchtime. The only time the family spent together was on a Sunday afternoon when he would go looking for pubs that were unofficially open. Sometimes on these trips out, he would stop the car in the middle of nowhere, take the key and leave May and the baby sitting in the car until he returned a couple of hours later. All May wanted was for him to come back, "then I'd be safe", and get home. Yet she was also afraid that when they did get home he would not stay there. When he came back to the car she did not say anything, otherwise he would do it again.

May "never refused" sex with Chris; there was "no point" and she said they had "a natural, normal sexual relationship". In spite of his womanising she was "so thrilled that he turned to me". She never refused because, like waiting for him to come home, "as long as he was there, he couldn't be doing anything else". She was "so afraid" of being on her own: "You don't think straight, you don't make logical decisions; you will cope as long as he's there, you are safe as long as he's there". May put up with all sorts of things in exchange for the little bit of time he spent with her. Divorce was unheard of and she thought divorcing him "would crucify him . . . you are constantly thinking of the other person and not of yourself".

They were desperately short of money and if May wanted some she would have to go to the pub and "shame" Chris in front of others into giving it to her. The pressure she was under was "chronic", she said: "You get very involved in what they do . . . coming home at lunchtime to cook their lunch, thinking that if you do not, they will start drinking; and invariably he would never turn up". Few people knew of May's problems: "I couldn't get anyone to believe me" and it was not always helpful when people did know. For example, if May was ill, doctors would say, "oh well, you live in a very stressful situation; you have a husband who drinks heavily" and would not take her health complaints or emotional state seriously.

Having continually been told by her father, "you are naughty and difficult", May thought that perhaps the problems were her fault. Her father would "openly" say, "I'm not surprised" and that May would "drive anyone to drink". She said "you carry that guilt with you". She used to wonder why Chris did not want to be with her ("why doesn't he want to be at home?"). She believed his "cover" that he was seeing customers, and when he returned from an evening out she did not speak to him or he would smash things up. She did not sulk as she was "so thankful he'd come back" and "so relieved" that he was not hurt and there were no signs of the police, or fighting, or other women. May never got angry because, as she said, "I'm not an angry person"; instead she "got frightened and lonely", although she also thought, "there must be something, he's come back to me".

Seven years after marrying, May became very ill and nearly died: "I didn't know which day it was". Her neighbour gave up work to look after May's baby and May was alone for most of the day and night. Being ill was "an absolute nightmare; I should never have been left like that; I don't think people realised how serious it was". It was "dreadful, so cruel . . . my baby was next door". People assumed that Chris was with her during the night and she did not tell them he was not.

Her whole life was "spent waiting for him to come home". Occasionally, Chris surprised May and stayed home, "and you would wait for those magic moments". His behaviour was a repeat performance of her father's, although Chris "never raised his hand against me", in spite of being violent and aggressive with other people. However, he did rape May when he was drunk and this was when she conceived her second child. The night the baby was born he was out drinking and May delivered the baby herself at home.

As May talked about Chris's behaviour she said, "I'm not exaggerating, it's the truth, but when you live with this, you are trapped". She could not work because of the children and had no family nearby. Her friends "avoided" her because "they couldn't work out what was going on". Chris would be "obnoxious" to them and they would go and as a result, May "ended up lonely". The only people with whom he behaved himself were their parents, so it looked as if May was telling tales when she tried to talk to them about what was going on. May "didn't know which way to turn" and in those days it was "totally different" as there was little information available about where to go for help.

Before May had her children, Chris "wouldn't let me out of his sight", but after they were born, he felt he could do what he liked and "be single again". May was "desperately tired" as her babies did not sleep for the first two years: "They were both traumatised although I didn't know it". On top of this, "the man you absolutely adore won't stop drinking, and you know he's sleeping with other women and yet your sexual relationship together is fine". It got to the stage where Chris could not hold down a job. He flew into towering rages and would "shriek and scream, bang the wall, break his fingers; things would get smashed . . . all this was masked by the feeling that I adored him; there was nothing I could do because I loved him". Sometimes, May felt hopeful because he stopped drinking for a while and would be "very loving, caring, supporting and charming".

On occasions May had said to Chris, "I've had enough; I'm not going on like this with you drinking all the money". He would deny drink was affecting the family, saying, "You have got your house, your baby, your garden; you love me; we go and visit the parents each weekend". He was in "an alcoholic haze" and did not realise until after he stopped drinking what he had done.

Chris tried to commit suicide several times, but May felt she could not tell the doctor because he would go to prison, as this was still an offence at the time. He would deny the frequency of his suicide attempts, as he did not remember: "They get to a stage when they black out". May thought these attempts were because he did not like what he was doing but could not stop. Chris attempted suicide after it was no longer an offence and for the first time May telephoned the Samaritans. He agreed to go into a psychiatric hospital voluntarily. He was in "a dreadful state" and May and the children visited him every day. It was a long journey by bus with a two mile walk and May was doing three part-time jobs at this stage, as well as trying to sort out Chris's business accounts. The doctors said that Chris was an alcoholic, and "then it began to make sense". May had "wondered vaguely" if this was the case but it was less openly known about in those days. Her understanding of Chris being an alcoholic as opposed to a heavy drinker, was that "his life [was] taken over by alcohol . . . it goes from social to heavy to beyond the barrier where they can't do without a drink, can't survive without a drink, they're addicted to it".

After leaving hospital he did not drink and his recovery was extremely stressful for both of them. They avoided socialising, and Alcoholics Anonymous became an important part of their life. May felt that Chris transferred going out drinking and womanising to going to AA meetings. AA people would often be at their house and the telephone never stopped ringing with people wanting help. May resented the amount of time that Chris was away and the intrusion on their life. She was working full-time and the children did not really understand what was happening with their father. He was physically unwell but would not take medication because people in AA were worried about substituting tablets for alcohol. May recalled thinking "this is just as bad" as when Chris was drinking. She felt he had his priorities wrong and this made her angry and caused a rift between them.

May described Chris's sobriety as an enormous achievement and respected him for it. He had told her that he could not have done it without her support and the support of AA. Although for a long time May was very anti-AA, she later became convinced that if someone wanted to stop drinking, AA was a wonderful support. She thought that going to Al-Anon meetings was helpful for partners, although she found it very difficult to go as it could be hard being forced to face the reality of the situation.

When Chris was drinking, May had to take charge of the family. "The theory goes that when he sobered up he didn't like the reality of me being in charge and he didn't like or love me". Nearly 25 years after they married, May got "the shock of my life" when he said "I'm going, I'm never coming back". For a month she did not know where he was. She was "devastated . . . I'd done so much for him and I wouldn't have put up with all that I did if I knew he was going to leave". May felt a lot of what had happened to her was "unbelievable" and thought if her story had happened to anyone else she would wonder why they stayed in that relationship for so long.

Chris subsequently told her that he fell out of love with her 10 years before leaving but stayed so he would not have to pay maintenance for the children. For the last year of their marriage they had no sexual relationship although May wanted to. He would be "too tired" and because they both led busy lives, May did not see this as any kind of warning sign. At the time he left, May felt they were just coming out of the tunnel and she had no idea he had stopped loving her.

Throughout her life, May's main support came from friends and from her child who had had a drink problem. She had little support from her family. When Chris left her, and she told her family the whole story, "I opened the can of worms". They "didn't console" her and their attitude was: "You have another 25 years to do something with your life". May's religion kept her going now and again, but because of all that had happened to her she was not actively religious. She felt that "him upstairs has forgotten I exist" and added, "I do find it very difficult that I should have had to go through all this and I haven't done anything wrong. I feel I've had more than my fair share".

## May's second marriage

When May met her second husband, Henry, getting involved with him "never occurred" to her as she was too busy "extracting" herself from her first marriage. Henry was attractive and "had a Peter Pan look about him". He was well dressed but had "no social graces whatsoever". They met at a divorce experience group and he asked her to go for a drink after the first meeting. They talked about how terribly hurt they had both been and how they did not want to be hurt again.

Henry had two small children from his second marriage and his ex-wife had an injunction against him. He told May he only once hit his ex-wife when she "wound him up" on purpose, in order to have grounds for the injunction. Within a week of their meeting, he asked May if she would drive him to fetch his daughters for his access visit. This became a regular event and May loved having his children at her house along with her own children: "It filled my Saturday . . . it was a family; it was wonderful, we became a family again". May found she was able to relive her own children's childhood again, but this time with money. She felt, "my goodness, aren't I lucky" and this feeling continued for some months.

Although he was very loving, caring, generous and supportive, Henry was also "very secretive . . . everything connected with him was very secretive". She did not attach any great significance to this, thinking that he was under stress because of his divorce and his work. At this time there was "a very strong bond" between them, and on the whole May did not feel there was anything wrong. Neither of her children were too sure about him, but they were coping with their own grief, their jobs and with May who was absolutely shattered. She also noticed he was "very sexually orientated" and felt that there was "something the matter with him sexually . . . he was a sexaholic". He would make sexual comments about other women, sometimes within hearing distance of the women, although with May he was "extremely loving and caring sexually".

A few months after meeting Henry things started to go wrong. As she was reading a letter he had given her to look at, he came up behind her and started to strangle her, saying he did not want her to read it. From then on, there would be "little fizzes" which developed into "frenzies". He would "scream and shout" if he was "prevented from doing what he wanted to do". The neighbours complained about his "foul language, and it was very foul, lewd, obscene". He attacked May at her home when his children were there, but "did his schizophrenic flip" and was very nice when they took the children home. After this incident access was stopped and the children never visited him again.

Once Henry got a divorce from his previous marriage, he began to battle with May as if he had "always got to be at war". He continued to be violent and would be in "a towering rage" if he was displeased. On holiday he "screamed" at her as she drove them around and May felt like "a wobbling jelly". When they returned to their hotel May felt ill but he wanted her to drink with him. He attacked May because she was not doing as he wanted and she fell. There was a crack "like a pistol shot" and she could not move. May was in hospital for three months and he spent most of his days drinking, neither remorseful or caring. He visited the hospital for food and even though May was so ill, "most days" he "would insist on oral sex".

When they got back to May's home, Henry left May on her own, "totally paralysed", complaining that her house was too untidy. He reappeared a couple of days later and carried on "as if nothing had happened". Although the atmosphere on their holiday had been really unpleasant, he had proposed to May and it was "a magic moment . . . when they are nice; they are nicer than the average person, and you hope it will stay like that". She said: "You think that if he can be nice you hope he can stay nice, and that if he loves me, he'll love me enough to be nice all the time".

As Henry had been trying to persuade her to marry him for three years, she thought that he would stop being frustrated and violent if she did. She also thought that his "bout" drinking, which he said he did from despair when he was not in control of events, would stop. However, he also threatened that if she did not marry him, then she would go into prison. He said she was lying about her health problems and was not entitled to the benefits she received. May believed Henry because he "brainwashed" her. She was "very much in love" with him "and I still am". During their "so-called honeymoon" he was "dead drunk all the time". He was "frightened" about being an alcoholic, but would also get annoyed with May when she would not drink with him.

The violence continued, and after another particularly nasty incident when May felt Henry was going to kill her, she saw a doctor and a solicitor who was "absolutely appalled" and advised her to take out an injunction against him. May would not do this, but not long afterwards, Henry attacked her again in a hospital waiting room and her friend telephoned the solicitor who arranged an immediate injunction. Later, a further injunction was ordered, but May agreed to telephone contact being opened. She asked Henry to drive her to a university reunion and he was "thrilled to bits". They stayed the weekend in a hotel where he attacked her and broke her fingers. May felt she could not go home and they stayed in the hotel for five days, where he constantly told May, "don't leave me; I love you more than life".

After this incident, May did not have contact with Henry for about 18 months although he wrote to her every month begging her to go back. She got a divorce but he wrote and asked if they could try again. A friend of May's who read the letter thought he sounded genuine and arranged a meeting. At that meeting Henry said that he was devastated by the divorce and had never wanted one. About a year after this he telephoned May in distress and she visited him and his new partner. He and May talked about getting back together, but the next day his new partner telephoned May to say that he was staying with her. May was "so angry" and stopped a cheque she had given him to pay a bill.

May had not got over Henry even though she had "no choice" but to end the relationship. Recently he had visited her and told her that since he had been in therapy he had learnt he could get what he wanted without violence. He told May he loved her, was very sorry and realised he had made "several dreadful mistakes". He also said he missed the sexual attraction between them, which May described as "an obsession", and she felt he was being honest about this and "still loves me dearly".

When May was still married to Henry she "got the opportunity to help start a group for women in violent situations", which she attended for a couple of years. May then started one-to-one therapy because she "couldn't unhook herself from him" and she knew she was "floundering and had to get help" to get rid of this "longing to be with him". She had become less afraid of succumbing to him again, because she felt herself slowly drawing away and could walk away from meeting him without crying. He wanted to be friends but she told him this could only happen if his current partner knew what was going on.

# What May felt about her experiences

All the men May had been involved with had drinking problems. After leaving Henry, May had another relationship with a man who was "a nice, placid, calm, caring man" but also "a liar" who "drank enormously". He was dirty and would not do anything about his personal hygiene. May did not love him but "used" him to try to "unhook" herself from Henry. Eventually, he got fed up with May's continued involvement with Henry. May did not feel life with her most recent boyfriend was for her, and would have ended the relationship anyway when she met someone else.

Although May did not agree with her parents' anti-alcohol attitude, she did agree alcohol can cause all sorts of problems. "It's strange that my whole life has been ruined by men who drink too much". However, May added she would "do it all again" although "it's taken its toll, especially on my health". The drinking of the men May was involved with neither increased nor decreased their attractiveness to her. Her second fiancé, second husband and most recent boyfriend had all been "magic" to be with and "idolised" her, which did her ego good: "you can walk on air for a time".

May did not think that she put up with Chris's behaviour because that was what she expected of marriage from her parents' experience. However, she did think that the enormous fear she had of being alone and abandoned stemmed from her relationship with Chris, and not from nightmares about her mother leaving or events in her childhood. May still worried about this and recently had "a terrible, terrible panic" when she felt there was no way she could stay on her own, which she described as "overwhelming depression and fear".

When she and Chris were married, May was afraid to challenge him because she thought that he would leave her and she was "an absolute stickler for my marriage vows . . . I had to stick in it no matter what happened". May felt "a hundred per cent loyalty" to her first husband and that it was "essential to keep the family together". When his drinking was at its worst, May said she "almost felt I was being punished for thinking of getting out of the marriage before the children were born" and this reinforced her feelings of having to stay with him.

A therapist had given May the book *Women Who Love Too Much*, and May said "that's me to a T . . . knowing that what he did, no matter what he did, I still adored that man. I never wanted him to go and I still would be there". She also felt that she had done so much for Chris that it was "unbelievable someone could be so cruel".

When May met Henry, she was "very vulnerable" after "being deserted after 25 years" and she was "desperately lonely". Because of the loneliness, "anyone who shows any kindness in any degree is better than nothing" and being with him got rid of "the terrible loneliness and the unbelievable fear" she felt. He was "charming and good looking" and to have "a toy boy" made May feel good: "you go out looking a million dollars". He told her no-one would ever love her like he did and May said, "you believe it because you are so insecure".

In spite of having doubts about Henry, even on their wedding day, May felt that she had "got to go through with it" because she did not want to be on her own. She never hated him: "That's the Quaker upbringing . . . I don't hate; I very rarely get angry . . . I am not a naturally angry person". She believed there was good in everybody and you should always forgive and bless those who have hurt you. May felt she could bless the men in her life: Chris for giving her two children; Henry for bringing her alive; her most recent boyfriend for his support; and her second fiancé because he was wonderful company. Henry had caused a lot of problems in her life but she felt this was because he wanted her completely for himself even if this meant injuring or killing her.

May had read a book about men who hate women and women who love these men. It described 'the hooks' that keep women in abusive relationships: the 'love hook'; the 'sexual hook' (i.e. the fear of not having a sexual relationship if you leave the one you are in); and the 'money hook'. May said she would add "the personality hook" to these and that although they applied in her relationship with Chris, he was not at all like the men described in the book whereas Henry was.

Although May was against divorce and thought it heinous, she had to admit there were times when there was no alternative. She would not get married again unless it was someone very special without a drink problem: "I have a habit of attracting the wrong sort of man".

# The Theoretical Perspectives

# CHAPTER 9

# A codependency perspective

## Liz Cutland

## A historical view

Having worked with codependent people for a number of years, my task is to interpret the six biographies of these women from that perspective.

I believe it is important to discuss how the term 'codependence' came about. The method of treatment that I represent is what has become known in the United Kingdom as the 'Minnesota' or 'Twelve Step' method of treatment. (The Twelve Steps of AA are published in the book *Alcoholics Anonymous*, 1967.) The first British treatment centre of this kind was founded in 1974 and modelled on Hazelden, a very successful centre in Minnesota in the United States developed to help alcoholics, other addicts and their families. Several other similar treatment centres sprang up and continue to treat large numbers of people who suffer from alcoholism (Spicer, 1994; Williams, 1995). This has happened despite the current trend in the helping professions to shy away from using the word 'alcoholic'. It baffles me that it is seen as politically incorrect to describe someone as having the illness of alcoholism. I mention this because I believe that the woolliness of terms like 'problem drinker' helps society avoid the seriousness of this problem and causes all sorts of confusion to the relatives of alcoholics. The effects of alcoholism on families (adults and children) is devastating and often ignored by the caring professions.

I cannot continue this overview without defining what I mean by alcoholism because that is what every one of these women in the six biographies has been living with. I have no doubt about that, despite the opinion of some of the professionals involved (e.g. in Lisa's case history in Chapter 4, her husband saw a psychiatrist who said that his problem was only habitual and was therefore "not a major problem").

In my view alcoholism is an illness; it is a progressive disease which gets worse and very often ends in death unless it is arrested (Jellinek, 1960). An alcoholic person no longer chooses how much he[1] drinks. If he does choose to drink (or take other addictive chemicals ) he cannot predict what will be the outcome. Sometimes he may appear to control the amount but at other times he ends up drinking much more than he originally intended. When he does that he loses control of his behaviour. Alcoholism is an addiction: it is an overwhelming compulsion to drink. The alcoholic is no longer in control of his drinking; it is in control of him. Fortunately, it is a treatable illness and many of those who find the right kind of treatment can have this illness arrested. Recovery starts with total abstinence from alcohol. Further information on the disease syndrome can be found in Blum (1991).

As self-help groups like Alcoholics Anonymous and Al-Anon grew, as the treatment centres which enveloped their 12-step programme developed, more and more professionals in this field began to be aware that some of the spouses of alcoholics exhibited similar symptoms. (Most of these treatment facilities involve the family in the recovery programme.) The relatives may not have been drinking like their partner but often their behaviour was similar. It is well known that someone who is alcoholic is obsessed by alcohol; he gives a huge amount of his time and energy fantasising about imbibing, planning his next drink, worrying about not being able to get it. Some wives (and husbands) can be as preoccupied by the alcoholic as he is by alcohol. Concerned persons can become obsessed by him, entering into a power game where no-one wins, where each person plays out a role, trying in vain to control the alcoholic's drinking. This pattern, with slight deviations, repeats itself across the board of a very large cross-section of families with an out-of-control drinker. Very often the extent of the wife's dependence on her husband needing her does not show until he achieves a period of time in recovery. Many are shocked to find themselves trying to sabotage what they have hoped and prayed for, for years: their husband's sobriety and health. Some others move on to seek another alcoholic relationship because, at some level, that is what they know, this is what they have become dependent on. In short, some wives become addicted to their alcoholic partner. The term that has evolved to describe this condition is codependence. The meaning of this word has grown to describe an addiction to any kind of destructive relationship, although it originated in the alcoholism field.

Not everyone who marries or lives with an alcoholic is codependent. Some don't see they have choices; others know that they have some options but are frightened to make the change. The most typically codependent person in the biographies is May (Chapter 8). She had a horrific life with several abusive relationships. In describing her first marriage, which seems to have been extremely painful, she said that her whole life was "spent waiting for him to come home". Occasionally, Chris surprised May and stayed home "and you would wait for those magic moments". That is addiction: the pursuit (often in vain) of an elusive magic moment; the denial of the reality of extreme emotional pain, of the destructiveness – in order to continue seeking that short pleasurable time; or the feeling of absolute powerlessness in not being able to change that pattern.

I found this chapter an interesting challenge to respond to, partly because I am used to having an ongoing professional relationship with my clients. Although I work in the field from which the term codependency has evolved, I believe that I am not typical in my approach to that condition, in this country, at this time. I acknowledge that there is such a state of being. Also, the overwhelming response to books like *Women Who Love Too Much* by Robin Norwood (1986) and *Co-dependent No More* by Melodie Beattie (1987) proves that there is a huge need in our society that hungers to be addressed.

However, I choose to stand back from a lot of what is happening in the treatment of codependence at the present time. I have witnessed some dreadful harm done to some of my clients as a result of the blame or 'parent-bashing' which has been encouraged by some practitioners in this field and other approaches to the problem. Families have been split by counsellors who have, I believe, overstepped their professional remit. The early response has been a powerful rage. It needs time for this force to settle down and the energy to be channelled more creatively. That process has started and many people are starting to heal because they are taking responsibility for their own recovery.

# How did these women find themselves in this situation?

## Lack of knowledge and education about alcoholism

Alcoholism is a family disease. As well as being affected by the obsessive drinker, partners often collude in an unacknowledged 'no talking rule' and enable the alcoholic to go further into the illness. They do not discuss the drinking because that would 'rock the boat' and often the primary rule in such a family is 'peace at any price'. "Over the ensuing months Lisa became used to her husband being violent towards her after he had been drinking. Occasionally she would hit him back although most of the time she was resigned to accepting the violence." The attacks often occurred for no apparent reason and Lisa would "just put up with it".

Denial is one of the main symptoms of alcoholism. Usually, the addicted drinker is blind to his problem. Denial is also the very powerful reaction of our culture to this problem. Many alcoholics die of this illness, and families suffer great stress. This happens so much because society is uninformed, shrugs its shoulders apathetically or buries its head in the sand.

What chance do the women in these biographies have against that background of poor information? Few received any kind of positive support in dealing with a partner with this disease. Most of them were struggling in the dark.

## The need to care for the self

We have been provided with a lot of information about the family of origin of each of these women. I do not intend to spend a lot of time studying this. At Farm Place, where I work, in treating codependence or alcoholism as an addiction, we spend little time considering why it has happened. While it is important to recognise patterns of relating to others established in childhood, it would be easy but not fruitful to point the finger and blame. Addiction is a no-fault illness; no one person makes it happen. The problem is a much wider social issue than can be explained away in terms of the problems in family dynamics. We believe that there are more important and more urgent questions to ask. Those are:

1. What are the destructive behavioural patterns caused by this condition (addiction or codependence)?
2. How have these patterns harmed you and your relationships with others?
3. What responsibility can you take to change your harmful patterns in relating to others?
4. How do you find some peace with yourself in this situation?

Carl Jung described alcoholism as the "spiritual thirst of our being for wholeness". This quotation came from a letter that he wrote to Bill W., one of the cofounders of Alcoholics Anonymous. Basically, what he was saying is that alcoholism is a spiritual disease; that people who become addicted to alcohol drink to feel 'normal', to feel 'good enough' as human beings. Recovery from alcoholism is much more than putting down the bottle. It requires finding a way of being at peace with oneself.

Codependence is also a spiritual disease. Robin Norwood says in *Women Who Love Too Much* "If you have ever found yourself obsessed with a man, you may have suspected that the root of that obsession was not love but fear. We who love obsessively are full of fear – fear of being alone, fear of being unlovable and unworthy, fear of being ignored or abandoned or destroyed" (1986, p. 2). Codependent people have little sense of their selves and are often attracted to alcoholics because of a powerful need to feel needed. That is what gives them a temporary feeling of completeness. The most important focus for these family members is usually the drinking alcoholic and his erratic behaviour. The more the wife becomes obsessed with the alcoholic and trying to fix him, the more she becomes caught up in a downward spiral of negativity and fear. This pattern of relating to others may have started in the family of origin. However, sometimes it originates as a way of trying to cope with the terrible chaos of living with addiction with no previous knowledge or experience.

I do not intend to make further attempts at deciding which of the women in the case studies is codependent or not. It may be interesting to know that in my 20-plus years of working with alcoholics and their families, very few of the drinkers have taken the initiative in presenting themselves for treatment for their alcoholism. It is usually the partners who have approached us first, and their assumption is that if the alcoholic is fixed all their problems are going to be over. Hidden behind the drinker, rarely do they believe that their personal problems are serious. Unless they have been receiving help from people who understand addiction, most spouses of alcoholics do not see themselves clearly. Often they lose sight of how they feel, become confused about what their responsibilities are, don't even know who they are. Before deciding if they are codependent, I think it is important to help free individuals to recognise the trap they are in (if they want to do that), to help them do what Al-Anon describes as "detaching with love". Only then can they step out from behind the alcoholic and see who they are.

## Accepting responsibility for blame

Ruth (Chapter 3) strikes me as fairly typical of someone who has found herself in the trap of an 'alcoholic family'. "She also felt very alone, isolated, angry at times, impotent, helpless, hopeless and guilty, as if she was 'responsible for the whole mess!' This feeling of responsibility stemmed from her uncertainty about being able to maintain a long-term committed relationship in the first place." Self-blame and accepting her partner's blame seems to keep Ruth hooked into a destructive relationship. "He had told Ruth that he wanted to kill her and that the children wanted to kill her. He also blamed her for ruining their sex life and said that was the reason he drank." Also, he would tell her parents "what an unpleasant person I was . . . how all I was interested in was the children. I wasn't interested in him, and I was selfish, and things like that".

Feelings of overresponsibility also kept her trapped. "Ruth mainly dealt with the problem by 'hiding it from everybody'. Sometimes she would ring work for James and say that he was ill; and she used to clear things up so others would not notice. She described it as 'a sort of conspiracy of silence' in that nobody worked openly to acknowledge his problem . . . At one stage, Ruth threw away all the home brew."

One of the sad things is that her partner did from time to time seek help, yet she herself had very little support and understanding from those professionals. "James left some information for her that he had been given at the clinic, specifically for partners to read and [she] got the impression that wives were held responsible for a lot of their husbands' drink problems . . . Ruth felt it was written by somebody who did not have much idea of what it was like for somebody who has already a very low opinion of herself."

"Ruth felt very guilty about much of what had happened and that if she had loved James more and better then he would not have needed a drink". This is the nub of the problem for many a family member: the belief that the problem is really the woman's inability to love her partner into stopping or controlling his drinking. Yet the irony is that her problem is really her inability to love herself, combined with her difficulty in coming to terms with the fact that she is powerless over his drinking. If she valued herself she would not tolerate the abusive behaviour, the blaming; she would not be trapped into waiting in vain for her partner to change so that life would get better. She would be free to choose to believe his taunts or to trust her own feelings, instincts or intuition.

May (Chapter 8) says she married her second alcoholic husband, who was violent, because she was "very vulnerable" and "desperately lonely". Because of the loneliness "anyone who shows any kindness in any degree is better than nothing . . .". He told her no-one would ever love her like he did and May said "you believe it because you are so insecure". Where is the self-love here? It seems non-existent.

Self-love begins when we start taking responsibility for ourselves. So many of the women described in this book have lost sight of themselves living with the trauma that addiction brings. It seems to me that Emily's own illness of manic depression helped protect her to some extent from her husband's alcoholism even though he justified his drinking by blaming her illness (Chapter 7). She had to move out in order to survive. Although he still attempts to hook her in I hope she cares enough about herself not to move back in with him unless he takes responsibility for his problem with alcohol and gets help. My fear for her is that she will continue to have poor professional help (if any). So many wives (and husbands) of alcoholics are left struggling on their own, blindly trying to find the answers.

## *The need to accept one's powerlessness over the alcoholic*

One of the many paradoxes that arises in living with an alcoholic is that many spouses rediscover their personal power when they accept their powerlessness over their partners' drinking. The greatest frustration for those who take on the role of caretaker is that all of their efforts to stop the drinking appear to be ineffectual. Eagerly, they keep searching for that elusive solution to the problem. Some family members really have to suffer, to hit some kind of emotional rock bottom before they can accept and admit complete powerlessness over the behaviour of the alcoholic. Sylvia (Chapter 6) finally left her husband on "a Sunday afternoon; we had just had lunch and I still had my apron on; something blew up; he couldn't find a particular piece of paper and (he said) it was my fault. He stood over me shouting and poking. It was the last straw. . . . He was very belligerent and stinking of drink".

Until a crisis like this arrives, often the efforts to control the drinking as well as the crazy actions of the addicted drinker are an attempt to install some security in the family. Instead of trying to find that comforting feeling within themselves, the wives can put all this effort into trying to get the alcoholic to change and provide the stability. Of course, he keeps rocking the boat, keeps letting them down. Obsessively they keep trying to fix him;

tidying him up, lecturing him, covering his tracks, rescuing him from the consequences of his drinking, hanging on to the omnipotent belief that they have or should have the right and the ability to change another human being. Fear stops them from yielding to their powerlessness, from standing back and letting go. To admit the truth is to feel the pain, the depression, the grief of being powerless.

## The effects of alcoholism on the children

What keeps most of these women trapped in these relationships is their concern for their children, without really understanding the effects of such a marriage on them. Ruth (Chapter 3) said that, "She had felt a strange sense of responsibility since having her children and thought they were largely the reason she had stayed with James. She imagined if she ever left she would take the children with her and she worried about how he would cope without them." It greatly saddens me that because there is so little support for families of alcoholics in this country, so many people suffer; not just the adults, the children do too.

Perhaps Dawn (Chapter 5) was the most fortunate of this group of women. She was able to get support for herself but also as a family they were able to get help. "She . . . felt that the family sessions were very helpful because they gave the children the opportunity to speak to their father about how they felt. Some of the feelings expressed were due to the frustration about his drinking, the feeling that he was not doing things that other fathers did and the feeling that he was causing disruption to their daughter's studies . . . Martin could not see the point of family meetings but Dawn felt she benefited from understanding the difficulties the children were having. This helped her cope better with the situation and also cope better with them." It happens so often in these families that the communications breaks down and the children get forgotten. It is rare that they get the opportunity to talk in a supportive environment as Dawn's family did.

Compare this with Lisa's situation (Chapter 4). Lisa has not received any help and she has four children under eight years of age. ". . . He had never been violent towards their children although occasionally they witnessed his violence towards Lisa. The children did not see anything unusual about his drinking as they had grown up with it. In later years, however, the elder children developed a negative attitude toward the police as a result of seeing their father arrested on numerous occasions. They would call the police 'pigs' and ask Lisa why they were always so horrible to him. They also played 'arresting games' imitating what they had seen happening to their father." What chance do these children have? Unless they get help, unless there is some intervention in the family it is almost inevitable that they are the next link in a destructive chain which already contains at least two generations of alcoholics.

Sylvia (Chapter 6), "also felt she had to stay because of the children and because Bill told her so many times she would never manage on her own, she believed him". Eventually, after much chaos and pain she did leave and as a result her relationship with her children is not close. "Recently Sylvia had told one of her children that her state of mind had not always been good when they were very young. This came as a surprise 'so they didn't realise what was going on at home.' Sylvia thought perhaps this had been a mistake because it meant that when she left, they did not understand why she was going. In retrospect, Sylvia wished she had left Bill sooner and felt she could have made a decent life for them . . ." Even though Sylvia did get help for herself and did break free from a very destructive relationship, she was unable to help one of her children. Again the 'no talking rule', the lack of communication that is usual in a family where there is an alcoholic, means that the youngsters did not really understand what had been happening as a result of the drinking. They must have been very confused.

There is not enough done to reach and help the alcoholics in this country – even less to help their spouses and partners. Sadly, the amount of understanding and support given to the children is almost non-existent. Children of alcoholics are the next link in a destructive generational chain. A very high proportion become addicted to alcohol or drugs themselves; it is becoming more widely acknowledged that alcoholism can be a hereditary illness (Fitzgerald, 1996, describes this). Others marry, or become involved in a series of relationships with other addicted people. This is the only kind of relationship they know how to cope with. Looking after addicts is how they have learned to feel like worthwhile people. An alcoholic family which receives no help is a hot bed for producing another generation of co-dependents and other sufferers of addiction.

I think that the main point these biographies have illustrated is how much alcoholism is a family disease and how much everyone in that family needs and deserves support. How sad that we live in a society which sweeps the extent of the problem under the carpet. Very few of these people get the professional help they need and deserve.

## What can be done to help these women?

As I read these case histories, I was uncomfortably aware of the appalling lack of support for these women. I work in an addiction treatment centre where we not only treat the person displaying the primary addiction but also the family. We do not blame; we help the relatives look at how they may have enabled the alcoholic further into the illness by being too protective. Also, we help them look at how this behaviour has harmed them and their children. As well as learning to 'detach with love' they are encouraged to build up their self-esteem. If partners are unable to 'let go' then we offer them residential treatment for codependency which is very similar to our treatment for alcoholism. We view them both as addictions.

I know that we do not even touch the tip of the iceberg. Farm Place (where I work) is a private treatment centre. Few of the women in the biographies could afford our treatment. Nevertheless, there are huge numbers of men and women in our society being pulled down into a destructive spiral, not knowing where to go for help. As I have said before, there is a huge denial of the extent and seriousness of alcoholism in our culture. There is an even greater blindness about the effects of that addiction on families. Subsequently there is very little help offered to the alcoholic and next to none for the wives and children.

At this time, there are few professionals such as psychiatrists, psychologists, social workers, therapists or counsellors that I would refer these women to. Again, because of the lack of knowledge, and the lack of training, only a small (although growing) number of people in the helping professions understand addiction and the effects on the family. Those who are able to offer constructive help have been willing to learn from the growing body of recovering alcoholics and codependents. Indeed I would encourage all of the above professionals to attend open meetings of Alcoholics Anonymous, Al-Anon and Co-dependents Anonymous.

My tendency is to refer partners of alcoholics to self-help groups like Al-Anon and Co-dependents Anonymous (Al-Anon Family Groups, 1967, 1972, 1975). There, the isolation of so many of these women dissolves because of the identification of being in a group where others have been or are going through what they have been experiencing. Although many women go to Al-Anon to try to find a way of fixing their alcoholic partner, they learn instead to 'detach' as in the case of Dawn (Chapter 5) and Sylvia (Chapter 6). They understand the need to focus on themselves, their desires, their feelings and their behaviour. They begin to appreciate that the addiction is not their fault and that they are actually 'powerless' over the alcoholic. As a result, self-esteem begins to flourish. With a greater self-awareness they are in a better position to make decisions about what it is they want from life or relationships.

Ideally, in accepting that addiction is a family disease, recovery should be for the whole family. May's (Chapter 8) first husband did recover, became very involved in AA and then decided to leave her, after 25 years of marriage. May got "the shock of my life". She was "devastated . . . I'd done so much for him and I wouldn't have put up with all that I did if I knew he was going to leave". Sadly, May did not get help for herself. She had the option of attending Al-Anon but "found it very difficult to go as it could be hard being forced to face the reality of the situation". Instead, she eventually married another alcoholic. Unwittingly, she had fallen into the same trap of relating all over again.

Recovery from alcoholism is more than putting down the drink. It requires a character transformation. This has very important implications in the dynamics of family recovery. It is the same when a codependent decides to change and recover. If rehabilitation of either addict resulted in him (or her) returning to his (or her) pre-addiction state, that would be no accomplishment because it was precisely that state which resulted in the addiction. Often, an alcoholic or a codependent is in that relationship because it is the addictive behaviour that attracts. For example, people in the early stages of alcoholism can be passive and leave the decision making to their partner. Family members can quite enjoy that role. Recovering alcoholics learn that in order to continue being well they have to be more responsible for themselves and as a result want to participate in the decision making in their marriage. Codependent partners who get their self-esteem by being in charge can feel very threatened by this change.

Living with alcoholism is usually about surviving endless crises. Until these women can stand back from the chaos and trauma, they are not going to be able to see themselves clearly. So many clients (partners of alcoholics) have come to us for help, having been in therapy before. Their frustration has been that they have been guided to discuss their childhood when the primary question was really: how do I cope with my alcoholic partner? When answers are found to that question then in time they may be ready and willing to look at patterns established in childhood.

In the short term, I am not optimistic about the help available for these women and their families. It really depends on luck and where they live, whether the right help is available for them. The United Kingdom has to wake up from a very deep sleep to face the reality of the extent of addiction in this country and the havoc it reaps in families. We also need to look at how we encourage addictions like alcoholism and codependency to grow and develop further.

In the long term, I believe future generations will have more opportunities of help. Books on addiction and codependency are flooding in from the United States (e.g. Black, 1982). The knowledge of the Twelve Step groups is growing and developing on both sides of the Atlantic (see e.g. Cutland, 1990; Ditzler & Ditzler, 1989 for UK books). People in the medical profession, social services and therapy are beginning to listen to what those suffering from addictions are actually saying. Sadly, there is a long way to go before we can offer adequate help for the whole family.

## Note

1. I also want to mention that although this is a project with the aim of focusing on women, my experience is that there are many codependent men who suffer just as much. Codependency is not just a woman's issue. Nor is alcoholism a problem that happens to men only. For the purpose of this chapter I describe the addicted drinker as "he", but it is important to acknowledge that there are many women alcoholics being pulled down with addiction, too.

# CHAPTER 10

# A psychodynamic perspective

*Barbara Cottman*

## What is a psychodynamic perspective?

When I was thinking about how best to answer this question for the purpose of this chapter, I was struck by a quotation which I heard on the radio during a programme about the nature of music. "It does not matter what music *is* – the most important thing is what it is *for*. What music is for is to give effective expression to some aspect of human experience." I was delighted, because this definition captures for me the nub of the thing – it does not matter what a psychodynamic approach is, the important thing is what it is *for*. For me, the point of a psychodynamic perspective is the possibilities for its use in the task of giving effective expression to our experience as human beings.

The idea of psychodynamic psychotherapy as art may seem a very strange one to be using in this technological age. The study of psychodynamics over the last 100 years or so has sought to advance scientific understanding of our relationships with ourselves and each other, and there is now an increasingly complex body of theoretical knowledge with which psychodynamically oriented workers can try to make sense of our diverse experiences, both of ourselves as private individuals and of our more public shared experience and behaviour. The conceptual framework provided by a psychodynamic way of thinking can help us think about our potentialities as human beings, about our limitations and, especially, about our sufferings both physical and mental. In this last context the use of a psychodynamic perspective to try to understand the human condition comprises a healing or treatment process.

Psychodynamic psychotherapy, which is the field in which my training and experience lies, is a joint project in which therapists and patients seek together to discover or develop ways in which patients can give more effective expression to their experience and hence alleviate their afflictions.

Many people nowadays prefer to use a word other than 'patient' in this context. I continue to think of the people I work with as patients, that is, 'those who suffer' and many of them choose to call me by my title, Dr Cottman. The implications of this for the work which they and I are able to do together need to be continually borne in mind. Increasingly nowadays questions of the location of authority and power in 'helping' professional relationships are, rightly, a matter for much concern. For this reason, those of us who use the psychodynamic approach, whether medically qualified or not, in our work as health care professionals have a responsibility to start with an attempt to identify and reflect on our own experiences and what we bring from that to our work.

## What do I bring to thinking about the subject of this book?

First, I was interested in contributing to a book which is an attempt at a dialogue in print between those who live with, and those who work with, problem drinking. Since a psychodynamic perspective, as I understand it, concerns first and foremost the attempt to establish a dialogue, I felt I wanted to see if I could contribute something useful from my own experience, both personal and professional, about the lives described in these six biographies.

Thinking about one's own life, and how it comes to be the way it is, is very difficult. When I was a student I was often asked why I chose to take up medicine. I had to deal with the uncomfortable fact that I did not really know at a rational level. All I was aware of was that I had 'known' since the age of eight that I wanted to be a doctor. This is hard to explain since there is no tradition of medicine or indeed any other profession in my family. When I found myself agreeing that I would write this chapter, as a psychotherapist working with people with all kinds of problems, I thought I had no particular experience relevant to the subject of the book. Then I thought again. I thought about the fact that my family has a tradition of seafaring going back three generations. I remember stories of the great-uncle whose problems with drink earned him the status of 'black sheep' of the family. I remember closer to home, my own uncle, who, after years at sea and a stormy family life, died an untimely death as a result of too much alcohol and too many cigarettes. I remember his children, my younger cousins with whom I had only occasional contact as a child, one of whom has survived (against all expectations) many years of drug misuse, and another who did not survive a suicide attempt in her early twenties. My cousins and I share much in common with respect to family background and ordinary social circumstances; how is it that our lives have taken such different directions?

How is it that at the age of eight, I developed such a firm notion that I must learn how to save lives? What was it that made it impossible for my cousins to protect their own lives from devastation? Questions such as these about the thoughts and feelings that we have and the choices we make or find ourselves making and what they might mean are central to the psychodynamic perspective.

Concern for the answers to such questions, and the belief that in such answers we find a basis for living our lives more effectively, differentiates the psychodynamic approach from others where the focus is more directly on problems of living and their solutions, what to do or how to cope, and so on, rather than reflecting on our subjective experiences, on our internal life and what that might mean and how it might influence the decisions we make in our day-to-day existence.

## Some ideas basic to a psychodynamic perspective

It is important to understand how much proliferation and diversity has developed over the last century within psychodynamic thinking and how much cross fertilisation has been occurring, especially over the last 10 years or so, between psychodynamic and other fields. The continuing use of old familiar terms (such as 'defence mechanisms') may give the misleading impression of a 'senior' perspective with an unchanging conceptual framework which can provide a solid backdrop against which new developments can be viewed for comparison and contrast. Closer examination of the literature will show the enormous range of meanings which so called 'basic' psychodynamic concepts now carry in different contexts. It is therefore more useful to try to identify key assumptions which are held in common by psychodynamically oriented clinicians.

The following four ideas characterise – in my understanding – the essentials of a psychodynamic way of thinking:

1. Early experience in relationships shapes later experience of ourselves and others and the ways of thinking and behaving that derive from that experience.
2. In trying to learn how this shaping works, the most useful field of study is the area of the interchange or interaction between people, in particular the interplay of felt or intersubjective experience, that is, the feeling or behaviour evoked in me by another and by me in them.
3. Those behavioural and emotional interactions which can be thus identified and observed can be thought about, reflected upon, and brought into the area of awareness and choice, for example "there I go sounding off again, is it really warranted by what is happening now? Even if it is, do I really want to let it get to me so much?" and so on.
4. This process of exploration of the intersubjective experience, and reflecting upon it, is itself the effective agency in promoting or facilitating psychological change rather than the 'successful' achievement

of particular pre-set goals or objectives, for example the pursuit and acquisition of 'insight' is itself less important in effecting change than the process of reaching or constructing it.

These ideas have informed not only my comments on the biographies in this book, but also the style of writing I have adopted for this chapter. Through focusing on my own process of subjective response, enquiry and reflection in relation to the material available in the biographies, I have tried to describe and model the type of engagement which I as a psycho-dynamically oriented clinician see as potentially useful. If I were to have the opportunity of working with any of the biographees, I would obviously have the advantage of their feedback in clarifying to what extent this was in fact useful for them and reorienting my efforts in the light of this.

# How do we establish our sense of who we are and how we can be in the world?

How do we get to be 'us' in the first place? The evidence is that we need an experience of secure attachment in our earliest months and years, to be able to develop a sense of safety and trust that we can be ourselves. This experience of security may be absent because our caretakers have not had it themselves and hence cannot provide it for us. Without this basic security, a sense of danger accompanies our efforts to explore our sense of ourselves and others and we tend to withdraw from experiencing our own feelings and ideas about life and just do the things that have to be done to get through life. Survival becomes an achievement rather than something we can generally take as given and 'being ourselves' is not even on the agenda.

In these circumstances, the 'self' that we present to the world is there as much to hide and protect us by ensuring that we fit in and adapt, as it is to represent who we are and what we need and want in order to get on and manage our lives as the unique individual that we could be.

## How do I know I'm still me?

Whether or not our sense of ourselves is rooted in a basically safe experience of the world, we inevitably become involved in a continuing process of emotional feedback or interchange – initially through our interaction with others around us in the family and beyond and later within ourselves – whereby we promote and maintain our sense of being someone with an ongoing existence. This sense of continuity of being is the emotional or psychological equivalent of the physical continuity of being alive which arises from our ongoing bodily processes and we normally take it just as much for granted.

Through this process of emotional 'learning' which starts with our earliest experience, we are all of us inevitably shaped by the pressures on us to fit into our allocated places in our own particular world. It seems that we then come to experience our continuity of being as if it were dependent upon our maintaining a sense of fit in the context of relationships with others and with ourselves which contain the same essential elements as those we have grown up with. By this means, I can recognise that I go on being 'me' living in 'my' familiar world.

# What happens when the relationships we grow up with contain elements which are restrictive, damaging or destructive?

We can explore this question by thinking about May and her story. May's account of a childhood marred by neglect and physical and emotional abuse, is both shocking and sad to hear. It makes us wonder how anyone could manage to survive such treatment, and we appreciate the courage and strength it must take to make a life out of such beginnings. Her early life, deprived of both material resources and affection, was dominated by a father described as "a bad-tempered evil man", "emotionally dead" perhaps on account of his war-time experiences. With him she was screamed at, beaten and constantly criticised, always "in trouble" and being told she was stupid. As well as this, with repeated moves resulting in her attending 10 schools in five years, there was no opportunity to establish a more positive sense of herself in a different environment. She came to believe that "father knew best" and "that was just the way the world was". When eventually she was able to move from home to make her own way through an apprenticeship, she is once again set back by poverty and life-threatening physical illness and we have a powerful sense of her suffering alone and living, as it were, "at death's door".

Although May did well at university and at work, with "very happy times" and a seven-year engagement to a well-balanced and reliable man which grew out of friendship into a love affair, she fell in love at "first sight" with her first husband. They were "desperately in love" . . . "on cloud seven" . . . "it was absolutely magic" and they were married within eight weeks of meeting. His kindness and concern toward her was a new experience and she found it "hurtful and unbearable" when he began seeing other women. She thought about leaving him but found herself unexpectedly pregnant with her first child and felt this was a punishment for this thought. Having continually been told by her father she was "naughty and difficult", May thought perhaps the problems were her fault – her father would tell her he was "not surprised" about her husband's drinking, that she would "drive anyone to drink". May explains, "you carry that guilt with you", recognising that she carries the idea that she is somehow bad and responsible for her own pain and suffering. Her husband's cruel desertion, criticism and neglect, even when she is seriously ill, are described as "a repeat performance" of her father's behaviour.

It is hard to understand how, after she is eventually abandoned by this man, May finds herself in a second marriage to another man and suffering violence and abuse; once again in a situation where they "always had to be at war" and "brainwashed" into believing she was at risk of being sent to prison if she tried to free herself. It is even more perplexing to hear that although eventually she found the means to leave him, she still felt she "couldn't unhook herself from him" and found it hard to be rid of her "longing to be with him". May explains how it is to be "so afraid of being on your own, you don't think straight, you don't make logical decisions, you will cope as long as he's there, you are safe as long as he's there".

May's sense is that she has an enormous fear of being alone and abandoned, stemming from her relation with her first husband (with whom we recall she had her first ever experience of being loved). She describes a "terrible, terrible panic when she felt there was no way she could stay on her own – a feeling of overwhelming depression and fear".

## What could this terrible fear be?

I would understand it as the experience of being annihilated in oneself, a kind of emotional death or psychic non-survival. It has been described to me in the course of therapy when a critical point is reached in terms such as "it's like reaching 'ground zero' – everything stops – everything is impossible" and – less catastrophic but still terrifying – "I feel myself disappearing". It seems that without something to hold on to, outside or inside ourselves, even if it is the 'wrong sort' of person, we can be exposed to an intolerable experience of losing everything we depend on for our existence, even ourselves, which perhaps amounts to a fate 'worse than death' in the ordinary physical sense of the word.

## How can this disastrous breach in our subjective sense of ourselves come about?

The existence of psychological trauma was first widely recognised when soldiers suffering from 'shell shock' were identified during the First World War. Since then we have become more familiar with the impact of extreme traumatic situations on people who find themselves rendered powerless in the face of life-threatening circumstances (e.g. train crashes, fires, hostage taking, as well as war zone experiences) with the sudden, overwhelming and complete overthrow of all their ordinary protective and coping mechanisms.

It is only in recent years, however, that we have come to realise that very similar life-threatening circumstances are by no means as uncommon as we would like to believe within families and other 'caring' environments where physical, emotional and sexual abuse has the potential for even more devastating impact because of the youth of the victims and the secrecy surrounding their plight. At the same time studies of the impact of early separation, loss and deprivation on 'healthy' (i.e. flexible and adaptive) emotional development have helped us to change practices such as banning parents from visiting or staying with children in hospital. We are also becoming better informed about the patterns of small child and carer interaction which are associated with the development of more secure or less secure or disrupted attachment bonds. Through this work, we are now aware of how difficulties in establishing a sense of basic safety and security can occur in many quite ordinary, loving families where actual life-threatening circumstances or incidents never occur. The far-reaching consequences of these difficulties might well be evident in my own very early 'choice' of a 'life-saving' occupation.

## What can we do about these areas of damage in ourselves?

My understanding of this is that the most effective measures we can take are essentially protective ones, that is, we cannot expect to be able to undo what has been done in the sense of achieving a 'cure' for the problem. We could see the measures that we might take as belonging to one of four main methods of protection:

1. Prevention,
2. Avoidance,
3. Relief through reciprocal relationships,
4. Recognition, reflection and revision.

### Prevention

In theory, we can imagine circumstances in which children could be so ideally cared for that they would never be exposed to feelings of loss, fear or shame which were more than they could bear. In this scenario there would always be someone available to the child to help him or her identify, understand and manage threatening feelings, and that person would have no areas of emotional vulnerability in their own make-up which could get in the way and interfere with this availability or capacity for attunement to the child's emotional needs.

In practice such ideal conditions do not, of course, exist and hence we must accept that all of us, as members of the human race, are subject to the ordinary vicissitudes and frailties of the human condition. What we can do is be aware of this and do our best to support parents, to enable them to support each other and if we are parents ourselves, to seek the help we need in protecting our children from unnecessary exposure to emotionally threatening situations.

## Avoidance

Given that all of us sooner or later will encounter situations in which the emotional demands on us are more than we can bear, what measures can we take to deal with this? Faced with overwhelming pain or danger which brings with it not only suffering and fear but also the experiences of weakness, incompetence and powerlessness, we have to find ways of maintaining our sense of control. The first and most basic method we find of doing this is by avoidance, by getting away from the overwhelming experience. There are many ways we can do this. Foremost among these is physical activity.

Screaming babies, toddlers having 'tantrums', 'hyperactive' children, young people and adults who 'lash out' at others or take action – overdoses or cutting – against themselves, may all be understood as individuals who are trying desperately to regain a sense of control. Sadly, when these desperate measures are taken by abusing parents lashing out physically or verbally against their children, the cycle of pain and terror is perpetuated.

Less dramatically, action in the form of work may also be an important method of avoiding pain as suggested by the use of the term 'workaholic'. Work seems to play a very important part in Dawn's story, perhaps for this reason. Another way we can gain control when we feel threatened is to abandon our own feelings and needs and tune ourselves totally to other peoples' demands or expectations. Through placation and compliance we can get away from our distressed isolated, vulnerable experience and feel safe as long as we 'do as we are told'. This seems important for Sylvia when she describes herself as a "bit of a people pleaser".

Another very important method of protection by avoidance is 'going to another place', not physically but in one's mind. We are all familiar with daydreams and the part they play in helping us 'get away from it all'. We can think of the same need being met in a more consistent ongoing way when we gain comfort from religious and spiritual ideas of there being 'another better place', or from social aspirations to get away from a position of poverty, disadvantage and shame through money, marriage or a successful career. We can also 'get away' inside our minds by the psychological process of dissociation. This involves a degree of detachment of part of the mind from what another part is experiencing.

Finally, and of particular importance for this book, we can use chemical means to 'get away' from our current internal or external situation. People who use alcohol or drugs are often described as 'out of it' or as getting 'out of their heads'.

A colleague of mine describes his understanding of alcohol use as a 'mode of transport' away from pain and finds that this idea is useful in helping people think about their drinking. With this in mind, we can appreciate that the point at which I might need and want to change my problem drinking habit will only come when the painful consequences of my drinking out-weighs the pain which I am trying to get away from through using alcohol. But supposing I have also found a way to protect myself from those painful consequences through my relationships? This question brings us to the third method of protection.

## Relief through reciprocal relationships

The avoidance method we have been considering above tends to be a rather general blanket approach to protecting ourselves from pain and fear which may be so severe that it is felt to threaten emotional 'death'. It is also pos-sible to identify particular, specific fears which may predominate, for example fear of 'death' by desertion, by violence or by shame or censure, and to then see how relationships can be set up or evolved which provide a form of relief from these experiences. The relief is never completely effective, but – like bailing out a boat which is taking on water – it can ward off disaster and become a way of getting by until, hopefully, conditions change for the better.

We can find examples of particular relationships focused around three specific fears – fear of 'death' of the self by violent attack, by desertion, and by shame or censure – in the life stories contributed to this book. We can also see how these relationships can be used to provide temporary relief from these fears by gaining control over them, by actively evoking the feared experience in others.

Let us look in turn at the stories of Sylvia, Lisa, Dawn, Emily and Ruth.

*Fear of death of the self by violent attack – 'living with the enemy'*
Sylvia's story, like May's, bears the imprint of war and its damaging con-sequences. Her father was unable to work, having suffered from 'shell shock'. Because of this, his life and that of the family must inevitably have been restricted in its potential, in various ways. His religious faith enabled him to look for spiritual comfort and perhaps reward in a life after death. How-ever, Sylvia's mother carried in her "unhappy" and "selfish" feelings, the pain and frustration of the loss of richer possibilities in this world. She sought comfort in the prospect of social advancement through her daughters making "brilliant marriages" whilst lashing out at her husband with her sharp tongue when she could not manage her feelings of disappointment. A family climate was created in which mother's 'attacking' and father's 'attacked' positions fitted together in a complementary or reciprocal rela-tionship and became 'the' world in which Sylvia grew up. She thus has two main ways of being with which she can identify, neither of which was useful as a basis for flexible emotional development, but which did provide her with a sense of continuity as a survivor in the battle zone. Sometimes

she protects herself by compliance with mother, joining her in attacking father, but she is often herself the target of mother's attacks, both verbal sarcasm and physical caning. At this time she is identified with father in the attacked position. When she was older she turned on her mother, becoming the attacker fighting back against 'the enemy' but this brief outburst left her worried and frightened about the effect she might have had on the mother she also loved and depended on. Sylvia is aware of the existence of a powerful tie between her and her mother – "a great bond; no matter how cruel you feel your mother has been to you".

We know little about Sylvia's second husband's background except that his mother had died and his father was alcoholic. We might speculate that he had suffered cruelty in his early life which expressed itself in his wish to "smash against the rocks" the heads of his children; in his actual violent behaviour smashing things in the house; and in his abusive treatment of Sylvia, making her stand to attention and hitting her if she shows any sign of defiance. He establishes a sense of control over his fear of death of the self by violence by becoming the attacker and making Sylvia the attacked: "so terrified that she is afraid to breathe". Sylvia bears this for years, almost like a constantly bombarded 'shell shock' sufferer, until the "turning point" she describes when she experiences a reversal of the positions: "I could have killed him with no compunction whatsoever. I knew I was capable of murder and this was a turning point in my life". When Sylvia at last finds a sense of her own autonomy and power it is not felt as a healthy protective assertiveness but as the murderous aggression of an enemy at war.

*Fear of death of the self by desertion – surviving abandonment*
There is considerable physical violence in Lisa's world but she can protect herself, as her mother strove to do, from this most of the time. As the first child of a young, struggling mother and "rarely around" father who left her with her grandmother between the ages of 10 and 20 months and also left her with no idea why, Lisa grew up in a world where abandonment is the expected predictable 'reality of life'. In such circumstances no child could escape the conclusion that somehow it is she who is unwanted, unloved, not important or somehow 'too much' to cope with, living on resources which are somehow bound to 'run out'. Inevitably, when she was left to look after her younger brothers, she became the one to abandon them in her turn.

After several sets of foster parents and spells in different children's homes, at the age of 13 she started to initiate the running away or "running out" for, as she says, "something to do" but also perhaps, as a way of perpetuating the abandoning world which by now was the one she knew best how to survive in by being the one doing the abandoning. This way she is not left in the terrible powerless position of the abandoned one. Perhaps her husband's early experience installed in him a similar familiarity with the reciprocal abandoning–abandoned relationship. He evidently felt abandoned in the sense of feeling betrayed by the way his mother "got him arrested" at his

15th birthday party and after that began – through truanting and challenges to unjust authority – to find himself more and more on the wrong side of the law and on the outside of the ordinary 'accepting and acceptable' mores of society. From this perspective we might see that it is Lisa's and her husband's mutual understanding of what it is to be abandoned which binds them together in abandoning and rejecting 'us', that is, society and its expectations and values.

We could see their use of alcohol as part of this shared reciprocal rejection of and by the world – it becomes unnecessary when both have jobs and can afford to have help with child care and transport to work. We can also see it as an example not only of avoidance of pain as described above, but in addition a more active abandonment of themselves and their potential in a continuation of their childhood world experience. The strengths in the relationship between Lisa and her husband are apparent in her acceptance of him as he is and her determination not to "throw away" what they have together. She understands from within herself and strives to accept and stand by, a husband who comes to a point where he "cannot eat because that meant parting with his bottle for 10 minutes and he was afraid it would 'disappear'", understanding what it is to experience total dependency and fear of abandonment. She understands that he cannot manage to use a place in a rehabilitation centre without full detoxification first "because he did not trust himself and would be happier with a doctor or nurses on the premises 24 hours a day, while he detoxified".

We might also try to understand Dawn's story in terms of fear of catastrophic loss or separation, with a sense of being left totally alone, resourceless and vulnerable. The most striking aspect of Dawn's story is the number of deaths which she and her husband have had to bear and how these have driven each of them into desperate states where they seem out of reach of one another. Dawn's hardworking, strict parents, coming themselves from larger families with many mouths to feed, may have passed on to her an expectation of uncomplaining stoicism and service which made it difficult to express her feelings of distress and need for help. No more than a factual mention is made of her time in hospital at the age of 10, but we might wonder how frightening that might have been and what part it might have played in her later choice of a nursing career.

Dawn's husband seems to have been frequently separated from his parents during house moves as a child. It could be important to try to understand what these were like for him. It is possible that the separation imposed on the two of them when he was transferred to a job which meant he had to live away from home during the week when their first daughter was six months old, could have been more difficult than it seemed. Perhaps both felt isolated and unsupported and carried this experience together in a reciprocal abandoned and abandoning relationship which sadly drove them ever further apart. It would be heartening to think that Martin's illness might help them both to accept their need of, and possibility to care about, each other and together think about and enjoy the new lives which their children are beginning to build.

*Fear of loss of status and self-respect – the threat of blame and shame*
Emily grew up feeling special but in a family where failure, criticism and blame were ever-present issues. Her father and her mother's father constantly argued about their business, each blaming the other for its eventual failure. Her father then preferred to work in a factory rather than work for his father-in-law and lose his self-respect. Emily blamed her mother for her father's problem drinking until she realised that his traumatic war experience might be the cause of this. Also there was an atmosphere of criticism and denigration at home because of her father's verbal aggression to her mother. Emily would nag her father, whom she eventually "wrote off", and her sister sometimes made offensive racist remarks. Whilst Emily felt special within the family, she was exposed to being laughed at and denigrated for her country accent in her "smart" school and for her "Sloaney" accent in her more ordinary school.

Emily's husband also felt central and "fussed over" by his mother at home but outside felt a loner, a misfit and generally inferior. Perhaps this was linked with his father's experience of having been illegitimate and brought up in an orphanage until the age of five when he was claimed by his mother presenting herself as his aunt. It might have been hard for him when Emily became more successful at work, but it was then hard for her to sustain this when she became overwhelmed with the amount of work she had to do.

Attempts to account for Emily's problems often seemed to involve finding things to blame: the pill, not having children, financial problems, the depressing "hemmed-in" house, living with her husband. In turn Emily's husband felt that the stress of her illness had damaged his career, and may have felt that the risk of conceiving an unwanted child was so great that he had to withdraw physically from Emily altogether. Emily eventually withdrew from her husband after his blackout in the car. After this, there seems to have been a re-creation between them of Emily's previous experience of an atmosphere of abusive behaviour, criticism, blame and shame about loss of dignity, self-respect and a capacity to manage life. Both feel resentful of the poor service they have been offered for their health problems and each needs the support of being with their own mother. Despite their present separation and painful reciprocal criticising–criticised relationship, it seems that both feel a tie to, and a sense of security in, the marriage in which they have invested so much of themselves.

*Only room for two? – Survivor guilt and confusion*
Ruth describes a happy childhood with a good relationship with both her parents, but despite this she felt lacking in confidence. Perhaps we can relate this to a family atmosphere in which it seems hard for mother and father to relate to each other as well as to their children, as if someone has

to be displaced if there is to be room for someone new. Ruth's mother was "caught up with her children" and unhappy when they left and her father was caught up in his work, functioning "more like two individuals than a couple", each seeming to displace the other with different interests, as if it wasn't possible to have both.

Perhaps Ruth was trying to avoid this dilemma in her shyness and reserve but somehow still felt liable to feel "judged" or "intimidated", as if she might be guilty of something – for example displacing her father in her mother's affections or her mother in her father's or her older sisters in the affections of both. The idea that she is "not good at long-term relationships" may be linked to a conviction deriving from this experience that somehow she cannot offer or claim real commitment in a relationship without this being at someone else's expense. This conviction would fuel a cycle of hesitancy to claim, and hence failure to get, what might meet her needs, leading to disappointment and thus further hesitancy and withdrawal in relationships. This might in turn help to account for Ruth's pattern of "always finishing something and then moving on to the next thing". In this there is both continuity for her in the displacing–displaced reciprocal way of relating and hope of escape from this unhappy cycle.

We do not know at what age Ruth's partner had the experience of being "forced together" with his mother after his sister's death in a horrific car crash and his father's death a year later. Evidently, he became the focus of all his mother's powerful feelings, both loving and hostile critical blaming ones, and was unable to have any help with his own feelings about the losses. If he experienced in this that he was both replacing in one sense, his father and sister and yet, in another sense, being totally displaced by them – in so far as his mother could not relate to him in his own right – this might help us to understand the desperate violence of his feelings toward Ruth when he felt catastrophically displaced in her affections by the arrival of children. One might expect that the younger he was, the more severe the confusion between past and present and between positive and negative experiences and relationships.

How can we move on from being caught in confusions and repetitive patterns such as these?

## Recognition, reflection and revision

As contributors to this book we have all accepted the challenge to take notice of and try to think again about the experiences described here in the light of what we have known before. I hope I have been able to explain, from the psychodynamic perspective, why it is that this process of recognition can be a lot more difficult than we might expect. It involves realising that we all have the power, however limiting our circumstances, to look at ourselves and our lives differently, at the same time as accepting that we all have our 'reasons' for having done things the way we have up until now.

To be able to reflect on our own experience involves holding a dialogue inside ourselves between an aspect of ourselves that acts, thinks and feels, and another aspect that can observe those actions, thoughts and feelings, as when Ruth comments on herself in a continuing process of 'I' considering 'me'.

Through this dialogue, which often needs to be supported by a trustworthy outside person in order to work well, we can survey both our past and present experience and sort out those things and events which we can't change from those things which do not hold in the present and are therefore open to being changed. We can then come to a position of being able to revise and amend our ways of responding to what life brings us and reconstrue ourselves and our capacities in the process. By the same token, with a different sense of ourselves we can then widen our options and find ways out of unproductive patterns of relating which are no longer necessary or appropriate.

## *Suggested reading*

I have not provided references for my statements in the normal academic manner. Instead, I suggest as further reading: Fonagy and Target (1997), Holmes (1996), Ryle *et al.* (1990), Stern (1985), Winnicott (1960) and de Zulueta (1993).

# CHAPTER 11

# A family systems perspective

*Arlene Vetere*

## Family therapy and systemic approaches

Family therapy has been defined as "any psychotherapeutic endeavour that explicitly focuses on altering the interactions between or among family members; and seeks to improve the functioning of the family as a unit, or its subsystems, and/or the functioning of individual members of the family" (Gurman *et al.*, 1986, p. 565). Systemic approaches are more broadly defined to include intervention in other groups and organisations, for example, networking and systemic consultation to teams, agencies, professional groups, and so on. The family systems models that underpin systemic interventions are based on patterns of interaction amongst individual members of a family group. They seek to describe and explain the organised complexity of interrelationships found in human social systems, such as family household groups, extended families and kin networks, agency and family systems, therapist and family systems, and so on.

Family therapy developed during the 1950s and 1960s. Early observations, such as difficulties in sustaining improvements in individually treated psychological problems, the possible role of interactions in maintaining individuals' difficulties, and the inability of some individual therapy approaches to address relationship problems, led some therapists to experiment with involving family members in treatment. Speculation as to the role of the social and relational context in the genesis and maintenance of individual psychological problems placed the family at the heart of therapeutic thinking. These early practitioners found that their practice had outstripped available theory and so they turned to General System Theory (von Bertalanffy, 1968) for its application to family process and family therapy.

General System Theory (GST) attempts to explain how a system, such as a family, functions as a system through the interdependence of its members. Within this model of organised complexity there is said to exist a hierarchy of system levels, with each level more complex than the one below and with emergent properties that are not reducible to explanation at a lower level of complexity, such as the ability to reflect on our behaviour. The major contribution from GST has been in the study of system adaptability, that is, the balancing of the need for stability in relationships with the capacity for change. Family systems theorists explore patterns in relationships, beliefs and behaviours, that is, organised complexity. They describe family rules that underpin observed interactional sequences, and identify hierarchies of feedback and control, where family members' 'output', or behaviour, is recognised as 'input' at some later stage. Thus explanations for behaviour embrace circular notions of causality, where family members respond to one another's behaviour in cycles or patterns, rather than the linear cause–effect sequences found in functional analyses of behaviour.

A number of schools of family therapy have developed over time. The different schools gave different emphases to family systems ideas and developed different methods of intervention, such that structural therapists focused on behavioural interactions and sequences within the family (Minuchin, 1974), whereas Milan therapists approached the family as a history-containing system with entrenched meanings (Selvini-Palazolli *et al.*, 1980), and transgenerational family therapists were interested in the intergenerational transmission of family members' beliefs and behaviours (Lieberman, 1979). The hallmark of the family systems approaches was in the development of live methods of supervision and consultation (Whiffen and Byng-Hall, 1982), whereby family therapy sessions were observed and supervised by a small team of family therapists.

Family systems models and approaches have been critiqued extensively (Vetere, 1987; Pam, 1993), mainly because the focus on interactions led to a perceived diminution of individual emotional experiences, and the emphasis on circular causality led to a diffusion of responsibility within family groups for violent and abusive behaviours. Feminist-led critiques gave rise to extensive revisions of working models and assumptions of family life. Whereas generation had long been recognised as an organising feature of family life, gender had been overlooked (Goldner, 1988). The concept of power and gender-based access to sources of interpersonal power enabled therapists to understand therapy processes as 'political', in so far as they dealt with the allocation and distribution of power among family members, therapists and family members, and so on. Gender-sensitive approaches to family therapy developed whereby individual and family system needs were negotiated in a context where therapists tried to be explicit about their ideas and values regarding gender, and the way in which gendered roles and stereotyping affect each family member, and so on. Similar critiques have been made with issues of race and culture, leading to examination within training and practice of how our respective cultural identities influence our understanding and acceptance of those who are both culturally similar and dissimilar (Lau, 1987).

Contemporary systemic approaches represent a knitting together of different theoretical positions and concepts. Recent theoretical developments have had a significant impact on thinking and practice, embracing issues of meaning and the use of language, narrative, and politics and practices of power. Family therapy increasingly attends to the interpretive meaning-making dimension of experience and the multiple contexts in which it occurs and evolves (Cronen and Pearce, 1985).

Thus family systems theorists and family therapists are interested in the connections between family members' beliefs and behaviours, family events and episodes, and family members' relationships with each other, and how these develop and change over time. They are interested in connections between the family and other systems, such as extended family, community groups, health services, and so on. Understanding of these connections and processes is considered crucial for effective problem solving and clearer communication between family members. In conclusion, and linking this wider discussion of family systems approaches to problem drinking, it is useful to note Edwards and Steinglass's (1995) review of 21 studies of family-involved therapy for the treatment of alcoholism, which found that family therapy is both helpful and cost-effective, and in particular seems to motivate individuals with drinking problems to enter individual treatment programmes.

## Systemic issues and themes in the biographies

Family systems theorists and therapists are interested in process and pattern; the sequences of connectedness between people, events, beliefs and behaviours. Looking for patterns can be seen as the way we make sense of the world (Bateson, 1973). Exploring patterns inevitably means we select certain sequences above others. The systemic notion of observer-created reality, and the associated idea of different descriptions of a system stemming from different observer positions, creates a dilemma for a systemic view of the biographies. Clearly the biographies are based on the views and reflections of the women for themselves and for their family members. This constraining effect of working here within one perspective will apply also to the final part of the chapter in which we discuss options and mechanisms for change. However, working systemically with individuals is a developing tradition within the field and represents a rapprochement between systemic approaches and both psychodynamic models (Wachtel and Wachtel, 1986) and cognitive behavioural models (Bandura and Goldman, 1995). This tradition of working systemically with individuals will be helpful to us here.

## Symptomatic behaviour

There is a long-standing debate in the systemic literature over the role of symptomatic behaviour in both maintaining stability within the family and helping to ward off fears of change induced by impending life cycle transitions. Some theorists think of symptoms as functional, helping the family to stabilise, such as when a child's symptomatic behaviour unites the parents in mutual concern for the child, thus distracting them from dissatisfactions within their own relationship, which if addressed, might lead to separation and disruption within the family (Selvini-Palazolli *et al.*, 1978). Other theorists think of symptoms as 'ironic consequences'; as proposed solutions to dilemmas and difficulties faced by family members, which in turn become problematic in their own right, and demand further reorganisation within the family to accommodate and adapt. An example of the latter view could be seen when drinking is used as an immediate solution to a problem or worry, or as a way of enhancing interpersonal affective spontaneity, and is reapplied as the solution even though it has no impact on the original problem, and so the drinking becomes problematic in its own right. The adaptation of other family members to the problem drinking over a period of time can be seen as an example of a problem-determined system (Anderson *et al.*, 1986), or another 'ironic consequence'. Ruth's biography documents closely how she sees this kind of adaptation taking place: "Nothing I said made any difference, and I got tired of saying the same things".

Steinglass and his colleagues have long been interested in documenting differences in interactional styles in families according to whether the person with a drinking problem is abstinent or drinking (Steinglass, 1981). Emily in her biography notes her partner's increasing verbally and emotionally abusive behaviour as his drinking escalates. Steinglass has noted a greater flexibility with emotional expressiveness, more disagreements addressed and resolved, higher levels of interaction and greater involvement in decision making among family members during periods of abstinence, compared to periods of drinking. Liepman *et al.* (1989) point out that the Steinglass studies do not compare the same families across these two periods. They review the limited research available and broadly conclude that couples and other family members do self-report differences in family functioning across these two periods of drinking and abstinence. The women's biographies show a mixed picture with some, like Emily's, describing an escalation of problem drinking, and others, like Dawn's, describing periods of abstinence, or Lisa describing her husband as non-violent when sober. The pragmatic question here is the extent to which the above two views of symptomatic behaviour (in this case, problem drinking, as either functional and stabilising or as maladaptive solutions which are powerfully reinforcing), are helpful to us in understanding the dilemmas raised in the biographies, and thereby point to some possibilities for change.

## Interactions and patterns in relationships

When thinking about interactional patterns, the systemic approach also explores the rules, both overt and covert, that can be said to govern interaction, and the different beliefs that might underpin them. Pattern in relationships, pattern in communication, and pattern over time will be explored, along with rules and beliefs, with the help of themes that emerge from the reading of the biographies. Ruth gives an example whereby she would be stressed and tearful when her husband returned in the evening, she would put the children to bed and then go to bed herself, whereas he would stay up, brew some beer, and drink and then go off in the morning, to come home to her at night where she would be tearful again, and so on. Clearly such patterns arise within a larger context of stress, resources, disappointment and unmet needs which need to be included in any understanding of a particular behavioural pattern. But as Ruth herself points out, these patterns that repeat day in and day out, take on their own meaning and significance, and often partners do not consider the wider contexts that influence their relationship when making judgements about the satisfactoriness or otherwise of their relationship.

Patterning in relationships can be conceptualised at the behavioural, cognitive and emotional levels. The language we have available for describing relationships is limited compared to the words and phrases we use for describing individuals and their traits and abilities, and so on. For example, Sylvia describes a pattern whereby her partner appears jealous of the time she invests in the children and behaves in ways that further distance her from him emotionally speaking, which makes it more likely she will spend time with the children and more likely he will believe his jealousy is justified, and so on. There have been a number of attempts to describe and classify relationships in interactional terms, necessary if we are attempting to help change relationships. Watzlawick *et al.* (1967) proposed three modes of interaction: symmetrical, complementary and reciprocal, based on notions of sameness and difference. Each mode is thought to have the potential for constructive and destructive functioning. Symmetrical relationships are based on the exchange of similar behaviours, for example, two people exchanging praise or insults, competing in order to have the 'last word' and maintain dominance in the relationship and exercising different sources of interpersonal power in order to define the relationship in their terms. Complementary relationships are based on sequential exchanges that involve difference. Examples of complementary interactions can be found between parents and young children, employers and employees, therapists and clients, and teachers and pupils. Problems can arise in complementary relationships if the exchanges between couples, as in most of the examples in the biographies, become entrenched and the women have limited access to sources of interpersonal power and external support, for example with Lisa's and Sylvia's stories. Reciprocal relationships are seen as a balanced mix of complementary and symmetrical interactions, with flexibility within the couple to exchange roles, recognise expertise in the partner, acknowledge and discuss differences, and negotiate and adapt to changing circumstances.

The reading of the biographies from a systemic vantage point reveals a preponderance of complementary interactions, with little evidence of reciprocity in relating, particularly in the later stages of the couples' relationships. Interpersonal power seems vested in the male partners, such as Sylvia's and Lisa's partners, who exercise physical strength and violence, and contractual power, such as threatening to leave the relationship or actually leaving the relationship for a while, to maintain dominance, in some of the extreme examples. Emily and Sylvia describe these processes of threatened and actual abandonment in graphic detail. Symmetrical interactions are usually described when the women decide to 'fight back' in an attempt to redefine the relationship and assert their views and needs, sometimes with long-term constructive consequences and short- and long-term catastrophic consequences in the women's eyes. Emily describes her current trial separation from her partner. Lisa talks about fighting back physically, but eventually giving up as she thought she had to accept her husband the way he was and that she could not change him.

Within what appear to be rigidly complementary interactions, one might observe covertly symmetrical sequences, such as a child's defiance to a parental dictat, or a woman partner's attempt to be powerful from a disadvantaged position. Mostly though, the women seem focused on keeping their families and relationships together, for example Lisa and Sylvia, with Sylvia struggling to understand why her grown-up children appear to blame her rather than their father for what happened in the home.

Sadly and ironically, most of the women in their biographies describe their search for reciprocity in relating, and a wish to negotiate a *quid pro quo* (Lederer and Jackson, 1968) in terms of the mutually agreed rules which constitute the definition of their relationship.

## Violence and abuse

Some of the biographies, such as May's, Lisa's and Sylvia's, include examples of abuse and extreme and prolonged violence towards the women, often witnessed by the children. May's story describes a closed family system, where outside influence is curtailed, secrets are kept in an enforced way, such that abusive patterns of behaviour become possible. Dobash and Dobash (1987) address the question asked by the women of why they stay in these relationships, and attempt an explanation that highlights intrapersonal, interpersonal and societal processes. They adopt the model of learned helplessness (Seligman, 1975) to describe a woman's sense of depression and acceptance within a situation she believes she cannot change. Her love for her partner and wish to believe the promises of reform and reconciliation, her concerns for the children and desire not to deprive them of their father's company and influence, and her financial dependence on her partner, can limit her choices and options. In addition, cultural and societal patriarchal beliefs about women's and men's roles in families, such as the woman's responsibility to make relationships work, often accepted by the women themselves, further restricts her perception of her options. Sylvia talks a lot in her account of how she believed that it was her responsibility to make the relationship work, and her sense of guilt if she was thought to be failing. Echoes of this view are found in the other biographies. May, for example, talks about her belief in marriage vows, loyalty and the rights of her husband. It is only much later in the accounts of some of the women that we see a sense of their own personal agency emerging and beliefs about their rights to be treated decently and respectfully, such as in Sylvia's account.

Dobash and Dobash's explanation can be seen as drawing on multiple levels of context, which is exemplified in the work of Cronen and Pearce (1985). Thus in May's example, violent behaviour might occur in the context of a drinking episode within the context of the couple's relationship. May's beliefs about marriage vows and loyalty to one's spouse and her husband's rights in the relationship might be reinforced by her perception of attitudes towards divorce and gendered patterns in behaviour held in the wider cultural system. These ideas can be seen as a series of layers, like the layers in an onion, which are connected through circular and reflexive processes, with each layer simultaneously influencing the layers above and below. Thus, according to Cronen and Pearce, for behaviour to be understood in an interactional sense, it needs to be seen in the context of the episode in which it occurs; the episode is viewed in the context of the relationship in which it occurred; and the relationship is influenced by prevailing family beliefs and cultural beliefs.

## Patterns of emotional closeness and distance

In addition to describing sequences of behavioural connectedness, systems theorists have also attempted to describe emotional connectedness as patterns of emotional closeness and distance. Minuchin put forward a continuum of emotional style of relating, which had at one end a pattern of emotional closeness called enmeshment and at the other end a pattern of distance called disengagement (Minuchin, 1974). Enmeshed patterns can be seen as having a positive and negative influence on the participants, for example, early infant–caretaker patterns are often described as enmeshed and extremely close, often to the exclusion of others. Closeness between mothers and children can become enhanced during episodes of the father's drinking, thus further distancing the fathers. We see this process occurring in Lisa's and Ruth's accounts. Closeness can become problematic when other styles of relating are not encouraged in developing children and the

children become overly reliant on the enmeshed relationship for information, experience and opportunities to define themselves and their opinions,
and so on. Emily described her husband's relationship with his own mother
in this way. By contrast, disengaged relationships are characterised by emotional distance and underinvolvement between family members, for example,
parents might be emotionally unavailable towards their children, partners
unable or unwilling to acknowledge and meet each other's emotional needs,
and so on. Sylvia talks of the emotional distance between herself and her
grown-up children and how she has to work hard to maintain contact with
them, believing they are not motivated themselves to ensure this contact. A
mixed style of relating would describe relationships which are flexible and
where participants constantly monitor and negotiate the balance between
closeness and autonomy, according to changing needs over time and in
different circumstances. Dawn describes her relationships with her children
in this way.

## Family roles

Family groups are often described as acting as if they are organised by rules
which govern the parameters of possible behaviour. These rules are said to
be overt, such as rules for children's behaviour, or covert, such as a rule that
conflict can only be expressed indirectly. Sylvia describes herself as being a
"disfavoured child" and how it was never possible to discuss her childhood
experiences with her own mother; the rules prohibiting such conversation
seemed strong.

The boundaries are defined as the rules that govern participation in the
family or its subsystems and the manner of the participation, such as family
members' roles and tasks. Boundaries are described as more or less open or
closed. Open boundaries, based on exchange of information and reciprocity in negotiation are said to be clear; closed and rigid boundaries between
the family and its environment describe circumstances with little exchange
and provide a climate in which secrets can survive (see the example of May's
biography referred to earlier). Diffuse boundaries between family members
describe enmeshed relationships in which there is little personal autonomy,
and individual decision making is less favoured. Many of the biographies
describe the effects on children, such as not bringing their friends home, as
described by Lisa, Ruth and Dawn; Emily describes her childhood of ruined
Christmases because of her own father's drinking.

All of the women believe themselves to be alone for extended periods in
struggling with the dilemmas raised by their partner's problem drinking.
May, Sylvia and Ruth describe the implicit and explicit sanctions on talking
to 'outsiders', such as extended family, voluntary and professional groups,
and so on, which prevent the women accessing high quality social support,
with its acknowledged role in buffering against depressive reactions. Sometimes when the women do 'break' the rule of secrecy, they encounter what

Carpenter and Treacher (1989) call 'dangerous professionals', workers who ignore, minimise or who fail to notice the consequences of violence and abuse for the women, and for their children. The effects on children of witnessing marital conflict and violence have been well documented (Rosenberg and Rossman, 1990). Sylvia went to her GP for help, and talks of how he told her she had "grace" to stay in the marriage and prescribed her tranquillisers. Ruth talks in her biography of her husband bringing home literature from an alcohol service that seemed to hold wives responsible for their husbands' drinking.

## Family behavioural patterns

Family behavioural patterns can involve two people, three people or involve multiple relationships. Descriptions of patterns in three-person interactions are helpful in exploring some of the dilemmas raised in the biographies. Coalitions, where two people join against a third in achieving their goals, described some of the alliances between parents and children in the biographies. This had the effect in some cases of 'excluding' one of the partners, such that they became disengaged within the group, locating their activities and meeting emotional needs outside the family. Exceptions occur in instances of prolonged periods of drinking where the drinking seemed to serve as a vehicle for reconnection to the family. Emily described a pattern in her family of origin of close and intimate connection between the generations of women in her family, and how her mother seemed relieved when her father went out to the pub to drink because it relieved some of the strain and tension at home. Triangulation is a process whereby conflict between two people which cannot be addressed directly for fear of the consequences, is detoured through a third person, thus diffusing the conflict, but not solving it. Examples within the biographies include instances of children becoming caught up in the marital dilemmas, such as Sylvia's descriptions of her children taking their father's side against her, mothers like Dawn and Ruth trying to bridge the emotional distance between fathers and children, and other examples of 'go-between' behaviours. Emily describes this most clearly when she talks of both her mother and grandmother being married to men with drinking problems, and how her grandmother tried to warn Emily not to repeat the patterns with her choice of partner, and how the marital patterns repeated in her marriage.

## Family belief systems

The behavioural and emotional styles of relating described in the pages above are said to exist within what is known as a family's belief system (Reiss, 1981). Beliefs are the premises that family members use to make sense of their world. They can operate like filters, mediating wider cultural proscriptions for how we think and behave in families. These beliefs may evolve over generations and will reflect such influences as gender and cultural expectations for behaviour as well as more idiosyncratic family experiences. They may be handed down via family customs, rituals, prejudices, and so on, and altered according to changing family circumstances, such as Sylvia talking about herself as a "disfavoured child". The women describe many beliefs about family-based loyalty and secrecy, such as Ruth's and Dawn's accounts of secrecy about the drinking meaning that they could not properly access support, the rationale and response to violence, such as Lisa's idea that she has to accept violence because she loves her husband and that is the way he is, beliefs about the acceptability or otherwise of prolonged alcohol consumption, such as Emily's childhood exposure to drinking in her family and her mother's apparent condonement for a "quiet life", the denial of the role of excessive drinking in their problems as a couple and a family, as we see reported in Sylvia's and May's accounts of their husbands' perspectives and in Ruth's account of not bringing people into her home because she was fed up and embarrassed about her partner's drinking, and so on.

Some of the women question what their children are learning within their particular family culture and the extent to which patterns will repeat or alter in the next generation and for some of the women themselves, in subsequent relationships with partners and their adult children. Lisa reports her concern that their children witness her husband's violence towards her and Sylvia rues the long-term impact on her children.

## Family life cycle and transitions

Family process, identified as repetitive behavioural sequences which evolve over time and based on shared belief systems, can be understood within the context of family life cycles. According to Carter and McGoldrick (1989), the processes for family members to negotiate are the expansion, contraction and realignment of relationship systems to support the entry, exit and development of family members in a functional way. Transitional events such as births, deaths, leaving home, retirement, cohabiting and marriage, separation and divorce, adoption and fostering, and so on, require adaptation at different stages of the family life cycle. Carter and McGoldrick remind us that household family groups are emotional subsystems, reacting to past, present and anticipated future relationships within larger three, four or five-generational extended family systems. Thus one generation may have a life-shaping impact on another, for example, changes in the grandparent generation on the household group. We see this most clearly illustrated in Emily's biography with her account of her relationship with her grandmother and mother. May talks about never getting over her own mother's death. Rigid application of stage theories is unhelpful as it might encourage viewing any differences from the model as deviation and not properly account for the rich diversity of living arrangements within household and kin groups.

The negotiation and timing of transitions in family life, both expected and unexpected ones, are believed to be stressful for family members. The interaction between vertical and horizontal stressors is said to determine in part how well transitions are managed. Vertical stressors are thought to be the patterns of relating and functioning transmitted down the generations of a family via myths, taboos, expectations, patterns of emotional triangulation, and so on; whereas horizontal stressors are those that arise within and outside the family, for example, predictable and unpredictable life events, and the social, economic and physical circumstances within which the life cycle is enacted.

Both Emily and Dawn talk about the role of life events in decisions to increase or stop drinking. For example, Emily believes her husband's drinking accelerated when she was hospitalised with major mental health problems, and Dawn describes her husband's abstinence in the face of a major threat to his health. The systemic view of symptoms and psychological distress emerging around the time of a transition is that they can serve the function of preventing change in the family and protecting family members. If family members are lacking in skills of negotiation and conflict resolution, it can make it harder to negotiate a transitional period; alternatively, solutions developed for family tasks at earlier stages of family life may not be helpful at another stage, for example, parenting older adolescents as if they were much younger.

All of the biographies refer to family transitions, such as the process of partnering and the joining of two extended systems, with the attendant needs to commit to the new partnership and realign relationships with extended families and friends to include the new partner. Emily talks of this at length and how she believes her husband never really separated from his own mother. Problematic experiences of family transitions are described in a few accounts of adaptation to the birth of children. Adjustment of the marital system to make space for children and the negotiation of coparental roles highlighted the different expectations of the marital partners, for example, who had primary responsibility for caretaking and whether it was negotiated or assumed, differences in beliefs over whether children or partners 'come first', and so on, and the continuing consequences of these different expectations and the capacity of the partners to negotiate further transitions.

Ruth describes how it was difficult for her and her husband to negotiate parental responsibilities and how he would accuse her of putting the children first. Clearly the safety and protection of children demands that both adults take their parenting responsibilities seriously. Sadly Ruth describes how these conflicts over parenting led to her experience of their relationship as "two ships sailing away from each other". The women describe the strains of parenting on their physical and psychological well-being, the burden of sole responsibility and their partner's lack of understanding of these changes and demands, for example, Dawn talks of becoming a "cabbage, dull and tired with the demands of child rearing". The women mourn the gradual loss of communication between themselves and their partners in the context of other losses to them personally and wonder to what extent these processes interacted with patterns of problem drinking. Dawn describes the gradual loss of communication between herself and her husband and Emily describes her sense of loss with the ending of her physical and sexual relationship with her husband, occurring in the midst of other losses, such as hospitalisation, job loss, house moves, and so on. Transition and loss were particulary evident in Lisa's biography with a childhood story of multiple placements and multiple carers in a context of abuse and neglect, repeating in the next generation with violence, drinking and known effects on children. Emily, when recalling her father's death, talks of her memories of the bad times in contrast to her mother's memories of the good times. The recognition of strengths, resources and competence, a hallmark of the systems approaches, can be seen in many of the women's stories as they recount their survival and that of their family members. This is seen especially in May's and Sylvia's accounts of their attempts to regain a sense of personal agency and self-worth. The search for competence will be discussed again when we examine options for change.

## Possibilities and options for change

Change in family systems can be conceptualised at the symptomatic level (often called first order change), at the level of family relationships (often called second order change), and at the level of family beliefs. The different schools of family therapy and systemic practice emphasise these different levels of change using different techniques and interventions. One model of change adopted is that change at the level of relationships will lead to changes for individuals in how they experience themselves and see their options in relation to other family members.

Edwards and Steinglass (1995) identify the role of relatives in confronting the problem drinking as crucial in the initiation of treatment for problem drinking. This finding raises questions about the role of relatives in families where violence and abuse is part of the pattern, and about the process of convening and engaging men in family therapy. Most of the biographies talk of the difficulties for men in acknowledging that their drinking is a problem, and the associated difficulties for women of trying to persuade their partners of this. Dawn talks of not being able to tell her parents about the drinking and the associated problems, and Ruth talks of not being able to tell her mother and when she did so of how her mother minimised the drinking, saying that's what people do at New Year's celebrations. A few biographies speak of the benefit of therapy sessions for family members:

(a) providing a constructive opportunity for the children to talk about the drinking, their reactions and feelings and for their fathers to hear as they speak; and (b) helping the mother to understand the children's perspective and helping the mother to cope at home. Emily mentions they had two couples counselling sessions which were ended without explanation and Dawn talks of the potential benefit of family counselling sessions.

It is not always clear within some of the biographies to what extent the women might be seeking first order (symptomatic) or second order (relationship) changes. For example, Dawn and Lisa seem to be seeking symptomatic change in their husbands' drinking behaviour, whereas May has sought a court order to stop the violence, and Emily is experimenting with a year's trial separation, although it is not clear to what extent she wants her partner's drinking to stop or she wants fundamental changes in the relationship. In pursuit of symptomatic change, solution-focused approaches to change in problem drinking hold promise (Miller and Berg, 1995). Solution-focused approaches assume that change is happening all the time, that there are always exceptions to the problem, and that small changes in one part of a person's life can be extended to others. Questions are used to introduce the idea of the possibility of change, such as the miracle question: "If there was a miracle one night when you were sleeping and the problem was gone when you awoke, what would be the first thing that you would notice? What would your life be like? What would your family/friends/employer notice about you? Who would be most surprised/delighted/disconcerted? How would they show it?" and so on. These approaches search for competence and solutions to problem drinking that already exist, even if in embryonic form in a person's life, and attempt to maximise on a positive wish for change even when people are ambivalent about the need for change in their drinking patterns.

When exploring possibilities for second order change in reciprocal patterns of interaction in the couple's relationship, such as Ruth's example of her husband's jealousy of the children and her responses over time, as well as in one partner's drinking patterns, such as Emily's description of the escalation of her husband's drinking around life events, couples can be helped to identify the different explanations and beliefs that maintain these drinking patterns, reflect on these patterns and their attachments to them, and develop other descriptions of themselves and their relationship, which are also grounded in their experience.

People are said to choose specific incidents from their past experience to justify and explain their present behaviour, constructing meanings which become small stories, scripts, myths and acting as if they were 'true' (Freedman and Combs, 1996). Emily describes how her view of herself is shaped by her understanding of her relationship with her grandmother, and the influences contained within, and how she thinks this influenced her responses to her husband. Some of these stories are problem-saturated and influenced by socialisation processes, cultural and economic conditions, and so on, as we see in May's and Lisa's accounts of their childhoods and in their accounts of how they think their childhoods impacted on their sense of self-worth. The systemic therapist is curious about how the problem drinking has influence over the partners, their lives and relationships. By broadening the questions, the couple can begin to notice 'unique outcomes', or entry points to an alternative account or story in which the partners have had some influence over the problem. Questions are asked that help them notice that when the pattern is escaped, they can experience something different, taking small steps away from the drinking and associated problems. The beliefs and their origins that may be supporting the problem story are explored, such as family-of-origin beliefs, then moving to bring forth experiences which represent the influence of alternative beliefs. Thus what begins as a focus on behavioural patterns or lifestyles shifts to focus on aspects of relationship discourse that have been around a long time. In situations of high conflict, the partners are often invited to work on their end of the problem for their own reasons and invited to take steps (and feel good about them) independent of what the other does.

More recently, the idea of the observer as part of the system has reminded us that the patterns therapists observe are only one of many possible sequences that could be identified. The perception and understanding of those patterns affects therapists' interventions and the family members' responses. A therapist observer who joins a family system with its shared history will inevitably notice patterns that those engaged in daily interactions with each other are less likely to notice. By choosing to identify and intervene in problematic patterns, family therapists can avoid blaming individuals, invite family members to be curious about their perceived attachment to particular behavioural patterns, and to consider what alternatives they might have. This might include speculating about what might happen if one of the participants in the interaction were suddenly to change his or her behaviour.

It is possible to work systemically with individuals, using many of the concepts and methods developed for working directly with relationships. For example, asking questions about the possible function of symptomatic behaviour, such as problem drinking, exploring whether the symptom is the result of a 'solution' that has backfired and itself become the problem, exploring how other family members would react to a change in drinking, and how drinking might serve to stabilise the family, and so on. Systems thinking and interpretations can be combined in an analysis of the family's structure and context, putting the individual's problems in a wider framework, and basing interpretations on vicious circles and patterns, and making use of interactional reframes. Tasks and interventions can be devised that are both individual- and systems-oriented, such as role plays and role reversals, devising rituals, predicting relapses and so on. Meeting the 'cast of characters' not in therapy can help in choosing therapeutic directions, correct the tendency to blame, provide additional information about the individual's interactional style and making the system more hospitable to individual change.

All the biographical accounts of the women seem to recognise the possibilities for change, alongside their recognition that the motivation of their partner to take responsibility for their drinking is important, if not essential, for starting the process of rehabilitation. Two of the biographies, particularly Dawn's, recognise the significance of health fears in motivating a change in their partner's behaviour. Lisa seems to believe that attempts to reason with her partner have failed and at the same time that resignation is therefore the only course left for her to follow. We see echoes of this resignation in all the biographies.

I hope the above reflections create a debate about the usefulness of systemic ideas and practice in helping create options for change, alongside the other approaches to the treatment of alcohol problems. Ruth comments that alcohol services focus on the drinker, with no consideration of the partner's perspectives or needs and thus exclude partners by not listening to them. I should like to see a systemic couples and family service as part of every community alcohol service. This would provide an opportunity for family members to explore and change the relational context for problem drinking, and in particular the impact of drinking on family members, family problem solving and communication style.

## A personal note

I am struck by the courage and endurance of these women. I am pleased to have had the opportunity to comment on their experiences, and in so doing, I hope I have not done them any disservice; rather I hope they can find something of use in my reflections.

# CHAPTER 12

# *The coping perspective*

*Jim Orford*

Of the many ways of looking at and trying to understand the lives of people who are intimately related to loved ones who have serious drinking problems, I believe the coping perspective is one of the best. Like all perspectives, or models of human experience, the coping perspective makes certain assumptions and draws certain analogies. Like all assumptions and analogies those made from the coping viewpoint are simplifications. They are not total truths, but rather working tools. They do the job well if they provide a good understanding, both for the participants themselves who wish better to understand their own lives, and for others who might be in a position to help if they understood better and who may certainly be a hindrance if they fail to understand. I believe the coping model does this job well.

The main assumptions behind the coping viewpoint are as follows. First, it assumes that when one person has a serious drinking problem, this can be highly stressful both for the person with the drinking problem (whom I shall refer to as the PDP) and to anyone who is a close family member (the CFM). This is because serious drinking problems are, by their very nature, associated with a number of characteristics which are very damaging to intimate relationships and can be extremely unpleasant to live with (see Orford, 1985, for a psychological account of the nature of excessive appetitive problems such as serious drinking problems).

The second assumption of the coping perspective is that CFMs come to this experience as 'innocents', perhaps with some general experience of alcohol problems and possibly some specific knowledge based on experience of family or friends, but essentially unprepared for the task of coping with living with a PDP and all the stresses that may involve. The third, and central assumption is that CFMs are then faced with the large and difficult life task, involving mental struggle and many dilemmas, of how to understand what is going wrong in the family and what to do about it. In particular, this task includes the core dilemma of how to respond to the PDP whose drinking behaviour is sooner or later likely to be seen as being a problem. The ways of understanding reached by the CFM at a particular point in time, and ways of responding are what are referred to collectively as 'coping'. The word is certainly not limited to well-thought-out and articulated strategies, nor to ways of understanding or responding that the CFM believes to be effective, although these are included. It includes feelings (for example of anger, or hope), tactics tried once or twice and quickly abandoned (such as trying to shame the PDP by getting drunk oneself), philosophical positions reached (e.g. "I've got to stand by him because nobody else will"), and 'stands' taken (e.g. "I'm not coming back until . . ."). 

Part of the assumptions about these ways of coping is that some ways are found by CFMs to be more effective than others, either in impacting upon the PDP's drinking, or in terms of the CFM's own health and well-being, or both.

A further assumption is that CFMs can be helped or hindered by other family members, friends, friends and associates of the PDP, neighbours, professionals and members of self-help groups. What is particularly important about the support which these others can provide, but surprisingly often fail to provide, is the support they give the CFM in arriving at and maintaining ways of coping. Like all human social support, the support received from these others may take a variety of forms, including emotional, informational or material support. But, from the coping perspective, the important ingredients are thought to be such things as whether the supporting person understands the stressors and dilemmas faced by the CFM, appreciates the ambivalence that the CFM feels towards the PDP and does not inappropriately "take sides", understands the difficulty of finding a way of coping, and reinforces the CFM in her or his chosen ways. The bare bones of this perspective, and these assumptions, are shown in Figure 12.1.

The appropriate analogies that can be drawn are with other stressful family circumstances which centre around the problematic behaviour of one person, which involve difficulties and dilemmas in knowing how to cope, and where the support of others could be important but cannot be relied upon. They include such circumstances as Alzheimer's disease (Matson, 1995), severe psychological distress (Birchwood and Smith, 1987; Kuipers, 1987), serious conduct problems in adolescence (Herbert, 1995) and regular violence (Dobash & Dobash, 1987), as well as close parallels such as excessive drug use (Velleman *et al.*, 1993), or compulsive gambling (Orford, 1985).

The coping perspective on women living with men who drink excessively has a history that goes back to the research and writing of women such as Jackson (1954) and Wiseman (1980), from the late 1950s onwards, who in the early days were concerned to offer a perspective that contrasted with the "wives' psychopathology" perspective which was prominent in the social work and other professional writing at the time. Since then the coping model has been taken up and developed by many individuals and groups of practitioners and academics in the UK, USA and Australia. Amongst the major published sources, in addition to those already cited, are the following: Barber and Crisp (1995), Holmila (1988), Love *et al.* (1993), McCrady and

**Figure 12.1** The coping model: main elements

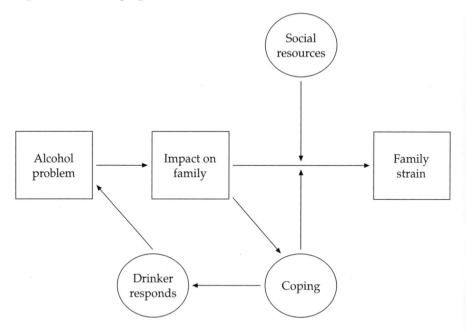

Hay (1987), Meyers *et al.* (1996), Orford *et al.* (1975, 1992, 1998d), Rychtarik *et al.* (1988), Schaffer and Tyler (1979), Thomas and Ager (1993), Yates (1988).

The present author and colleagues have been studying, from the coping perspective, the accounts of their experiences given by the young adult sons and daughters of parents with drinking problems (Velleman and Orford, 1990, 1998), close relatives of people with drug problems (Orford *et al.*, 1992; Velleman *et al.*, 1993), and of partners, parents and other relatives of people with alcohol or other drug problems in England and Mexico (Orford *et al.*, 1998b).

Some specific findings from this programme of research are displayed in Figure 12.2. The figure shows the three broad ways in which we have found that CFMs cope (Tolerating excessive drinking; Engaged in trying to change the drinking; Withdrawal from the drinker) and eight more specific ways of coping that we have identified (Orford *et al.*, 1998d). Whilst trying not to be constrained by it, this "map" of the terrain of coping was in the present author's mind when reading the six biographies. The biographies them-selves may help to confirm or to challenge parts of this picture.

The coping perspective, adopted here, contrasts with the alternative per-spectives taken by other authors of chapters in this book, in a number of ways. It rejects, for example, the "systemic" idea that the PDP's excessive drinking is likely to be a "symptom" of a more fundamental problem else-where in the family system, and that the excessive drinking may be serving a function for the family in maintaining the status quo (albeit with discom-

**Figure 12.2** Three general and eight more specific ways of coping

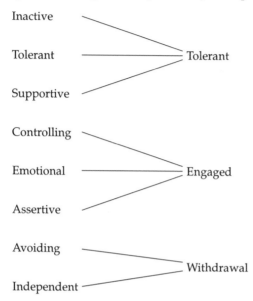

fort) or by diverting attention from the more basic problem (Steinglass *et al.*, 1987). From the coping point of view a serious drinking problem in the family is an unmitigated disaster and serves no functions. It is a serious hazard to the health and happiness of CFMs as well as PDPs and ways need to be found to deal with it and its consequences. Indeed to suggest otherwise, as the systems perspective does, is to run the risk of obscuring the real problem (the PDP's drinking) and to be seen to be blaming CFMs by suggesting that they are part of the problem.

The issue of blame is central and unavoidable. A risk for the coping perspective is that it may look as if it places blame fairly and squarely upon the PDP. This might be highly counter-productive since PDPs mostly carry a large amount of self-blame already and this is likely to be one of the factors that maintains their problem drinking. The answer to this is really quite simple: from the coping perspective blame attaches to the drinking but not to the drinker. The drinker is not to blame for his or her problem drinking. The causes of drinking problems are multiple, many of them now remote in the individual's past history or external to the individual in the form of the sale and promotion of alcoholic beverages, past stressors, the drinking habits of friends and colleagues, and the laws and social mores of the individual's cultural group. Like CFMs, PDPs did not voluntarily seek out their drinking problems but came upon them 'innocently'. Both PDPs and CFMs are victims of an uninvited and unwanted hazard.

Some of the central coping dilemmas that can be identified in the biographies turn out to be dilemmas that are not confined to families where

there are drinking problems and might particularly be thought to be dilemmas faced by women living with men, or generally by the less powerful
living with the more powerful. On the other hand, the coping perspective,
unlike the feminist, assumes that the essential task facing the CFM is that of
coping with the stresses and dilemmas associated with a serious drinking
problem. It is the case that such problems are more common amongst men
than women, and it so happens that this book is about women, but the task
of coping with drinking problems is not confined to women, and CFMs are
often husbands, fathers, brothers, sons or other male relatives. Although the
stressors they face, and the ways they find to cope, are partly fashioned by
their maleness, they are in most respects the same.

There are a number of respects in which the coping perspective parts
company with the codependency perspective. The codependency view is
that the CFMs, particularly women partners of 'alcoholics' (a term which
itself is often avoided by adherents to the coping model), are suffering from
'codependency' which can be thought of as a kind of abnormal condition,
almost an illness. The coping position, in contrast, is that CFMs, such as the
women whose lives are told in this book, are ordinary people caught in
unpleasant and difficult family circumstances and struggling, as any of us
would, to find ways of managing (e.g. Moos *et al.*, 1990). Although the
women's stories are often dramatic, in considering how they responded we
are looking at the ordinariness of people's lives, not at abnormality.

Both the codependency and psychodynamic views place much emphasis
on personal history[1], seeking for the origins of a CFM's present behaviour
and feelings in her (or his) past history and particularly in relationships
in the family of upbringing. The coping model is deliberately silent about
past history. If CFMs are ordinary folk coming naively as adults to a set
of circumstances for which they are unprepared, just as one might if a close
relative develops Alzheimer's disease or the family breadwinner became
unemployed, then past history is irrelevant. Indeed, to rake over a person's
past history in an effort to discover why a person might have partnered
someone with a drinking problem or why a woman continues to love her
husband or stay with him when all around her are advising otherwise, may
constitute a particularly stark example of what Ryan (1971) called 'blaming
the victim'. It is exactly for this reason that Howells (1997), working from a
coping perspective, has recommended that counsellors working with CFMs
should steer well clear of asking people about their personal histories.

Finally, unlike the 'community' perspective, the coping view has little to
say about the wider sociocultural context in which CFMs find themselves,
nor the larger collectives of which they are or could be a part, nor the
complex arrangements of affiliation and power relations that surround and
interact with their family lives. This chapter will touch upon the question of
the work and educational opportunities open to the six women, but this is
not central.

# How 'the six' coped: Main themes from the biographies

## The experience of severe, chronic family stress

All six women described to their interviewers marriages that had declined in quality, and which had become for them unsupportive and abusive. This state of affairs had in all cases existed, continuously or off and on, over a number of years. Their stories are full of descriptions of how their husbands became incapable of supporting the family emotionally or financially. There is much mention of secrecy, deceit and infidelity. Most remarkable of all is the theme of aggression which occurs in every one of the six accounts. In Lisa's and Sylvia's biographies this amounts to repeated and severe physical violence. In Sylvia's account this is described graphically. All of the others described their husbands' aggressiveness or abusiveness. May described how her husband would come home "seething with hate", and Ruth's husband had told her that he wanted to kill her. The word 'stress' may be too mild to apply to these stories. 'Torture' is a word that springs more readily to mind.

Such experiences are not at all uncommon in the lives of CFMs. But it should be pointed out that some of the six biographies collected in the present book are representative of the more severe end of the spectrum of drinking problems, which are not always associated with violence and abuse (indeed, violence is not a central feature in three out of the six biographies here: Ruth, Dawn and Emily). It is interesting to note, also, that the husbands of four of the six had had a parent with an alcohol problem, and that the husbands of the other two described childhoods that were troubled in other ways (Emily's father-in-law had been adopted and felt a misfit, and May's husband had experienced his parents' divorce as traumatic and his father as cruel). Although such family backgrounds are often found in the biographies of people with severe alcohol problems, they are by no means universal.

## Looking back at tolerance

As May said, ". . . it's incredible what you will do looking back on it". The single most impressive thing about these six biographies from the coping perspective is how full they are of descriptions of ways of coping that can be described as *tolerant*. At the core of the coping model are the actual ways in which those who are stressed, abused or tortured as a result of a relative's excessive drinking respond to the PDPs. Let us examine closely some of the 'tolerant' ways of responding to their husbands described by the six women.

Tolerant ways of coping include some that are more *inactive*, some that are more *accepting*, others that are more *sacrificing*, and yet others that are more *supportive* of the PDP. All have in common, however, a lack of challenge of the PDP's drinking behaviour, and a lack of asserting independence.

Sylvia provides an example of the inactive form of tolerance when she says that, although she was obsessed with looking around the house for her husband's drink, she would never dare throw it away when she found it. Meanwhile, her feelings alternated between despair when her husband was drunk and violent, and feeling in a fool's paradise when she thought he had given up drinking. May provides a textbook example of tolerant inaction when she describes how she would not speak to her husband when he came back after an evening out because she was afraid he would smash things up. She wouldn't even sulk, since she was so thankful that he had come back and so relieved that he was not hurt and that there were no signs of the police, fighting or other women. She never got angry but instead got frightened and lonely.

Emily illustrates the accepting form of tolerance, recalling that she used to block out or deny things because she didn't want to know about them. This was the case even when her husband did totally unacceptable things like urinating in the corner of the room. The next morning her husband would refuse to talk about it, so Emily kept quiet.

There are many examples in the biographies of the sacrificing form of tolerant coping. Ruth, for example, described the sacrifices she made in her social life because she was embarrassed to bring people home because of her husband's drinking, how she would take care how she spoke to her husband when he had been drinking, and how she hid the problem from everybody, sometimes ringing her husband's work to say that he was ill, and clearing things up so others would not notice. Similarly, Dawn sacrificed the support she might have received from her parents by not telling them about her husband's drinking – she later told her mother but her father never knew, and by remortgaging their house, for the second time, because of her husband's drinking debts.

Lisa's interview provides some of the best examples of that form of tolerance which has a strong element of supporting the PDP. Lisa describes how she took her husband's side, not only against the police with whom he was often in dispute, but against the view of her friends who doubted whether her husband really did not remember his violent outbursts, and who could not understand why Lisa did not get rid of him. In answer to her friends saying that she should not have to put up with his behaviour, Lisa said that she loved her husband and didn't want to throw away what they had together. She even took the blame for things being broken around the home so as to protect the children from realising what their father had done when drunk.

The foregoing are merely some examples. Many further instances of tolerant behaviour taken from these six biographies could be cited. Even looking back at the worst times, however, the six describe other ways in which they tried to engage with their partners' drinking and unacceptable behaviour associated with it. Amongst these alternative ways of responding are those that, from a coping perspective, might be termed *controlling, emotional* or *avoiding* the PDP. But in most cases, the behaviour described failed to provide an effective challenge to the partner's behaviour, nor did it help to create independence from the PDP. Sometimes this was because attempts to control a husband's drinking were tentative, secret, or just too weak to be effective. In other cases confrontation took an emotional form and was found to worsen rather than improve the situation. Other examples show how women on occasions "took a stand", but under pressure quickly reversed it.

For example, Ruth described how she would cover up for her husband but would then confront him about his drinking. He would agree and say he would stop drinking but didn't do so. At one stage she threw away all his home brew, and realises looking back that this was naive because from then on he simply bought his drink.

Lisa tried to talk to her husband about his drinking and violence, but he remained silent or acted bored and eventually she gave up trying to talk the problems over with him. At one point Lisa was so fed up with her husband's verbal abuse that she took her three children to a women's refuge where they spent a night. But she had no long-term plans and found the women's refuge disturbing, so she returned home the next day. Her husband begged her to stay and promised that he would change his behaviour, so she stayed. Some months later police had pressed charges against her husband for assaulting her and a court injunction was placed on him preventing him from entering the home. The following day, however, Lisa broke the injunction by allowing him back into the house, saying that she was prepared to give him another chance.

Dawn had used a number of strategies to try to control her husband's drinking. She had tried to ensure that he ate regularly and had tried to keep him busy, thinking that in that way he would not drink so much. She would not lend him money. She would try to find where he had hidden his drink and at one stage poured it down the sink when she found it. In retrospect none of these strategies had worked.

Looking back, Sylvia realised that she was giving all her attention to the children as a way of coping. She felt this was good for the children but it also served to help her avoid the situation with her husband, to whom she said she was giving almost nothing because she had become afraid of him. This example provides a good illustration of how CFMs may cope in what we call an avoidant way (i.e. avoiding the PDP) but a way that is inactive with regard to the PDP's drinking, and which creates no real independence for the CFM.

Emily, like Lisa, had taken a stand at one point and refused to have her husband home after he was hospitalised, having had a blackout in the car.

She even took him to the station so that he could get a train to go and live with his mother. Next day Emily went and picked him up and took him home. 'More fool I', she now comments.

May's description of having to go to the pub and 'shame' her husband in front of others into giving her money that she desperately needed, provides an illustration of the controlling tactics to which CFMs sometimes have to resort in order simply to survive, but which do not provide a challenge to the drinking or independence for the CFM. May had thought of leaving her husband, but these plans for independence were thwarted, as I shall outline in the next section.

## The struggle for independence

From a coping perspective the six stories told earlier in this book can be read as accounts of the struggle for *independence*. These women's accounts are full of images of abject and impotent dependence. For instance, the image of Sylvia in her kitchen, and her husband coming in and making her stand to attention and look into his eyes: "If I said anything out of place or defiant at all he'd hit me; I was frightened". And May sitting in the car with the baby in the middle of nowhere, her husband having abandoned her for a couple of hours in the middle of a weekend trip out – all May wanted was for him to come back, "then I'd be safe", and to get home.

All six describe elements of struggle for more independent ways of coping. Ruth had been to university and established a satisfying career before she married her husband. Later she mentions wanting to get back some independence as the children got older. But, despite this background of being her own person, it was only after some time that:

> She became more independent, both with and without her children and got involved with activities which were separate from James. Eventually she stopped covering up for him. Every now and again things would flare up and they would have a row but on the whole she avoided this and thought, "If you really want to talk to me about it you will be sober and then we can have a proper discussion about it; but unless you are going to sober up then it is pointless me trying to talk to you".

The foregoing paragraph illustrates well the way in which independent coping contrasts with tolerant coping of the sacrificing kind.

Lisa's background was very different to Ruth's. She met her husband-to-be when she was sixteen and living in a children's home, and her plans to get a college qualification had been obstructed by her early pregnancies. But the main theme is the same: tolerance appears to come easily, and independence only with a struggle. One night at a women's refuge is the greatest independence that Lisa had achieved to date, and although at the time of interview her husband was in prison it was expected that he would return to live with Lisa and the children.

Although Dawn was only 21 when she became engaged and 23 when she was married, she had trained as a nurse and had already had experience working as a senior staff nurse. After having three children she became bored at home and felt she wanted to use her skills to do some kind of work (she said she began to feel like a "cabbage"). She worked at a playgroup and did a relevant course, helped out at her youngest child's school, and later on, in the later stages of her husband's excessive drinking, she described holding a responsible job and getting very involved in her work. Once again, however, independent ways of coping with her husband's drinking did not come easily, and this appears only to have been through her contact with Al-Anon.

Sylvia had put up with a great deal of violence from her husband, and it was only after one incident, when something in her had "snapped" and she had realised that she had homicidal feelings towards him, that her position started to change. Like Dawn she had started to attend Al-Anon meetings and found them "quite an eye opener", and learnt a number of tactics for dealing with her husband's aggression.

Although at the time of giving her story Emily and her husband were having a year's trial separation, Emily felt cross with herself that she had only been able to make a stand and break away from her husband by being ill. She thought she was particularly foolish looking back on the earlier occasion when she had taken him back home just a day after sending him to his mother's after he had come out of hospital.

Quite early on in her marriage to her first husband, when he began seeing other women, May had thought about leaving him and had planned to get some further career qualifications. But May became pregnant, unplanned, with her first child and gave up her job once she had the baby. Thereafter, there is very little in May's biography that is recognisable as an indication of independent ways of coping. Indeed, May herself thought it was "incredible" that she had been so loyal to her husband, and "unbelievable" that she stayed in the relationship for so long. It was her husband who left May in the end, leaving her devastated, and May described further relationships of her own with two men with drinking problems.

Whether or not to leave their husbands, which may be thought of as the ultimate independent act of coping with living with a PDP, was a major dilemma for all the other women as well as for May. Sylvia had finally left her husband, although she described the separation as very difficult and unpleasant, and with hindsight thought it might have been better to have left him some years' earlier when her children were small. Emily and Lisa were both temporarily separated from their husbands at the time of the interview, Lisa while her husband was in prison, and Emily living with her mother on a year's trial separation from her husband, who remained in the marital home. Despite her husband's violence to her, and her very brief attempts at independence through the women's refuge and a legal injunction, it appeared that Lisa and her husband would be reunited when he came out of prison. Emily's biography, too, also ends with her outlining the advantages of continued marriage and the unattractiveness to her of becoming a single person. This was despite the fact that she had regretted not making a stand earlier, her husband had continued to drink away a lot of money and Emily was still paying the mortgage, and she had been advised by a psychiatrist that living with her husband was bad for her mental health and always would be. Ruth was still living with her husband but the question of separation was clearly on her mind. Over the years Ruth's feelings for her husband had died, and she said that she had begun to feel, "We're together now but I can't quite foresee us being together in, say 20 years time". Even Dawn, who of the six women seems the most likely to stay with her husband, said that she used to think a lot about separating from her husband and remembered looking through the papers wondering whether she would be able to find a job that would pay her enough money to live on her own.

At the time I was drafting this chapter Anne Brontë's *The Tenant of Wildfell Hall* (1848/1996) was serialised on British television. The parallels between the struggle for independence of the central character, Helen, and those of the six women whose biographies have appeared in this book, are all too obvious. It is particularly relevant here because there is every reason to suppose that descriptions of the behaviour of Helen's husband Arthur are based upon Anne Brontë's observations of that of her brother Branwell (Davies, 1996). The form of the novel is also particularly interesting since the central, largest section of the book is written in the first person in the form of Helen's diary. There are many points of similarity between Helen's diary and the present six biographies, but a brief comment on Helen's ways of coping with Arthur will have to suffice.

Very soon after their marriage, Helen becomes increasingly conscious of Arthur's inconsiderate behaviour and his excessive drinking. At this point Helen's diary includes an almost textbook description of *engaged* coping:

> . . . though I could not prevent him from taking more than was good for him, still, by incessant perseverance, by kindness, and firmness, and vigilance, by coaxing, and daring, and determination, – I succeeded in preserving him from absolute bondage to that detestable propensity so insidious in its advances, so inexorable in its tyranny, so disastrous in its effects. (1996, p. 260)

Almost three months later, Helen appears to have moved to a position that is not one of independence, but one in which she has achieved some personal distancing from her husband's behaviour, a kind of tolerant acceptance, with lowered expectations of his conduct, and less worry and emotion on her own part:

> . . . I have found it my wisest plan to shut my eyes against the past and future, as far as *he* at least is concerned, and live only for the present; to love him when I can; to smile (if possible) when he smiles, be cheerful when he is cheerful, and

pleased when he is agreeable; and when he is not, to try to make him so – and if that won't answer, to bear with him, to excuse him, and forgive him, as well as I can, and restrain my own evil passions from aggravating his; and yet, while I thus yield and minister to his more harmless propensities to self-indulgence, to do all in my power to save him from the worse. (1996, p. 269)

Helen does finally resolve to leave Arthur, and the rest of the book describes her life, in effect as a fugitive, attempting to live incognito and independently of her husband.

## Why does tolerance come so naturally and independence with such difficulty?

How did these six women find themselves tolerating for so long marriages that were unsupportive and abusive, and struggling for so long for independence. Their accounts provide many clues. From the coping perspective they are ordinary people trapped in a social context that invites tolerance and which puts up many barriers in the way of independence. There is nothing abnormal about these women that needs explaining in terms of their own personal biographies or characters. Indeed to ask the question "Why did these women tolerate their husbands' behaviour for so long?" might be construed as suggesting some abnormality or deviance on their part. From the coping perspective the question should be reformulated as: "What is it about the particular circumstances that CFMs find themselves in that makes tolerance seem so natural and independence so difficult to achieve?" Let us take the biographies one by one and see what answers they suggest.

Central themes in Ruth's account are excusing her husband's behaviour and blaming herself. Early on in their marriage Ruth formed an alliance with her husband against his "unfeeling, hostile and critical" mother who Ruth believes knew of her son's drinking and who had said to Ruth, "I shan't blame you if you leave him". This form of alliance with the PDP against criticism from a third party is not at all uncommon amongst CFMs (Lisa provides an even clearer example). Its function, for coping, is that it encourages the tolerant-supportive way of coping. Even more strongly encouraging of tolerance, however, is self-blame, of which Ruth provides one of the clearest examples amongst the six. Looking back she describes how incredibly tired she was with two young children and how this interfered with their sex life: "That's where it all started to go wrong really". Later, "I didn't feel that I had anything to offer, because I wasn't an interesting person anymore. I was just a mother". Her partner would sometimes tell her that it was all her fault and that he would stop drinking if only she did not put the children first, or if their sexual relationship was as it used to be, or if she cared for him more (the parallel with Arthur in *The Tenant of Wildfell Hall* is striking here). Ruth's response was indeed to try to change her behaviour towards him but this never lasted and she thought they were

139

both responsible for this. No wonder she dealt with the problem, "by hiding it from everybody", clearing things up so other people would not notice, and contributing "a sort of conspiracy of silence". The responsibility for her husband's excessive drinking which Ruth accepted for herself made it difficult for her to achieve the clarity of understanding of her husband's responsibility that would have been necessary for her to make a clearly independent stand. It is very noticeable that the last three paragraphs of her biography, under the heading "Ruth's understanding of her situation", focus almost exclusively upon what Ruth herself has done wrong and how she needs to change.

A minor theme in Ruth's account, but one which is quite common, is uncertainty about the future and the perpetual keeping alive of some hope. Because addiction problems, including excessive drinking, run a very uncertain course, and because CFMs often have the experience of good times as well as bad, it is very difficult to take an independent stand which may be thought to be rejecting of the PDP. Ruth said, "I am not really sure where we are going now . . . I think he is trying very hard, when he is at home with the children, to stay sober".

In Lisa's case the theme of self-blame is absent but the theme of excusing her husband for his behaviour is a strong one. This can be traced in Lisa's story to the strong, early alliance that they formed as teenagers in care in a children's home. They were in alliance against children's homes, against Lisa's husband's mother who had allowed him to be arrested, against the police, a college to which they both applied, and even against Lisa's friends who could not understand why she did not get rid of him (Helen, in *The Tenant of Wildfell Hall*, staunchly defends Arthur early on in the face of warnings from her aunt, her best friend, and her maid). Although there are signs in Lisa's biography that Lisa's understanding of her husband is wearing thin, the impression gained is that their relationship is founded upon solidarity in the face of a hostile environment. Like Ruth and her partner, Lisa and her husband have had some good, stable periods, and Lisa is prepared to give her husband another chance. By the time she gave her biography, Lisa appeared to have reached a position of resigned optimism.

Dawn's account of the earlier years of her husband's drinking problem, before he received any treatment for it, is, like Ruth's, full of uncertainty and confusion. The uncertainty in Dawn's case, however, is not about how much she is responsible for her husband's excessive drinking, but rather about the seriousness of the drinking in relation to other problems including her husband's excessive gambling, deaths in his family, and Martin himself developing diabetes. It is very significant that Dawn says that she still did not see his drinking as problematic at this time, but saw it more as a reaction to his emotional grief and the resentment he felt about his diabetes. Her husband would pass out, Dawn would worry a lot about this, but did not know whether it was the effect of alcohol or due to his diabetes. The picture was complicated still more by Dawn's own health problems.

This theme of confusion is a common one for CFMs and is there again in Sylvia's story. When they were first married Sylvia used to drink quite a lot herself with her husband, and get drunk, so much so that "people seeing us may have thought I was the one with the problem". Later, when the pattern of her husband's violence towards her became established, Sylvia explains that it was some years before she began to make a connection between her husband's violence and his drinking. When someone from Social Services called, she had responded by feeling that she didn't need any help. Although she "knew life was an absolute nightmare", at first she had thought it was probably normal, and later that it was "fated". Until she heard about Al-Anon, Sylvia "didn't know about alcoholism". It was a long time before Sylvia could admit to herself that her husband had a problem, and she used to think up reasons to defend his behaviour. This statement links the theme of confusion with the theme of loyalty which is also strong in Sylvia's account. Sylvia said, "for years and years I felt I had to stay faithful to my marriage vows", particularly as she had not done so in her first marriage. At her first Al-Anon meetings she had felt disloyal talking about her husband.

Emily was another who reports drinking heavily with her husband when they first met, and later on she reckoned herself a hopeless judge of whether people had been drinking or not. But the main theme of Emily's biography is her own depression, psychiatric diagnosis, hospitalisation and medication with Lithium. In relation to her husband's excessive drinking, the function of Emily's own mental health problems and treatment seems to have been to mask her husband's problem and to confuse Emily. Indeed in her account there is more information about her own problems and treatment than about his drinking problem, although eventually her husband's excessive drinking emerges as a significant problem and the cause of the year's trial separation that Emily and her husband were having at the time she gave her biography. As was the case for Ruth, problems in their sex life were blamed on Emily, and at one stage they had gone to a sex therapist and to marriage guidance. Not only did her own mental health problems confuse the picture, but Emily believes the medication she was receiving blunted her emotions, making her quieter and more accepting of her husband's behaviour than she would otherwise have been. Even when she was not on Lithium, however, Emily ignored unacceptable, drink-related behaviour because her husband denied it, and she too used to block out or deny things because she didn't want to know about them.

Many of these same themes are to be found in May's account. She too drank heavily in the early years as part of an intense relationship with her first husband with whom she was very much in love and with whom she shared a childhood background involving cruelty from their fathers. She "never took a lot of notice of what he drank", and rather like Dawn, when he did drink heavily, she felt he was basically "drowning his sorrows". May is particularly eloquent about the various factors that, she felt, "trapped" her into staying with her husband and tolerating his womanising and excessive

**Figure 12.3** Why tolerance comes easy and independence with difficulty: main themes

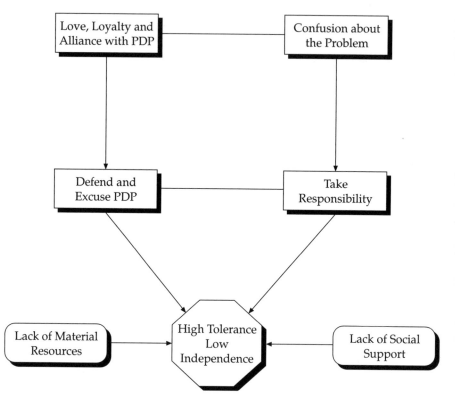

drinking. These factors included loyalty, love, and self-blame, as well as practicalities of finances and responsibilities for childcare, the latter being elements that are implied rather than highlighted in other women's accounts.

Also present in May's account is the theme of confusion about the nature of drinking problems, plus the perpetual hope for change. May said that she had "wondered vaguely" if her husband was an alcoholic, and "it began to make sense" when the doctors said that he was. Sometimes she had felt hopeful because he stopped drinking for a while and would be "very loving, caring, supporting and charming". She said something very similar about her second husband.

The main themes of the foregoing section are shown in Figure 12.3. According to these six women's accounts, the forces that make for continued tolerance in the face of the effects of excessive drinking, and which make independence so difficult to attain, are those of love, loyalty and alliance, plus uncertainty and confusion about the problem. This powerful combination supports a position in which a CFM excuses and defends a PDP and even takes much of the blame and responsibility herself. Lack of social, occupational and financial resources further delays the process of moving towards a more independent position.

## Lack of social support for independence

It might be expected, given their circumstances, that the six women would have been supported by other people in their struggle to gain some independence and to overcome the pressures for continued tolerance. This, however, was mostly not the case. Each woman described how such support was lacking.

Ruth, for example, described how until quite recently her partner's mother had been the only other person who knew about his drinking, but Ruth had not felt close enough to her to talk about it. She once talked to her own mother who had been staying with them when her partner got very drunk, but her mother thought it was just because it was New Year's Eve. Ruth thought her mother had "found it too hard to cope with then". In general Ruth had not felt that she could talk to other people about the problem because it was unacceptable and other people would not know how to deal with it. She would not say anything to others unless they had noticed it for themselves, "because it is something which is rather shameful and embarrassing and needs to be kept quiet". Even if someone in Ruth's position does talk about the problem to someone else, what other people say is not always helpful, as Ruth explained. For one thing, "sometimes people's support can be rather strongly advice-giving". Even when people are generally helpful, sympathetic and supportive, as some of Ruth's work colleagues had been once they knew about her situation, Ruth had thought that, if anything, they had taken her side too much. This is an interesting comment, and it fits with what we know about the sensitivity of CFMs about other people mistakenly thinking they are being helpful by "taking sides" against the PDP. Most family members say that this is not what they want (Orford *et al.*, 1998c). Like Ruth, Lisa had also not found it helpful when friends of hers had tried to support her by taking a strong line against her husband, in this case by casting doubt on whether he really did not remember his violent outbursts, and by failing to understand why she did not get rid of him.

Family members often feel very unsupported by professional people. In Ruth's case it was something that her partner's GP had said to her partner that she had found really unhelpful. The doctor had said, "You've got a lot more drinking to do before you are going to be ready [for treatment]". Emily was also critical of professional services, both for being unempathic about her point of view, and failing to follow through on the treatment that was offered to her husband. Lisa also felt let down by a psychiatrist who told her husband that his problem was only habitual and therefore not a major problem. Lisa viewed this reasoning as stupid, and it meant that the psychiatrist was unwilling to get her husband into a detoxification unit which was what he wanted at the time.

Like other women, Dawn referred explicitly to never speaking to her own father about her husband's drinking problem, even though she was close to her father and described having very deep talks with him before he died. Al-Anon had been Dawn's main support in achieving some independence, and this will be discussed again in the final section of this chapter.

Sylvia had also found Al-Anon positively supportive, but otherwise her account contains a number of clues about how other people fail to provide support for independence. In the case of her neighbours, for example, Sylvia stated that she had thought that none of them knew what was going on, and in any case she did not like to go "and land on neighbours". In fact once Sylvia spoke to people about her problems, she discovered that all her neighbours knew and that they were sympathetic. Sylvia's sister would have been an obvious person from whom to obtain support since she shared with Sylvia the experience of excessive drinking and violence in her marriage. Sylvia did not turn to her sister for support, however, it seems because they had different moral values, and later perhaps because her sister might have been a bit jealous about Sylvia's growing independence.

The position of Sylvia's GP in relation to tolerance or independence is an interesting one. Like Sylvia herself, he was a Christian who believed in the sanctity of marriage, saying to Sylvia that she must have a lot of "grace" to put up with her marriage. At the time Sylvia had found this a "comfort" but on reflection had thought that his attitude had possibly contributed to her staying with her husband. At a crucial point, when Sylvia "snapped" and had developed homicidal feelings towards her husband, her GP had put her on tranquillisers.

The role of religion in relation to Sylvia's tolerance and independence is a complex one. Although her own and her GP's Christian attitudes of tolerance may in some ways have made independence more difficult for her at a certain stage in her married life, religion had also allowed her to feel that ultimately God was keeping her safe and her faith had grown strongly. Emily was also of the opinion that the Church may have influenced her to stay with her husband. In fact Emily was very explicit that a combination of guilt, induced by the Church, and her own Lithium medication, had made her accepting of her situation: "This is a cross you have to bear, you've made your bed and you have to lie on it". Unlike Sylvia and Emily, May in the end felt let down by religion: "Him upstairs has forgotten I exist . . . I feel I have had more than my fair share".

Like other women, May was able to explain why support that might have been expected was not forthcoming. As May said, "I couldn't get anyone to believe me", and when other people did know it could often result in reduced support. For example, if May was ill herself doctors would dismiss her health complaints, saying, "Oh well, you live in a very stressful situation, you have a husband who drinks heavily". Her friends avoided her because "they couldn't work out what was going on". He would be unpleasant to them, they would leave, and she would end up feeling lonely. On the other hand he behaved himself with their parents, so it appeared that May was telling tales when she tried to talk to them about what was going on. All in all May felt trapped and "didn't know which way to turn". Even worse, her own father and brother directly blamed her for causing her husband's problems.

## Can we ignore the women's histories prior to meeting their partners?

When outlining the coping perspective at the beginning of this chapter, and contrasting it with other perspectives, a very definite and deliberate stance was taken towards looking in detail at CFMs' personal histories. The viewpoint adopted in this chapter is that the women's personal lives, prior to meeting their partners, is immaterial to solving the dilemmas that they, and other CFMs like them, face in deciding how to respond to someone whose excessive drinking deeply affects them and about whom they are concerned. Of course personal-developmental hypotheses can be formulated for individual women, for example linking deprivation of affection in childhood with tolerance of a partner's bad behaviour in adulthood. But the argument here is that to do so is to displace attention away from attempts to solve a very difficult, but very common, family dilemma, towards attempting to unravel a CFM's (in this case a woman's) personal history. This inevitably implies, however strong the protests from developmentalists such as those espousing the psychodynamic or codependency[2] perspectives, that CFMs have in some way contributed to the problems they now face.

There is an even greater danger in the personal-historical approach. The lives of some CFMs are particularly seductive for those who wish, retrospectively, to trace developmental links. This is particularly the case for women such as Lisa, whose caretaking as a child was very fragmented, who formed an alliance with her future husband when they were both teenagers, who later married her husband although he had already shown evidence of excessive drinking and violence, and who struggled for independence. A developmental hypothesis is particularly inviting, also, for women like May, whose father was violent towards her, and who as an adult married two men with drinking problems and then had a relationship with a third. The danger, then, is that these particularly noticeable 'cases' become the prototypes for a general theory about the experience of CFMs. Indeed that is exactly what has happened in the past. At one time, not long ago, women married to 'alcoholics' were thought to have a characteristic 'psychopathology' (Jackson, 1954).

The coping view, adopted here, is clear on this point. What matters is the current experience of CFMs and not their past histories. What they can benefit from most is understanding of their current experience and support in solving the dilemma of what to do. If anything, they need help with current problem solving, not personal-historical therapy.

The family childhoods described by the six women are very varied. Whilst Lisa, May, and possibly Emily, whose father was a heavy drinker, described adversity in childhood, this was not the case for Ruth, Dawn or Sylvia who described happy, sheltered, or at worst strict family upbringing. Hence, an adverse childhood is not a regular theme, and cannot therefore be part of a general account of the experience of women who live with men with drinking problems, let alone of CFMs more generally. Nor can it be argued that adversity in childhood is necessary for women to put up with a partner's excessive drinking and the violence that is sometimes associated with it. Sylvia disproves that argument. She lived with a heavy drinking and extremely violent husband for many years before leaving him, despite a sheltered childhood and a gentle, religiously devout father. So strong is the inclination to search for remote causes in childhood, that Sylvia even wondered whether her childhood had been "too sheltered".

Naturally enough, given the events of their married lives, all six women had much to say about the process of meeting, getting to know, and marrying their partners. Almost all (Dawn is the only exception), with the benefit of hindsight, now compare their partners unfavourably with other men they might, or should have, married, and/or describe early warning signs of impending trouble which they ignored or were blind to at the time.

One of the signs that might have been missed is the sign that the intended partner is a heavy drinker. Much is made of this by 'psychopathology' theorists who tend to see it as a clue that women are attracted to problem drinkers for personal-historical reasons of their own. These six women's accounts suggest a different explanation in terms of naivety. Most describe drinking heavily themselves, with their partners, when they first met, and none thought their partners' drinking was a problem at the time. Even Lisa, who rather reluctantly married after her partner's heavy drinking and violence had become apparent, and after they had their eldest child, had not thought her future husband's drinking was a problem when they first met, and they had drunk secretly together as teenagers.

## What can be done to help close family members become more independent?

Many CFMs, given the sheer passage of time and the accumulation of stress, are likely to move in the natural course of events towards a new position. This new position may not be one of healthy independence, but may be one rather of 'resigned acceptance' or one in which there is an unhappy sense that 'love has died'. Perhaps, for a real move towards independence, there has to be a challenge to one or more of the forces, shown in Figure 12.3, that impede the natural move to independence. The availability of outside occupation, new and absorbing leisure activities, or improved finances, may constitute one kind of challenge.

But ideas constitute another. For two of the women, Dawn and Sylvia, Al-Anon had been a main source of challenge to ideas such as, "I'm crazy", "it doesn't affect me much", "I'm to blame", and "I can control his drinking by reasoning or other means". "Knowing about alcoholism" was the vehicle for "realising" what was going on and "seeing things differently". Although Ruth does not mention Al-Anon, she does mention a counsellor friend who had helped Ruth clarify some of her feelings. Like this good friend, Al-Anon can combine the possibility of fresh thinking with the provision of social support, which is so often lacking for CFMs.

Primary healthcare workers (PHCWs) such as GPs are well placed in the British healthcare system to provide CFMs with support and the help to challenge the barriers to independence. We know, however, that PHCWs often lack a grounding in the coping perspective and often feel they are not in a strong position to provide the help that CFMs need (Howells, 1997). From the accounts of the six women in this book, we know that GPs may inadvertently fail to be supportive by making pessimistic or critical comments, by dampening down discomfort by prescribing psychoactive medication, or by congratulating a CFM on her tolerant attitude. Fortunately there has been a recent and welcome development in the form of approaches for responding to CFMs (e.g. Barber and Crisp, 1995; Howells, 1997; Meyers et al., 1996; Thomas and Ager, 1993; Yates, 1988). In the UK this approach is currently being piloted in the Birmingham and Bath areas using a 'package' of a written manual and supporting materials for PHCWs plus the provision of specialist training, support and back-up (Copello et al., 1996, Copello et al., 1998). Amongst the aims of this approach are the following:

- To help CFMs share the problem with someone who has specialist knowledge and no personal involvement with the drinking problem. This may bring a sense of relief and a more positive attitude, especially when a CFM has been bearing the problem alone.
- To provide reassurance that there is a genuine drinking problem. This can help overcome CFMs' fears that their own assessments may have been exaggerated, and may give them the confidence to confront the problem and bring it into the open.
- To provide accurate information using, where appropriate, good quality information leaflets about alcohol problems and their effects on the family, which may allow CFMs to voice their fears and address misunderstandings or lack of knowledge.
- To discuss ways in which CFMs may have been acting in a tolerant and self-sacrificing manner in the face of the drinking problem, and to

discuss other options for coping, including taking distance and maintaining some independence from the problem drinking.

The first two steps are the most fundamental from a coping perspective. If people who come into contact with CFMs, and that includes other family members, friends, neighbours, work colleagues, health workers, police and potentially many others, grasp the coping viewpoint and respond to CFMs accordingly, then women like those whose biographies are told in the book would feel heard and that their position was understood. They would know that people were not judging them or holding them to blame, nor that they were thought by others to be making a mountain out of a molehill. The fact that they were facing a variety of coping dilemmas, including to what extent to create some independence for themselves, would be understood. Others would not rush in with condemnation of the PDPs or with direct advice about what to do. They would, on the other hand, listen more carefully, allow CFMs to tell their stories and to express emotion associated with their current lives. This has rarely happened for CFMs in the past, but when it does it is much valued by them and appears, in itself, to provide much relief.

Conversations that friends, family and professionals find themselves having with CFMs can then move, as the list of aims given above suggests, to a stage in which the ways CFMs are coping is discussed. Howells (1997), who has reported on the success that she and her colleagues have had in using an approach very similar to the one described here, warns that such conversations should not move too quickly to the point at which ways of coping are being discussed directly. If the pace is forced too rapidly there is the risk that CFMs feel, as has so often been the case, that they are being blamed for getting it wrong. Most CFMs, on the other hand, once they know that they are not being judged and that their position is basically understood, are only too ready to discuss how best to cope and to acknowledge that there are options for doing things in ways other than those they have been used to. The aim here is to open up options for coping, to discuss the pros and cons of each, and to help a CFM make an informed choice of what to do. Howells' (1997) results suggest that, offered this approach, women like the six in this book report very rapid reductions in symptoms of anxiety, nervousness and depression. They also report changes in the ways they are coping, in particular a rapid reduction in what Howells calls 'self-sacrificing coping'.

If help for CFMs had been more easily accessible and well-publicised, in the form of well-prepared primary healthcare workers and self-help groups such as Al-Anon, Anne Brontë might have found some useful help in coping with her brother's behaviour, and Ruth, Lisa, Dawn, Sylvia, Emily and May might have been helped earlier to achieve some measure of healthy independence.

# Acknowledgements

The ideas expressed in this chapter, as well as being based on the six biographies, draw heavily upon the results of a collaborative, international research project on alcohol, drugs and the family. I should like to acknowledge the contribution made to that research by many women and men, in England and Mexico, who gave their accounts of living with excessive drinking or drug taking in the family; colleagues at the Institute of Psychiatry in Mexico City, at the Universities of Birmingham, Bath, Portsmouth and Exeter, and at Northern Birmingham and Bath Mental Healthcare Trusts; and the Mental Health Foundation who funded the research in the UK.

# Notes

1. Editor's footnote: although most codependency writers do this, Liz Cutland in this book does not in fact place much emphasis on past history.
2. Editor's footnote: again note must be taken of the fact that Liz Cutland in this book does not see codependency as historical and developmentalist in this way.

# CHAPTER 13

# A feminist perspective

*Jane Ussher*

## Introduction

> Feminism: The principle that women should have political, economic, and social rights equal to those of men; the movement to win such rights for women. (*Websters New World Dictionary*, 1978)

Commenting upon these six biographies, and the topic of women living with drink, from a feminist perspective, one must of necessity start with a definition of feminism. However, the general dictionary definition of 'feminism' given above could arguably encompass the majority of academic theorists and practitioners today, regardless of whether they define themselves as 'feminist'; only the most reactionary or misogynistic would surely openly declare that women *should* be subordinate to, or subjugated by, men. What differentiates a 'feminist' perspective is the centrality of the critical analysis of gender relationships and the focus on the detrimental impact of patriarchal power and control in both academic theory and professional practice. There are many different schools of feminist thought which differ in analyses of how and why gender inequalities occur, resulting in different solutions being put forward for intervention, prevention or change (see Humm, 1993). The standpoint that I will adopt here is that we need to take account of *material, discursive* and *intrapsychic* factors, and of the relationship between these different levels of analysis and experience, in any analysis of women's lives.

In this chapter I will outline how a material-discursive-intrapsychic approach can be used to inform a feminist analysis of the situation of women 'living with drink', starting by briefly describing each level of analysis in turn; then go on to discuss the way in which these three factors interact in both the accounts of the interviewees themselves, and in my own understanding of this issue, drawing on examples from the six biographies.

*150*

# A feminist material-discursive-intrapsychic analysis of living with drink

## The level of the discursive

To focus on the 'discursive' is to look to social and linguistic domains: to talk, to visual representation, to ideology, culture, and power. There is now a burgeoning field of 'discursive psychology', which draws on disciplines as disparate as semiotics, poststructuralism, sociology, film theory, history of art, psychoanalysis, anthropology and sociology (e.g. Potter and Edwards, 1992). This has been used to examine aspects of experience as wide-ranging as mental health, sexuality, violence, science, political power, or consumerism. However, what is arguably of most relevance here is the analysis of the relationship between representations of 'woman' and 'man' and the social roles adopted by individual women and men.

Rather than gender being seen as pre-given or innate, here it is seen as something which is performed or acquired. In the process of becoming 'woman', it is argued that women follow the various scripts of femininity which are taught to them through the family, through school, and through the myriad representations of 'normal' gender roles in popular and high culture, as well as in science and the law (see Ussher, 1997a). They have to choose between the contradictory representations of femininity which are available at any point in time, in order to find a fit between what they wish to be, and what is currently allowed (Ussher, 1997a). The fact that many women take up the archetypal position of 'woman' – always positioned as secondary to 'man' – is attributed to the dominance of patriarchy, and the fact that gender is constructed within a 'heterosexual matrix' (Butler, 1990).

Within a heterosexual matrix, the traditional script of femininity tells us that women live their lives through a man. To have a man, and keep him, is the goal of every girl's life. Girls are weaned on fairy stories that reinforce the importance of this tale (and remind them of the terrible fate of women who fail): Cinderella and her ugly sisters, Snow White and her wicked stepmother. In adulthood women are reminded of it through romantic fiction, women's magazines, television soap opera or Hollywood films: the good wife and the femme fatale, who in film noir always meets an unseemly end. The good girl is invariably self-sacrificing, but she always gets her man. In the late twentieth century, 'getting' still means monogamy, and usually marriage or motherhood; this is the script for the 'respectable' woman. *Not* getting means being positioned as sad or bad: the spinster on the shelf, or the shameful whore. And the sexual woman, the whore, is always deemed to deserve all the condemnation that she gets (see Ussher, 1997a).

In the traditional discursive construction of heterosexuality, 'man' is positioned as powerful, and 'woman' as passive and beholden to man. The institutionalised couple they form together is positioned as immune from scrutiny or intervention from outside. At the same time, 'man' is idealised as the answer to a woman's dreams: the fairy-tale prince who will sweep her off her feet; 'Mr Right' who will bring happiness, contentment and fulfilment of her heart's desires – the 'happy ever after' ending we are promised at the end of romantic fiction and fairy tales. Yet it is also acknowledged that this relationship can result in violence, oppression and neglect. The traditional discursive representation of heterosexuality provides an explanation for this which ensures that many women stay: the myth of 'Beauty and the Beast'. We are taught that a good woman can always tame or transform the monstrous brute or beast; through her ministrations or example the frog will turn into the prince, the violent man into the charming thoughtful lover. The woman who *can't* enact this transformation is positioned as being to blame; she must try harder, be more self-sacrificing, or attempt with greater vigour to be the 'perfect woman'. Yet even if she fails at this, and the beast is never transformed, we are reminded by the fairy stories and by romantic fiction that underneath it all the brute is a vulnerable and needy man, and that he is the most sexy or desirable partner a woman could find (Mr Rochester, Rhett Butler . . . ). And if all else fails, women still have the hope that motherhood will provide true fulfilment, as will the security of knowing that they are safe within the boundaries of a 'normal' heterosexual life (see Ussher, 1997a).

This isn't merely an analysis of fairy stories, or of an outmoded script of heterosexual femininity that many women have rejected in their quest for a more autonomous life. It is one of the explanations put forward for why women stay in unhappy, neglectful or violent relationships with men (Dobash and Dobash, 1979), and arguably one of the explanations for why women continue to 'live with drink'. For it is not the drink that they are living with, but a particular man, as is evidenced by the six biographies provided here.

## The level of material practice

To talk of materiality is to talk of factors which exist at a corporeal, a societal or an institutional level: factors which are traditionally at the centre of biomedical or sociological accounts. In this context, what is of relevance are material factors which institutionalise inequalities in heterosexual relationships, legitimating masculine power and control. This would encapsulate economic factors which make women dependent on men; presence or absence of accommodation which allows women in destructive relationships to leave; support for women of a legal, emotional and structural kind, which allows protection from further harassment or abuse. It would include issues of social class which lead to expectations of 'normal' behaviour for women and men, and which are implicated in educational or employment opportunities available to both, as well as in the way individuals are treated by external institutions such as social services or the police. The fact of whether children are present in the relationship (or are withheld in custody battles), and the material consequences of being married (or not) are also part of this level of analysis. Equally, previous history of abuse, or of bereavement, is partly a material event; as is family history, such as the number of siblings, parental relationships and factors such as parental divorce or separation from parents in childhood. There are also many material consequences of alcohol misuse, in terms of intoxication, illness, psychological effects, increased likelihood of violence, or even premature death. The social isolation which can be a consequence of alcohol misuse, or which can act to exacerbate its effects is also partly a material issue. Sex, ethnicity and sexuality are also associated with materiality: with the reproductive body, with gendered or sexual behaviour, and with physical appearance. Within a feminist perspective it is recognised that material factors often mitigate against women: women are often economically, physically and socially disadvantaged in relation to men.

## The level of the intrapsychic

Intrapsychic factors are those that operate at the level of the individual and the psychological: factors which are traditionally the central focus of any psychological analysis of women's lives. This would include analyses of the way in which women blame themselves for problems in relationships, and psychological explanations for why this is so, incorporating factors such as low self-esteem, depression, the impact of previous neglect or abuse, guilt, shame, fear of loss or separation, and the idealisation of both heterosexuality and of men. It would include an analysis of splitting as a psychological defence, and a mechanism for avoiding acknowledgement of difficulty or of pain: for example, the way women see themselves, or their man, as all good or all bad, with no acknowledgement that everyone can exhibit both positive and negative characteristics at the same time. It would also include women's internalisation of the idealised fantasy of motherhood, and of the expectations of being 'woman' in a heterosexual social sphere.

'Material-discursive' approaches, which integrate both of these levels of analysis, have recently been developed in a number of areas of psychology, such as sexuality, reproduction, and mental or physical health (see Ussher, 1991, 1997a, 1997b; Yardley, 1997). This is as a result of both a frustration with traditional psychology which has tended to adopt a solely materialist standpoint, thus serving to negate discursive aspects of experience, and a dissatisfaction with the negation of the material aspects of life in many discursive accounts. This integrationist material-discursive approach is to be welcomed, yet arguably does not always go far enough, as the intrapsychic is often still left out, for the reason that it is seen as individualistic or reductionist, or not easily accessible to empirical investigation. Equally, when intrapsychic factors are considered (e.g. in psychoanalytic or cognitive theorising), they are almost invariably conceptualised separately from either material or discursive factors.[1] It is time that all three levels together are

**Figure 13.1**  A material-discursive-intrapsychic approach

## MATERIAL FACTORS

- Physical effects of alcohol misuse, death in family, physical or sexual abuse
- Social support, accommodation, income, treatment options offered, law
- Family relationships, presence or absence of children

## Living with Drink

## INTRAPSYCHIC FACTORS ←——→ DISCURSIVE FACTORS

- Impact of past experiences
- Psychological defences
- Current mood/well-being
- Self-esteem
- Attributions
- Ways of coping
- Idealisation of men
- Insecurity: can't live without a man

Discursive representations of:
- Alcohol use/misuse
- Femininity/masculinity
- Sexuality/sexual violence
- Heterosexual relationships
- Acceptable ways of expressing distress for women and men
- Love and romance

incorporated into academic theory and practice, in order to provide a multidimensional analysis of women's lives – the central concern of any feminist critique.

To illustrate the way in which these three levels of experience interact, I will now turn to the six biographies, and in particular to the interviewees' explanations for how they found themselves in the situation they are in. For, as was argued above, these are not factors which can be considered separately from each other. It is the interaction between all three that makes the whole, as is illustrated in Figure 13.1.

## *Exploring the heterosexual matrix*

Arguably, each of the women described in the biographies is living life within a traditional heterosexual matrix, a fact which goes much of the way towards explaining why they are 'living with drink'. This is partly a material issue, in that they are economically dependent on men to various degrees, physically living with a man, and dependent on their partner for emotional support or for help in the raising of children; an example is when May describes feeling "trapped" into staying with her first husband, "because she had the children, no money and nowhere to go". It is also an intrapsychic issue, in that psychological defences act to maintain their position within what is often an unequal relationship, and arguably partly led to their entering the relationship, or choosing a particular man, in the first place. It is also a discursive issue, in that each of these relationships conforms with much of that deemed 'normal' within the dominant constructions of heterosexuality which we all see around us.

There is clear evidence in the biographies of women seeking happiness, fulfilment and a sense of self through a man, and of marriage being one of the key events in their lives. There is also evidence of *any* man being positioned as being better than no man at all. Emily is described as having agreed to marry her husband because she was "certain that no one else would propose to her", and despite unhappiness in the relationship, she describes feeling secure in "the role of a married woman", with the thought of being single being "devastating" to her. Likewise, Sylvia said she was "anxious to get married; I never felt happy about being alone for the rest of my life", and May felt she had "got to go through with" her second marriage despite her misgivings, because "she didn't want to be on her own". This could be partly due to fear of being positioned *outside* the heterosexual matrix, and of being seen as sad or shameful as a result. The spectre of the denunciation of the woman who is sexual outside of marriage was certainly evident in Sylvia's account. Her first husband divorced her when she was caught paying "attention to another man", and she lost the custody of her children when her second husband said she was a prostitute. This denunciation of active or autonomous female sexuality pervades phallocentric cultural discourse, most commonly seen in rape trials (Lees, 1996), but also in the mass media, science and the law (Ussher, 1997a).

It is also undoubtedly partly due to intrapsychic factors, such as low self-esteem, sometimes resulting from previous loss, neglect or abuse, that leads women to have very low expectations of what they can hope to receive in relationships with men, resulting in a need to be in a relationship regardless of the costs. Thus May described her first husband as "kind and considerate", which she says was a new experience for her, yet arguably this is the minimum any person should expect from a partner. She said of her second husband that, because of her loneliness, "anyone who shows any kindness in any degree is better than nothing" and that despite his violence he got rid of "the terrible loneliness and the unbelievable fear that she felt".

Many women negotiate the tension between their need to be in a heterosexual relationship, and the difficulty of finding (or keeping) 'Mr Right' through denial of the difficulties in the relationship: Emily is described as saying that she "used to block out or deny things because she did not want to know about them", and she "used to ignore his behaviour even when he was doing totally unacceptable things". There is also evidence of splitting of the good from the bad aspects of men: Dawn describes her husband when sober as "a different person" whom she really cared for. Some of the women arguably learnt this splitting in childhood: Sylvia describes her mother as a "harsh disciplinarian" but "loving at the same time"; Emily saw her mother splitting off her own husband's "awful side", which was the only side she herself could see. Childhood experiences can also teach the internalisation or somaticisation of distress, which are not uncommon within an archetypal feminine role: Ruth's sister's anorexia, and Sylvia's mother's headaches are two examples.

The discursive construction of the heterosexual unit as private and invulnerable is evident in these biographies. This is a factor which is central to the silence, secrecy and shame which surround many of the damaging aspects of family or marital life. It is partly an issue of discourse, as 'woman' is positioned as coping, long-suffering and silent on the subject of problems with her man within traditional constructions of heterosexuality. Yet it is also an intrapsychic and material issue, as women blame themselves for problems, and there is little institutional or material support for women who choose to challenge or to leave. Ruth, Dawn, May, Sylvia and Emily all report an absence of support from friends or family when they needed it most. There is also much evidence of competition, ambivalence, or absence of solidarity between women: such as Sylvia blaming her son's girlfriend for his violence; or Ruth's reports of her relationships with her mother and her sisters. Difficulties between women are partly a discursive phenomenon – representations of women's envy and competition circulate in fairy stories and popular culture, and are evident in the discourses drawn on by women and girls when describing their relationships with each other (see Ussher, 1997a). But it is also an intrapsychic and material issue (see Orbach and Eichenbaum, 1985), in terms of the literal separation between women, the further isolation of women from others who are in similar situations of distress, and the location of problems in the individual family, or the woman herself.

We also see evidence of male violence and alcohol misuse positioned as culturally 'normal' within these biographies – within dominant constructions of heterosexual masculinity neither are unexpected, if not officially condoned. If these behaviours are criticised, this is done so on an individual basis, with violence or alcohol misuse not seen as aspects of gender relationships or of masculinity, but the problem of an individual man, or of his family. This means that many women often feel shame when violence or alcohol misuse occurs, and it is rare for neighbours or family to want to intervene: so Sylvia was offered negligible support in the face of her husband's violence; Lisa became resigned to her husband's violence after his drinking; and Ruth dealt with her husband's drinking "by hiding it from everybody because it's something which is rather shameful and embarrassing and needs to be kept quiet". In the pub, on the football terrace, or in certain strands of corporate culture, masculine aggression and excessive alcohol intake are not merely normal behaviours, but necessary for survival in a hostile world, serving as signs of what it is to be 'man'. It isn't surprising that these behaviours continue in the home, but for the women who live with it on a daily basis it is not a sign of masculine power, but a source of their own oppression and abuse.

These are all factors which arguably contributed to the interviewees staying with their men, regardless of the quality of the relationship, even when others were telling them to leave, or when they themselves were unhappy or subjected to violence. Many of the women drew on a romantic discourse to explain this, where 'love' is positioned as the most important thing which cannot be cast off: so Lisa says she "loves her husband and does not want to throw away what they have together", even when her friends tell her to "get rid of him". May says she was "very much in love with" her husband "and still am". Ruth, May and Sylvia explained that they stayed because of the children: because of the desire to offer children two parents, feelings of responsibility and the need for financial support discussed above. One of the other major reasons put forward by the women was their own feelings of guilt or self-blame. As Ruth said, she felt "very alone, isolated, angry at times, impotent, helpless, hopeless and guilty, as if she was 'responsible for the whole mess'".

# The traditional scripts of femininity and masculinity

Self-blame is central to the traditional script of femininity. As was outlined above, 'woman' is positioned as the force that acts to transform man from beast to prince. Is it surprising that women blame themselves if they can't? So Ruth believed that "if she had loved James more or better then he wouldn't have needed to drink"; May says that "if he loves me, he'll love me enough to be nice all the time". Women are also blamed by others: Emily by her husband for causing his drink problems through her own mental health problems; May told by her father that she would "drive anyone to drink"; Ruth by the clinic which treated her husband's alcohol problems, and by her husband himself, who said he would stop drinking if their sex life was better or if she stopped putting the children first.

The self-sacrifice familiar from fairy tales is also clearly evidenced, as when May describes her reaction to her first husband leaving after 25 years: "devastated . . . I'd done so much for him". She describes herself as having stayed partly for the security of having and keeping him: "I wouldn't have put up with all that if I knew he was going to leave". This self-sacrifice is arguably reinforced by the depression, anxiety, and feelings of hopelessness which many women report, conceptualised by some as part of a maso-chistic feminine role (see Kaplan, 1991). It is often only extreme factors which allow many women to step outside of this role: Emily "had to have a psychiatric crisis" to leave her husband; Lisa left when her neighbours finally called the police as a result of witnessing domestic violence. There is a point when all women have had enough.

The discursive construction of masculinity, and the notion that difficulty in relationships is what heterosexual women should expect, also serves to ensure that women stay 'living with drink'. This is evident in the idealisa-tion of the unreachable man, reflecting the myth of the illusive romantic hero: May describing her ex-fiancé as "the love of my life", and "a wonderful person"; Sylvia describing her father as "so close to me since his death; I can't wait to get to heaven to cuddle him"; Ruth describing her relationship with a married man as "very important at the time but it was doomed". The idealisation of man also sets up an impossible standard for most men to live up to, which arguably contributes to the disappointment and discontent which many of the interviewees report, where early expectations of relation-ships are not borne out. Yet the myth that 'Mr Right' will someday shine through is also evident: as May says, "when they are nice they are nicer than the average person, and you hope it will stay like that". This is a sentiment commonly expressed by women who live with violent men (Dobash and Dobash, 1979).

The evidence we see in these biographies of men externalising unhappi-ness, anger or discontent – expressing it through violence, through alcohol abuse, or through blaming problems on a woman – is again a commonly observed phenomenon. It has been argued that within dominant discur-sive constructions of 'madness', to openly express distress or mental health problems is to be at risk of being positioned as feminine (Ussher, 1991; Busfield, 1996), and thus potentially to undermine masculinity for men. At an intrapsychic level, men may experience feelings of shame or inadequacy if they are unhappy or distressed, and as a result find it difficult to admit to their feelings or to seek help. Projecting these problems onto women, who as a result are pathologised themselves, is a common consequence, found in a number of these biographies where the women themselves admitted to and were treated for depression.

Yet paradoxically, many of the interviewees implicity positioned their men as vulnerable and insecure: this is a strategy which arguably functions to allow them to overlook or forgive violence or neglect, and to attribute their partners' behaviour to unhappiness rather than to more malevolent factors. So Ruth says about her partner finally seeking help, "It must have been very difficult for him, and he must have been feeling very apprehen-sive about doing it"; and Sylvia saw her husband's drinking as an illness that he had inherited. This discursive strategy has been observed in many other contexts (see Hollway, 1989; Ussher, 1994), where women will adopt a discourse of male vulnerability as a means of explaining why they themselves adopt traditional gender roles in relation to men – not expressing their sexual desires, or appearing too autonomous – as they say this will frighten or threaten men.

## Conclusion

In summary, the explanations given by the interviewees appear primarily to focus on the individual man, or on themselves as the source of problems (or on themselves as a potential saviour to their man), with little attention to wider social or discursive factors, and little acknowledgement of the repetition of cycles of behaviour, or of commonalities with other women. My own analysis would focus much more strongly on the discursive construction of heterosexual masculinity and femininity, and on how this is reinforced and maintained by both intrapsychic and material factors; with a recognition that we cannot examine or conceptualise one level of this equation without the other. For reasons of brevity I have focused on a number of specific issues here. However, one could extend this analysis to include the material-discursive-intrapsychic analysis of factors such as social class, extended family relationships, or cycles of abuse, amongst other factors.

## Ways forward: how to effect change

The way forward, in this analysis, is not simple. I would hope that much of what is necessary to effect change is implicit in the critique provided above, and therefore I will end with a number of explicit suggestions for change. Taking a material-discursive-intrapsychic feminist standpoint means that there are no quick solutions, no unilinear fixes. Changing deeply embedded patterns of relationships that have served a dominant group for so long (in this case men) will never happen overnight. 'Feminism' has been an active movement for decades. Some changes have been made, but there is still a long way to go. The changes which are needed for women 'living with drink' are not unique to this group even if there are some problems specific to their lives. What is needed is a change in the wider social sphere, empowerment of individual women (and arguably some men) and a reconceptualisation of masculinity and femininity, leading to more egalitarian relationships between women and men.

At a discursive level, we need to change the accepted notions of gender inequalities in heterosexual relationships, the notion that woman cannot exist without a man, and that 'man as monstrous brute' is an exciting proposition which women should embrace. We need to challenge the dominant representations of masculinity and femininity which circulate in the symbolic sphere, and develop more egalitarian models of gender relationships for both women and men. However, it is important to acknowledge that power imbalances are not unique to heterosexual relationships: many lesbians also encounter problems associated with violence or alcohol use, and indeed in other contexts it is *men* who live with drink in either gay or heterosexual relationships. So it is not simply heterosexuality, or indeed men *per se*, that are being positioned as to blame. It is relationships that encompass power imbalances, be they heterosexual, lesbian or gay, as these relationships are inevitably prone to a greater degree of problems, with, in the cases presented here, the problems being related to alcohol misuse. We also need to challenge the dominant discursive constructions of madness and badness which prevent many men from expressing distress in any way other than through violence or alcohol abuse, and which encourage women to internalise distress or to blame themselves. We need to make it more acceptable for men to seek and receive help for a range of mental health problems, as well as for alcohol misuse, and for this not to stand as a threat to their masculinity.

At a material level, we need to facilitate women's economic autonomy or at the very least their ability to leave violent or abusive relationships with men. We need to provide greater material support for women and men who are attempting to develop egalitarian relationships, in terms of couples counselling or advice. We need to educate women about what is unacceptable in terms of violence or abuse, and provide legal or social support for those who are subjected to it. We need to provide alternative means of solving problems which will make alcohol one option amongst many, and make it easier for it to be rejected as the option of choice. Specifically, in relation to alcohol use, we need to provide facilities for intervention which do not blame individual women or men. At an individual level, women need to be heard when they attempt to express distress or concern about 'living with drink'. Friends and family may find it difficult, but they should avoid turning a blind eye, or maintaining secrecy or silence, when they may be able to help. For we now know from the vast body of research on social support that it is a key ingredient in both physical and psychological health.

At an intrapsychic level, if women are empowered to seek satisfaction and selfhood from factors other than their attachment to a man, they will be less likely to accept anything they can get. Self-sacrifice and self-blame should be replaced with assertiveness in acknowledging and meeting one's own needs. Equally, if those who turn to alcohol to solve their problems can find alternative means of resolving their distress, they may be less likely to drink. Increasing self-esteem, developing a stronger sense of self, and dealing with issues of attachment or loss may be a step forward for many women and men. This can be achieved through counselling or therapy, or through the development of relationships which strengthen rather than detract from a positive identity.

As each of these levels of analysis must be conceptualised in relation to the others, there is little hope of change without movement in all three: we must effect change at a discursive, a material and an intrapsychic level if we are to achieve any progression at all. Yet as each level of analysis is irrevocably connected to the others, small changes in one area can have a carry-over effect. So whilst a multifactorial approach is the ideal scenario, no change is too small to be worth implementing. So a woman going on holiday on her own for the first time and realising it is the best holiday she ever had, as Emily did, or a small gesture of support from family or friends, or the provision of a safe house to allow a woman to leave, may be the first break in the cycle which allows a woman to change herself or her life. Breaking the cycle is the most important step, and it doesn't matter where this starts; the important thing is that it happens.

# *Note*

1. There are exceptions. For example, the feminist psychoanalyst Karen Horney (1935/67) developed theories of sexuality and gender relationships that encapsulated material, discursive and intrapsychic levels of experience.

# CHAPTER 14

# A community psychological perspective

## David Fryer

What is a community psychological perspective? Indeed, what is community psychology? The term 'community' has been claimed by so many differing interest groups that it has become devalued. In any case, it would be difficult enough to find two people who can agree on what the term 'psychology' means, let alone agree on the hybrid term 'community psychology'.

To complicate matters, the British Psychological Society, the UK's main academic and professional organisation, has neither a section nor a division of community psychology. In the UK, community psychology can currently only be studied at one or two universities at either under- or post-graduate level and at post-graduate level only in combination with clinical psychology. This is in contrast with the United States, Australia, New Zealand and many European countries, where community psychology is a flourishing professional and academic subdiscipline.

However despite its low academic and professional profile in the UK, it could be asserted with some justice that community psychology is, in terms of both understanding and helping, by far the most widely practised psychology in the UK as well as worldwide. By comparison, academic psychology could be lampooned as the ritual pursuit of a tiny minority of zealots preoccupied with their own arcane lore, surviving only under institutionalised professional and academic protection in sterile environments isolated from the 'real' world.

To try to define the word 'community' is little more help in understanding what community psychology is than to attempt to understand what impressionist art is by trying to define the word 'impression'. It is better to attempt to develop an understanding of community psychology by describing the practices, and the assumptions and values which underlie them, of those aligning themselves with community psychology.

Even here there are difficulties though, for in common with many community psychologists, I believe that the form and preoccupations of community psychologists are specific to the cultures in which they develop: particular manifestations of community psychology are inseparable from the traditions and perceived problems of the culture of origin. Thus community psychology takes different forms in differing places and time periods. Today community psychologists in differing countries are variously preoccupied with social change, multicultural diversity, public health, citizen participation, the limitations of clinical and social psychological perspectives and the community mental health consequences of labour market experience.

What follows may be usefully viewed, therefore, as one community psychologist's personal credo. However, because it developed out of, and is inspired by, recent advances in community psychology in the UK (e.g. Orford, 1992), the USA (e.g. Albee and Gullotta, 1997) and Australia and New Zealand (e.g. Thomas and Veno, 1996), it may point to a number of assumptions, preoccupations and value orientations held in common by many community psychologists.

## Social causation

In emphasising social causation, I assume as a community psychologist that not every psychological problem has a psychological origin or has a psychological solution. Accumulated research persuades me that unemployment, job insecurity, occupational strain, exploitation and social stratification by income, class, sex, race and a host of other societal level factors are intimately responsible for the social causation of much, probably most, mental and physical ill-health (Fisher and Reason, 1988; Fryer, 1995a; Smail, 1993; Wight, 1993; Wilkinson, 1996).

However, I seldom regard claims of single cause–effect relationships as plausible and this is especially so in the case of social causation (Winefield and Fryer, 1996). Rather I assume that most psychological states result from a reciprocal interaction over time of many factors on many levels from micro, psychophysiological processes via individual, family, organisational and neighbourhood, to macro intra-, inter- and multinational structural factors. I therefore believe that prolonged investigation and analysis simultaneously over time at many levels is necessary to understand these processes (Fryer and Fagan, 1994) and I therefore spurn inter- and intradisciplinary demarcation disputes.

## Personal agency

I assume that community psychology is also fundamentally about persons who actively strive for purposeful self-determination, and attempt to initiate, make sense of, influence and cope with experienced events in line with personal and culturally sanctioned values, constructions of the past, appraisals of the present and expectations of the future (Fryer, 1995b).

I therefore place a person's subjective experience alongside sociostructural forces at the centre of my approach. I regard subjective experience not as a source of error to be excluded from research by procedures based on outdated models of science borrowed from early physics and mechanics, nor as a dangerous black hole into which systematic social science may disappear for ever, but as a defining characteristic of what it is to be a person and as a fundamental resource for informants, investigators and change agents alike. Indeed as a community psychologist I assume that the social world affects people largely through their subjective experiences of it.

In common with many community psychologists I am sceptical of the conceptual preoccupations of orthodox experimental and clinical psychology: subjects, behaviour, associations, precise measurement, standardisation, representativeness, consistency, replication, error and truth. In my work I find myself more often preoccupied with: persons, actions, experiences, meanings, reasons, dense descriptions, sensitivity to the uniqueness of individual cases (whether person, family, organisation or community), cultural specificity; ambivalence, ambiguity and inconsistent beliefs as ways of coping with the multifaceted nature of human experience; authenticity and multiple 'realities'.

## Agents-in-context

My assumption is that the appropriate place to focus for both understanding and action is the person in the context of his or her community. To strip persons of their habitual social context and to substitute a temporary, socially impoverished and often bizarre context, as so often happens in experimental and clinical psychology with the relocation of the informant/client in the laboratory or the consulting room, renders the meanings of people's experiences and the intentionality of their actions largely opaque and inaccessible. Studying people removed from their community context, or the community devoid of the persons who enact it, is like the reductionism which breaks water down into its component parts, hydrogen and oxygen, and studies each separately. Water may be 'made up' of hydrogen and oxygen, but only in the combination of $H_2O$ do they have the emergent properties of water. Likewise, as a community psychologist, I am interested in the emergent properties of persons-in-community and believe that further reductionism loses the very phenomena in which I am interested, those where an understanding of psychological distress relevant to action to reduce or prevent that distress may emerge.

Perhaps the greatest current challenge to community psychology is to try to reconcile the *external* determination of our mental and physical states by powerful social forces, with the *internal* self-determination of our mental and physical states by ourselves as subjective social and moral agents. We experience ourselves as making constrained but nevertheless real choices.

It is vital that personal agency is not neglected. To de-emphasise the person and overemphasise the network of structural factors is to render the individual a mere cipher of social forces and to end up with a simplistic and naive parody of sociology. However, it is also vital that structural factors are not neglected or one renders societal factors mere accumulations of individual behaviours and ends up with a simplistic and naive individualistic parody of psychology, exemplified by Margaret Thatcher's notorious claim (*Woman's Own*, 31 October 1987) that there is "no such thing as society".

I believe that personal agency is sometimes, in some ways, enabled and facilitated by community contexts but is often restricted, undermined, disabled and frustrated by powerful formal and informal constituting and regulating forces at societal, social institutional, community, organisational, peer and family levels; by inadequate personal, family, peer group, community and societal support and resources; by minimal individual and collective rights and entitlements; and by overwhelming and oppressive duties and obligations (Fryer, 1986).

## Power and social support

I believe that power is intimately bound up with mental health. Psychologists seldom engage seriously with issues of power and when they do they usually conceptualise it as an individual/personality (e.g. bullying) or organisational/interpersonal (e.g. leadership) variable. However, in Western industrial societies power is most effectively structured through relative wealth, socio-occupational stratification, gender, dominant (especially ethnic) group membership and age.

I assume that reduced power (i.e. disempowerment) is implicated in the causation of many if not most mental health problems and that increased power (i.e. empowerment) is implicated in the promotion and enhancement of positive mental health.

I believe that social support, whether material or emotional; of affirmation, advice or companionship; and whether one-to-one, many-to-one or many-to-many, is intimately involved in the enhancement of mental health. I also believe that inadequate social support is a major contributor to many, if not most, mental health problems (Brown and Harris, 1978).

## Competence and expertise

Community psychologists believe that it is at least as important to look for and facilitate competence, resources and strengths as to look for and ameliorate deficits, needs and weaknesses. The resources to solve problems are often to be found within communities rather than outside them. Classic community psychology research concludes that para- and non-professional helpers belonging to communities are usually at least as effective as external professional helpers and, not infrequently, more effective (Cowen, 1982; Durlak, 1979; Hattie *et al.*, 1984). I assume that there is an informal ecology of power and support within rather than outside communities and that these are central to solving many mental health problems.

In my work I have experienced growing disquiet in relation to 'expert' status. For many people, professional experts are part of the problem rather than part of the solution (Holman, 1988). Viewed from the perspective of many disadvantaged people in our communities, the 'experts' are the professional architects who design their damp, cold houses; the social workers who take their children away into 'care'; the psychologists who are brought into schools to label their children as failures with behaviour problems (McCormack, 1988). After one group of experts has destroyed their employment in the interests of 'efficiency', other groups of experts tell them that they are not looking hard enough for non-existent jobs, that their 'employment commitment' and 'job-related attitudes' are wanting and that they have not only lost their jobs but are in danger of losing their minds (Fryer, 1985).

Some expert 'solutions' are more problematic than the original problem. Indeed, community psychologists question conventional wisdoms about who is in the best position to define behaviour as problematic. What looks like maladaptive behaviour to one, may be seen as problem solving to another (Fryer and Fagan, 1993). I believe psychology should be problem driven (rather than theory, method or statistical package driven), and I prefer the problems which are to be tackled to be identified and defined by people experiencing those problems in the context of their own communities.

## The biographies

I have now highlighted and attempted briefly to explain concepts central to my version of community psychology. Let us now turn to the moving stories of Ruth, Lisa, Dawn, Sylvia, Emily and May, women who are the real experts on living with problem drinkers. Let us see whether anything in this community psychological framework complements the wisdom embodied in those accounts to help us increase shared understanding and, through that understanding, to empower intervention to reduce or prevent the appalling psychological distress so eloquently and painstakingly disclosed.

Given the appalling nature of the psychologically toxic situations within which these women found themselves, I was humbled and impressed by the extent and variety of ways in which they were managing to make sense of, influence and cope with experienced events, to find – and to give – support in their communities, to continue to find authority and power not only to survive but also to cope, to determine their own lives, to exercise personal agency within extraordinarily hostile and restrictive circumstances.

However, I was also forcibly struck by the ways that the women had been undermined and disempowered as persons within their families and communities. Their capacity for self-determination – for making sense of, influencing and coping with the events they experienced – had been restricted and undermined by social dislocation, by being positioned as the parties responsible for the plight in which they found themselves whilst, in contrast, their partners tended to be positioned as innocent parties, by the trivialisation of their own conditions as 'only psychological', by the medicalisation of their partners' behaviour as 'illness', by their experience of chronic helplessness, by collusive secrecy and by absent or deficient social support from family, partners, friends, professionals and the labour market.

# Disempowerment

## Social dislocation

Most of the six women talked of severe social dislocation in early childhood. Several of them spoke of being looked after by, or living with, their grandmothers for long periods of time as young children. Before she was one year old, Lisa lived with her grandmother for 10 months. Later, whilst her father was in gaol and her mother was in psychiatric hospital, Lisa went to a succession of foster homes, assessment centres and children's homes. Emily also spent much of her childhood with her grandmother but this was a happier account: she described her grandmother as the most important person in her life, who made her "feel special and loved". However, to keep this in context, it has to be noted that Emily's grandfather (like Emily's father) was a problem drinker and that Emily spoke poignantly of missing out on part of her adolescence at boarding school. May moved school very frequently – ten different schools in five years.

Many of the adult women and their partners moved house frequently. In connection with moving round after her third child was born, Dawn commented that 'she had no real support and had to cope on her own'.

## Responsibility and innocence: psychological and medical complaints

Ruth's partner brought home literature from the clinic for her to see which gave her the impression that wives were being held responsible for their husbands' drink problems. Indeed, her partner would openly tell her that what had happened was all her fault, and even her older son blamed her for their predicament – this time for choosing the father!

Ironically, however, having 'a problem' protected Ruth's partner himself from blame for his behaviour. Ruth's parents, for example, did not get angry with him because they regarded him as having "a problem", that is, not able to help himself. Emily, in similar vein, noted that her husband had a vested interest in staying "sick" in order not to lose his sickness benefits. Ruth's and Emily's partners were thus positioned as innocent parties, their unacceptable behaviour redefined through a medical model as 'illness' for which they were not responsible.

On the other hand, May observed that if she felt ill, doctors were likely to say, "Oh well, you live in a very stressful situation; you have a husband who drinks heavily" and they would not take her health complaints or emotional state seriously. May's condition was thus 'psychologised': her psychological strain rather than his abusive behaviour was positioned as the problem. Likewise, Emily's diagnoses were made by a collusive trinity of husband, family doctor and psychiatrist, resulting in her medication and hospitalisation. Emily tellingly noted that she "felt her husband was happy to have her in this situation". In a breathtaking combination of sexism and religious bigotry, Emily's psychiatrist had also told her that she was "depressed" due to being a "Catholic on the pill" and that she would "get better" if she stopped taking contraceptive pills and had a baby! We are told that Emily's husband subsequently stopped sharing her bed and their sex life stopped. Emily, who clearly had more insight than her psychiatrist, traced her husband's distancing to the suggestion that her depression would lift if she had a child, clearly implying that her husband wanted her to remain depressed. May and Emily were thus positioned as people whose health problems were 'mental' rather than 'real', who were in any case to blame for their psychological conditions and whose conditions conveniently offered excuses to partners for their own behaviour.

Ruth accepted responsibility for much of what had happened – admitting she was not really sure of her partner in the first place, fearing she may have pushed him out emotionally for the children leaving him with only the means of coping by drinking.

However, Dawn and Emily took a very different line, shifting the responsibility back to the drinking partner. Dawn noted that she found "life became easier when she understood that drinking was his choice" and Emily noted that her husband's eligibility for sickness benefits was "delaying him making the decision to give up drinking".

## Experience of chronic helplessness

Ruth felt that "nothing I said made any difference". She never got clear answers from her partner. He never told her the whole story, only revealing, selectively and manipulatively, enough information to maintain or extend his power and diminish hers. Lisa, too, had given up trying to talk things over with her husband. He appeared either not to hear what she said or to be bored, but in any case he seldom replied. Lisa came to feel there was just nothing she could do to make her husband stop drinking. She even dropped charges against him for assault, letting him back into her home, because she felt "she had to accept Kevin the way he was as she could not change him".

May captured the sense of an underlying theme of many of the interviews when she said, "I am not exaggerating, it's the truth, but when you live with this, you are trapped".

## Secrecy

Secrecy is a motif running through the accounts. Sylvia's husband "drank at home and in secret" as well as at pubs with friends, Ruth's partner drank mainly in secret, Emily's husband wanted "a hermit's existence". "Everything" about May's second husband was secretive.

The women who lived with these problem drinkers were frequently sucked into this secrecy. As Ruth put it, "It's something which is rather shameful and embarrassing and needs to be kept quiet". Ruth and her son were both so embarrassed by her partner's behaviour that they stopped inviting friends home. For a long time, Ruth tried to hide her partner's drink problem "from everybody", ringing his employer for him to say he was ill, clearing up the mess he made after him. Lisa "protected the children from realising what their father had done by telling them that she had knocked things over or broken them". Although Dawn says she did not hide her difficulties from people at work or lie to them about problems at home, she never spoke to her father about her husband's drinking problem and only told her mother late on. Ruth and her partner's mother were the only people who knew about his drink problem, but even they could not talk about it together. Sylvia's relatives were surprised when she split up with her second husband "because Sylvia had never spoken about problems with him before", and Ruth "put up barriers with her friends" because she found it so hard to talk about her partner's problem drinking.

Attempting to keep such behaviour secret is of course, as Ruth said, "a big strain . . . it's an awful lot to carry . . . an awful lot to keep secret". Ironically it is also seldom successful. Sylvia thought her neighbours did not realise what was going on but in fact she discovered they all did: they had even seen her partner "shaking her through the window". Because there was a "conspiracy of silence . . . nobody wanted to acknowledge [the] problem", neighbours and friends were likely to collude with the secrecy by pretending not to know, reducing the support available to the women and increasing the power of the men.

# Social support

### . . . from families

"Throughout her life, May . . . had little support from her family" and, with the exceptions of Ruth, who felt very loved by her parents, and Dawn who "was devastated and found it hard to cope" when her mother died, parents were seldom recalled as warm or supportive in these accounts. When Sylvia called on her parents for support they would shift the conversation to her sister's marital problems. Although Sylvia recalled missing her mother "very badly" when staying away from her, she spoke of her mother as a selfish, harsh and cruel disciplinarian, who beat her with a split cane and had always made it clear that Sylvia's sister was her favourite. Sylvia's mother had not only provided little support herself but had actually blocked other potential sources of support for Sylvia: not allowing her to play with local children, for example. Only later could Sylvia express her rage and hatred openly. May's mother was timid and arrogant, pressuring May to do well at school but never intervening to stop May's cruel beatings by her father, who May recalled as an evil man who struck her savagely. Sylvia could not recall her father ever cuddling her as a child, and Emily had difficulty remembering her father as other than difficult, aggressive and "fickle with his affections".

Parents in law were spoken of even less often as supportive. A combination of conflict between Dawn's partner and her father and jealousy on the part of her mother-in-law meant that Dawn saw less and less of her own parents. Lisa's father-in-law actually made things worse by, for example, encouraging Lisa's husband to drink when he visited them.

For many of the women their sisters and brothers were little support. Ruth gradually lost touch with her sisters; although she felt they would have been supportive if she had seen more of them, the "relationship sort of drifted into a bit of disuse". Sylvia did not approach her sister for support because she had been disgusted by her sister's graphic accounts of her own relationship. Emily, whose sister is described as totally lacking in social skills and drinking excessively, "did not have the sort of relationship with her sister that would make it easy to talk to her . . ." about her problems. Although Emily's brother was easy-going and sociable, she had enjoyed little chance to build a supportive relationship with him as he went away to school when he was only seven years old. Emily remembered him as "a lost little boy whom they used to take out of school for outings". May was close to her brother when they were children but later felt he disapproved of her. Certainly he refused to give her help when she asked for it, saying that it was time she "got herself together".

As regards these women's own children, "Sylvia feared she would lose touch with them", and in the event neither of Sylvia's children had kept in touch with her after her nervous breakdown. May felt her children had both been "traumatised" as babies by events at home although, ironically, it was one of these children, who went on to develop a drink problem, who provided a source of lifelong "main support" for her.

Even where one of the woman, Ruth, did feel very loved by a family member, her mother, she was barred from gaining support *from* her by the need to be supportive *to* her. Ruth minimised her partner's drink problem as just a temporary Christmas aberration because she believed her mother could not have coped with the reality.

*170*

## ... from partners

According to the interviews, these women received very little support indeed from their partners. Only Emily describes her partner as "very loving, caring, supporting and charming", but this was only when he had stopped drinking for a while and Emily noted that her partner had a drink problem for most of their marriage.

Lisa recalled getting no support at all from her partner, remembering that her husband only asked her out in the first place to stop someone else taking an interest in her. Dawn said that "her husband was no support to her whatsoever" during the time she was ill in hospital, that she "felt very unsupported" by her husband when her father died, and the best thing she could find to say about the period her husband had in-patient detoxification followed by a six-week day programme was that she "was relieved that this gave her some respite from her husband being at home". Ruth received less and less support from her partner after their second child was born and she "felt he did not really understand what she was going through". As far as communication was concerned she graphically described her partner and herself as "two ships sailing away from each other". Sylvia felt her husband poisoned their children's minds against her.

Not only were partners providing deficient support themselves, but some even blocked other potential sources of support for the women who lived with them. Ruth and her son got so fed up with feeling embarrassed by her partner's behaviour that they stopped bringing people home. May's husband was so obnoxious with her friends that they stopped visiting and Emily's partner, never sociable, became more and more antisocial. Emily's husband was himself "very supportive when she was in hospital" but he would not let Emily's family and friends go to see her in hospital on the implausible grounds of sparing their feelings.

Despite the lack of adequate support *from* their partners, some of the women were assiduous givers of support *to* their partners. Ruth was concerned about how well her partner would manage if she left him, taking the children with her, and despite feeling excluded and resentful about the process of his treatment, Ruth "tried to be very supportive", reassuring him, asking him how he was, and so on. As part of her partner's legal defence against an accusation of a sex offence, May agreed to perjure herself by saying falsely that she had refused sex with her husband and threatened to leave him. May's husband admitted that he could not have given up drinking without her support but in a stroke of cruel irony, having used her support to help him recover, he left home – leaving her unsupported.

## ... from friends

May's friends started avoiding her because "they couldn't work out what was going on". Lisa and her partner became a "fairly insular couple" and

Ruth was lazy about "keeping up contacts", feeling it was not "appropriate to sort of drag friends along with you". Both Ruth's younger son's fear that "Daddy might be funny" in front of his friends, and her own embarrassment at her partner's behaviour, meant they both stopped inviting friends to visit them at home. In general Ruth found she was putting up barriers with her friends because it was so hard to talk with them about her relationship with her partner. Whilst these barriers potentially cut her off from some sources of social support, it is worth noting that Ruth was aware that the barriers were protective in other ways: although trying to be supportive, some of Ruth's work colleagues were prone to give intrusive unwanted advice. Nevertheless friends were important sources of social support for most of the women. Emily was still close to one childhood friend and several friends from school and college. Ruth had a particularly valuable friend with counselling skills who helped her clarify feelings and Lisa had friends who supported her in considering leaving her partner.

## . . . from health professionals

Only May speaks favourably of her family doctor, finding that after his labelling of her husband as alcoholic, "it began to make sense".

Ruth is more typical in considering her family doctor unhelpful when she went to see him about her child's insomnia and its effects on her sex life and "really unhelpful" when he told her partner he had a lot more drinking to do before he would be ready to stop. In general, like many of the women, Ruth got "little support and understanding from professionals". Sylvia's family doctor, who was a Christian, seemed to her unconcerned about her abusive relationship. Sylvia felt her doctor's underlying attitude was "silly woman, what's she doing here?". His 'treatment' was to tell her that she had a "lot of grace" to put up with the marriage, which Sylvia thought "possibly contributed to her staying with her husband" and thus continuing the abuse. After one violent attack on Sylvia by her partner, Sylvia's doctor put her on tranquillisers! As mentioned above, Emily felt her doctor colluded with her husband to have her medicated and hospitalised when the problems lay not inside her head but outside it in the external stressors of her work and domestic arrangements.

Emily's psychiatrist, who had told her that her depression was due to being a Catholic taking contraceptives, admitted her to hospital after an incident at work which Emily clearly related to stress. The consequence? – "being in hospital was a nightmare for both her and Paul". Lisa's psychiatrist effectively barred Lisa's partner from a detoxification programme by insisting that his problem was "only habitual". "Lisa saw this reasoning as stupid".

Emily did not find the NHS alcohol treatment service empathic, found its course literature on recovery misleading and considered its detoxification programme ineffective. Ruth objected to the service's "excessive" sympathy to the problem drinker and lack of consideration of the perspective of the drinker's partner. This made Ruth feel excluded, unheard and resentful though her partner was "lapping it all up". Lisa's husband attended an alcohol advisory service but this was unsuccessful.

Community psychiatric nurses, social workers and police officers were mentioned infrequently, but when they were mentioned were more positively regarded as professionals. Dawn found sessions as a couple and as a family with a community psychiatric nurse "helpful", social workers were mentioned as providing helpful backing several times by Lisa and police officers were mentioned favourably as providing practical support by Sylvia.

## ... from non-professionals

Dawn found Al-Anon a great source of support, providing relief, encouragement and help in making sense of her own and others' experiences. She particularly valued the practical details, coming from people with real hands-on experience rather than merely theoretical knowledge. The group became an important part of May's life too and Emily got support from the Samaritans when her husband became more and more abusive. Reciprocally, by herself providing non-professional support, May helped to start a group for women in violent situations and Sylvia stayed in Al-Anon in order to "be able to help others who come".

The Church was a source of support for Sylvia, a frequent churchgoer, who said "I have my faith". Emily, a committed Catholic, went to mass regularly and "felt it was a great comfort" in spite of her reservations about Church dogma. May's religion "kept her going" although now and again she thought "Him upstairs has forgotten I exist".

## ... from the labour market

Satisfactory employment can fulfil important deep-seated human needs and make available a network of support. It is clear that many of the women had found employment very satisfying. Dawn, Emily and May all made a point of saying how much they had enjoyed their jobs. Although her self-confidence had crumbled in general, Dawn had kept her confidence inside work situations during her partner's heavy drinking periods and found a lot of support in her own work. She spoke of managing to switch off from her worries whilst at work, though she did not hide her difficulties from work colleagues or lie about the problems she was facing at home.

However, for many people stressful employment is a major problem and this was also part of the picture for many of the women here. Dawn had needed to take sick leave from her job due to psychological strain. Emily had performed so "very well at work" that she had been "head hunted" for a new job but then after recession took its toll with colleagues made redundant in her new company, she became overloaded and suffered severe work stress. Ruth thought she may have become pregnant in order to get away from a stressful job, though later she found herself insufficiently stimulated by her job and would have enjoyed a more challenging one.

Excessive demands of a job can also spill over into the home. Interestingly, both Dawn and Ruth referred to this. Ruth found her involvement in her partner's job was so great that it was necessary to move house in order to give her partner and herself "some space from work". Dawn's family mealtimes were adversely affected by her shiftwork. Again interestingly, both women mentioned spillover of work stress into home life in the same breath as alcohol problems. Ruth spoke of alcoholism when she meant to speak of workaholism and Dawn implicitly compared the family consequences of shiftwork with those of binge drinking.

Expectations about the significance of employment and unemployment for a person are, of course, fraught with gender issues in our society. Dawn's husband did not want her to work full-time and she gave up work completely after her daughter's birth. Ruth did not become re-employed until her second baby was at nursery. Lisa had to give up her job because she could not rely on her partner getting their children to school in the mornings, whilst Emily's husband complained that his career had suffered due to his taking a lot of time off work because of her illness. The assumptions underlying these issues are clearly consistent with the pervasive sexism in our society.

Not only the stress of employment, but also the distress of unemployment, are motifs running through these accounts. Lisa's husband was unable to keep jobs for long and drank more heavily when unemployed. When he had been employed he only drank on his day off and then seldom too heavily because of work the following day. For Lisa that had been the most stable period of their marriage. Lisa attributed her husband's excessive drinking when unemployed to boredom but Ruth's partner also drank more heavily after he became unemployed. In his case Ruth attributed this to his taking up home brewing due to shortage of money. Whatever the particular routes in individual families, large longitudinal studies clearly show that unemployment causes alcohol-related problems for many people who lose their jobs (Dooley *et al.*, 1992; Janlert and Hammarstrom, 1992).

Here though, I am primarily interested in the impact of unemployment upon the women themselves. Sylvia, who had not been employed while she was married, was daunted by the difficulty of finding and keeping a job. For Ruth, unemployed motherhood seemed to have brought about a loss of independence, social status, identity and self-confidence. As she put it, she "didn't feel that I had anything to offer, because I wasn't an interesting person any more. I was just a mother". Similarly Dawn commented that a couple of years after her third child was born she "began to feel like a cabbage".

# Treatment, intervention and prevention

Psychiatric research suggests that less than 7 per cent of people with psychological disorders in the community actually receive specialist psychiatric treatment (Goldberg and Huxley, 1980). More specifically, Orford estimates that of the 250,000 people living in a typical UK health district, about 20,000 adults are likely to be drinking more than the recommended amount and 7,500 are likely to be experiencing problems related to excessive drinking, but only 125 (less than 2% of those experiencing problems) are likely to be receiving specialist mental health service treatment (Orford, 1987, and summarised in Orford, 1992, p. 43).

I believe that the extent and severity of socially caused mental health problems in Western societies is just so great that one-to-one treatment on the scale required dramatically to reduce or eliminate them could realistically never be provided (Fryer, 1995a). In any case, research evaluating the outcomes of many forms of individual level one-to-one professional treatment, counselling, psychotherapy and so on raises grave doubts about their effectiveness.

Moreover, even if one-to-one treatment were effective, if people who had been successfully treated were then sent back into the psychologically toxic environments which caused their mental health problems in the first place, psychological problems would be likely to result again. Even if successfully treated people were not sent back into the circumstances which originally caused their mental ill health, there would be a constant stream of new cases arising out of the conditions, which had remained intact and which threaten the mental health of others who find themselves in them.

Beyond these considerations, I believe that one-to-one treatment can collude with victim-blaming ideologies. If the mental health problem is to be treated by a therapist, both problem and solution appear to be found at the individual rather than the structural level. The victim of problematic social arrangements is repositioned as the cause of social problems. One-to-one treatment in these circumstances is offensive and unjust as well as naive and myopic.

For all these reasons, and others, as a community psychologist I prefer non-individual intervention and prevention to one-to-one treatment wherever possible. In common with many community psychologists, I regard prevention as three-pronged: primary prevention addressing incidence (new cases), secondary prevention addressing duration and tertiary prevention addressing impairment (Caplan, 1964). Of these, primary prevention is most radical, potentially most effective and most frequently advocated by community psychologists. (Holland, 1988; Kessler et al., 1992).

Albee has offered an incidence formula which has been described as "a foundation for primary prevention's alternative health care paradigm" (Gullotta, 1997, p. 23). Albee presents his formula in the form of an equation where incidence of mental health problems is said to be a function of the (social and physical) environment, stress and exploitation (the numerator) divided by the product of coping skills, self-esteem and support (the denominator). New cases are predicted to rise when the environment impinging on the organism deteriorates such that it has a negative impact on mental health, when psychological strain increases, when disempowerment occurs, when coping resources become ineffective, when self-esteem is reduced and when social support is inadequate or missing. Conversely, new cases can be prevented, according to Albee, when the environment improves, strain and exploitation are reduced, coping resources enhanced, self-esteem built and adequate social support found. At the beginning of this chapter I claimed that most mental health problems result from a reciprocal interaction over time of many factors on individual, family, peer group, organisational, neighbourhood, broader social contextual and political levels. Effective prevention requires simultaneous engagement at any or all of these.

At the individual level, the importance of Albee's self-esteem building and the celebration and enhancement of competencies have been highlighted in the women's accounts. "A commitment to competency enhancement goes hand in hand with a commitment to social change" (Dusenbury and Botvin, 1992, p. 192).

At the family level, severe social dislocation for long periods as young children was noted in the accounts. Community psychologists have highlighted the importance of emotional security and nurturing in childhood and the consequences of "psychological subdeprivation" where a child suffers from "emotional neglect in a malfunctioning family", a condition documented both in children who are the outcome of unwanted pregnancies and in children growing up in families where the father is alcoholic (David *et al.* 1992, p. 180).

Children born to women who had twice been refused abortion for the same unwanted pregnancy were not distinguishable at birth in terms of birth weight, length, malformation or malfunction and at nine years old were scoring at the same level on the Wechsler Intelligence Scale for Children as a comparison group of 'wanted' children. However, by nine years old the 'unwanted' children were achieving poorer grades at school, were significantly more rejected as friends and were rated as behaving less well by their teachers and mothers than the 'wanted' children. By age 15 these differences had widened and consolidated; by 22 the 'unwanted' children were significantly more likely to report dissatisfaction with their jobs, to be in conflict with their co-workers and supervisors, to have unsatisfying friendships, to have sought or had psychological treatment, to have started sexual relations earlier, continued with more partners and be less happy with their marriages. At 27, the partners of 'unwanted' babies were "markedly more often on file at the alcoholics and drug treatment centers and crime register" than were the spouses of 'wanted' children.

Despite these distressing findings, David and colleagues note the research also shows that "there are inner forces in the family and in society that operate in a positive direction" (David et al., 1992, p. 180), with some children born to mothers who had twice been refused their abortion overcoming all the obstacles. The researchers write that it "is time to identify and strengthen those preventive strategies that are most likely to counteract the handicaps of unwantedness in early pregnancy and subsequent psychological subdeprivation" (David et al., 1992, p. 180).

At the peer group level, the importance of supportive friendships was made clear in the biographies. Community psychologists have emphasised the supportive nature of social networks both at any one time (Hall and Wellman, 1985) and over time (Kahn and Antonucci, 1980). The latter conceive of dynamic social support networks as like convoys, with some people (close family, friends and partners) travelling with the core person over much of their life span and others (co-workers, neighbours, professionals, etc.) joining and leaving the convoy again at various times. The socially dislocated nature of the women's lives as recounted in this book suggests turnover and loss of potentially supportive others. Strategies which increase opportunities for longer term and more intimate social support are required.

Support groups and self-help groups are effective here. "Self-help organisations in the USA, Canada, Australia, West Germany and many other countries . . . now provide collectively one of the principal resources for the prevention and treatment of psychological distress" (Orford, 1992, pp. 222–3). Holland (1988, p. 126) believes that the "issue of mental health is both profoundly subjective and profoundly political. Prevention must therefore be addressed to both the internalised social structures . . . of the human psyche and the external social structures . . . of society and State". Holland pioneered 'social action psychotherapy', which aimed to provide conditions under which the depressed women with whom she worked could move themselves seamlessly:

- from individually coming to cope with their symptoms,
- to understanding via group work some of the cultural and historical factors responsible for their psychological distress,
- to collective action at the structural level to provide solutions to their problems.

At the organisational and neighbourhood levels, limitation of the damage done by higher status professionals (especially GPs, psychiatrists and treatment centre workers), recognition and facilitation of the support provided by lower status professionals (psychiatric nurses, social workers, police officers), non-professionals (voluntary groups), and indigenous helpers (acquaintances with non-judgemental attitudes, co-workers, etc.) is a priority.

At the broader sociopolitical level, effective campaigning to increase the availability of satisfactory employment, to reduce insecure employment, to reduce levels of unemployment, to redesign jobs and carry out organisational development to reduce occupational strain and to reduce the glaring inequalities of income and participation in our society are clearly called for. Community psychology blurs the distinctions some like to make between social science and social activism, between the personal and the political. Political activism can legitimately occur, not only alongside but also as an integral part of our practice as community psychologists. Albee (1984) wrote that in the USA:

> most forms of psychopathology are more prevalent among the very poor and the powerless; among those subject to the stresses of prejudices like sexism, racism, and ageism; among the economically exploited like the migrant farm workers and the vast underclass; and among those involuntarily unemployed, underemployed, or exploited by an economic system oriented primarily to the maximisation of profits. (Albee, 1984, p. 83)

These are powerful words whoever they are uttered by, but the fact that they were spoken by one of America's most distinguished social scientists, a man who has been President of the American Psychological Association, gives them an added interest.

## Concluding remarks

In this brief chapter I have attempted to present an overview of community psychology and, within that perspective, to offer a useful reading of the six interviews. Ruth, Lisa, Dawn, Sylvia, Emily and May are six individual women but I assume that their experience and psychological health is a product of their individual agency and common social causation processes within their community contexts. Alertness to the roles of power and support lie at the centre of my readings. The roles of disempowerment through social dislocation, social construction of responsibility and innocence, learned helplessness, secrecy, labour market experience and deficient social support provided by family, partners, friends and health professionals have been emphasised.

Community psychologists are distrustful of 'expert' status. It was striking in these accounts that, whilst the influence of partners and family appeared to be regarded as pernicious, those least expert (friends, low status professionals and non-professionals) were seen by the women as the most supportive and empowering and those most expert (doctors, psychiatrists) were seen as least supportive and most disempowering.

Where do I stand myself as an 'expert' commentator in this book? Sylvia recalls how, after their second date, her second husband-to-be stayed the night. In the morning he found a reason to stay behind in her flat when she went to work. "He read Sylvia's diary and afterwards kept accusing her of different things based on what he had read. She felt that he was 'inveigling his way into my life; trying to find out about me in underhand ways' . . . She thought he had taken advantage of her vulnerability".

I felt the force of Sylvia's outrage as I thought about and wrote this chapter. Although Ruth, Lisa, Dawn, Sylvia, Emily and May have generously provided accounts and given their consent to have these interpreted from a variety of perspectives, there is a risk that I too, after a relatively superficial acquaintance with a brief written record, have allowed myself to be positioned as an expert intrusively prying into their lives, taking advantage of their disempowerment and distress to advance my career through publication of a glib, formulaic and ultimately self-serving commentary. I have tried to avoid this and instead to collaborate with the women in breaking down the walls of the secrecy hiding the appalling problems and offering a reading which emphasises the role of structural factors and the shortcomings of current provision of 'professional help'. To what extent I have succeeded is for the real experts, the women themselves, to judge.

Collectively in this book, it seems to me that we need to go beyond engaging in token advocacy. In 'giving a voice' to women who live with problem drinkers, we should not deceive ourselves into thinking we have done much, if anything, about the structural factors which result in women who live with problem drinkers being normally invisible, voiceless and powerless. Although the pen is mighty, the mightier structural factors which render these women powerless and voiceless are still in place after writing this book. The real task is to tackle these structural factors to prevent and reduce distress and injustice, not just to document it.

# Participants' Responses and Conclusion

# CHAPTER 15

# The participants' perspective: Comments from the biographees on the commentators' perspectives

In order to create this chapter, the six participants whose biographies were commented on were asked if they would like to read the various commentaries, and produce a written response. Two participants (Emily and May) agreed to do this. We provided (at their request) some guidelines for their responses, and asked them to consider six questions, which are outlined below:

1. Do you actually recognise yourself and your situation when reading through the different perspectives?
2. Do the different comments offered by the authors make sense to you? Please describe how they do or do not.
3. What are your views on the value of the different perspectives?
4. How do the different perspectives make you feel?
5. Do the views of the different perspectives fit with your own view? In what ways are they similar or different?
6. Would any of the ideas in the different perspectives have helped you deal with your situation at the time or have helped you move on?

Both Emily and May sent us full responses to these six questions. Emily commented purely by answering our questions. May did the same, but she also wrote as if she was having a conversation with the authors, using many examples from her own story to respond to each commentary. The different styles complement each other well.

This chapter has been edited by us from these answers, using primarily the words written by these participants. Editors' additions and comments are in brackets, and italics.

# The codependency perspective

**Emily:**
Best of the bunch! Most readable and understandable. I recognised myself and particularly her plea for help for people like myself who can't afford private therapy.

*[Emily also had some criticisms:]*
- I can accept codependence, but codependence does not just apply to alcoholics: it applies to *all* relationships.
- I do not agree that Al-Anon is a self-help group: it's very prescriptive and the 12-steps approach is far too rigidly enforced. 'Twelve steps' should not be thought of as the panacea, it does not help everyone and there must be choices. Cocounselling is a *lot* better; and Relate helped me more.

**May:**
Yes, *[I recognised]* almost every word here: yes, it all makes sense. Until I'd read this perspective, I hadn't heard of codependence – or at least I hadn't realised that I was, could have been, codependent on the drinking husband. That never occurred to me. 'Attached' would be a word I'd use, but on reflection, yes it could be codependency. Perhaps that explains why at times I felt 'safe' with them. An eye opener for me! On page 90 Liz writes: "May is the most typically co-dependent person in the biographies" – I wish someone had told me that in 1959, not 1997.

Yes, I would be as obsessed with the alcoholic as he was – how true, Liz – his whole life was geared to alcohol, for example, work 9 a.m., pub 10 a.m., Sunday rides to the country via this pub and that pub, all night drinking seven nights a week with 'customers', dinner parties, heavy drinking, non-stop planning *[about drink]*. I often warn young men: "Make sure you are in control and alcohol is not!" They laugh and assure me "they are in control"; I usually say "Yes, I've heard that before, many times, and often that is the first step on the slippery slope." Not acknowledging the truth, not *realising* the truth: I can see it, they can't or won't. I sow the seeds, leave an AA leaflet, look them in the eye and say: "If you want to talk, you know where I am. Remember my son"; he is a recovering alcoholic and has helped numerous youngsters, but sadly lost his partner to drink and drugs – she died earlier this year.

I've read Robin Norwood's *Women Who Love too Much*. It's me, or it *was* me, to a T: I couldn't believe it. I couldn't believe a book had been written because there are so many of us. I felt relieved to know I wasn't going crazy. *[But it is also true that]* codependence is not just a women's problem.

I can remember my first AA meeting: "I am an alcoholic" said everyone. My God, what do I say, I thought. I didn't know what to say so said nothing – unusual for me! What I now know I should have said is, "I'm a codependent". Do you know, that might have saved my marriage!

There are many truths in this chapter. For example,

- In the 'Need to care for the self' section: you, I, have to be told how to do this. I found it hard and still do. To me it seems selfish and in Quaker eyes that is a huge sin, I'll never get to Heaven. Its true, oh so true: "a downward spiral of negativity and fear", yes I see that now, but not then.
- In the 'Accepting responsibility for blame' section, the last bit on p. 93 describes my ex-husband to a T. Liz says, "If she valued herself she would not tolerate . . .", but you lose yourself, Liz, you are lost, lost, lost. You have no money, nowhere to go, you are cold and lonely and have to feed the children on nothing. The fear of being left alone is overwhelming, still is. I'm scarred for life with that. The actions of the drinker, the womanising, the violence, the fights, the debts, the lies, the thieving, all have to be coped with, or so I thought. I should just have walked away but I couldn't live with myself if I had done that. Your mind is too full of this and you can't even *think* of yourself.
- In the 'Need to accept one's powerlessness over the alcoholic' section: (a) I never knew he was an alcoholic; and (b) I thought that as I could control a class of 40 children, he would comply, change, obey etc. at some point in time!
- In the 'Effects of alcoholism on the children' section: yes it's all true, it all makes sense. Every word is true. I have one child, aged mid-thirties, never drinks – it fills him with horror; I have another child, early thirties, a recovering alcoholic. They understand, but the older one doesn't want to know about it; whereas the younger child faces reality, but hopefully will never drink again. But the 'no talking' rule applies even today.
- [*Again, in the*] 'What can be done to help these women' section [*there are some important points*]: [*it is*] good [*that you state*] "detach with love": had I done that I may still have had a marriage. But though I could do it now, I doubt if I could/would have done it then because I wouldn't have believed it would work. I would have been fearful of change, so stayed in the status quo – it's familiar, it's safe!
- Liz, yes the professionals need courses from AA and Al-Anon. I was perhaps unlucky: no AA [*in the*] 1950s, 1960s, 1970s: too late for me. I did get help for myself, [*but that was*] 10 years and another marriage later and, as you say, too late. Oh dear – I see it now, it hurts to see it there on the page, but it's true.

*[There are also things that I disagree with:]*
- I'm surprised Liz spends little time on considering why it has happened. To me what has happened in the past has a reflection/influence on today – a bit like geology.

- I don't agree entirely that the "the problem is a much wider social issue than can be explained in terms of family dynamics". I think the history of a dysfunctional family is the *crux* of it.
- I wonder if the alcoholic *is* blind to his problem? Years after my first marriage, I found something Chris had written, a cry for help, but no-one heard.

Liz has worked with codependent persons. It shows. She knows what she is talking about. I wish I'd met Liz in 1959. Would it have helped at the time? Oh yes, oh yes. But better late than never.

Reading this perspective makes me feel sad that I couldn't work it out.

## The psychodynamic perspective

**Emily:**
I think this is possibly the most insightful of all the authors. I liked this perspective, particularly the looking at the therapist and how their training and background is likely to influence their way of looking at your problem. *[Having read the chapter,]* I understand more what is meant by this perspective, but I still do not understand how it is put into practice to help people understand why they feel about things the way they do. What coping strategies are they given?

Reading this perspective has made me feel understood. It certainly fits with how I now feel about the situation. How can I avoid it happening again?

In terms of helping me deal with the situation at the time, I think the ideas would have helped: it would have been helpful to have this context pointed out to me. *[But I'm still left feeling:]* how would she *[i.e. the author]* have done it *[i.e. helped me using psychodynamic psychotherapy]* and how long would it have taken?

**May:**
Yes, I recognise myself all the time. These comments were easy to read, and written mostly in layman's language.

There was much to agree with here:

- Reading "The conceptual framework", I thought: thank goodness that psychotherapy is "to try to understand the human condition and comprises a healing or treatment process". So often counselling offers no hint, no hope of healing/treatment and so you feel still in the wilderness.
- She writes about a joint project in which therapist and patient work together – how I wish I'd even had one opportunity to do this. *[One of my concerns is]* about the power in "helping" professions – *[even]* some members of Al-Anon can be unhelpful by being so dictatorial.

- Her "attempt at a dialogue between those who live with and those who work with problem drinking" is an important link that needs emphasising.
- 'Our early experience bears on our later functioning' – so true.

I presume the writer is a lady[1] – a very helpful lady, prepared to work on people's problems. [Her view of] digging under the surface to search into the background of patients as the real causes of the problem, makes good sense: a lot of illness, accidents, road traffic accidents, crime are the result or side- or after-effects of 'alcohol abuse' or too much drinking.

This chapter jogs my memory of things I'd rather forget. All this is very upsetting as it's in the past, but it affects me now – very definitely. It's like a scar in a hot climate, never heals. It's just so awful that the six of us have gone to hell and backwards so many times and in so many ways. My 'ex number 1' still delights in trying to manipulate me, taunt me – so I avoid his presence to avoid still being victim material.

In one of her key paragraphs she states that we can overcome blocks; that we make choices, as life goes on as a continuous process. This is key, in that I'd say that nothing ever remains the same, things are always changing. BUT – when you are trapped, it seems as if nothing ever really changes. Similarly, every word she says in the 'How do we establish our sense of who we are . . . section, is absolutely true: I know I rarely feel safe, most of my life I spend in terror, and feel unsafe. I read about me marrying a second husband because I felt 'safe' with a hostile, angry, violent man. I knew no different – father, brother, first husband, all lovely people but violent. I didn't know any other possibility – that's how they all were.

Would this have helped me? Yes, anything would have helped. Reading pages 103–4, I thought – at last, someone is giving me an explanation, but it tailed off like lots of explanations did. Almost as if she didn't know, or didn't want to tell all. It's a trend I found happening time and time again in counselling, which left me in mid-air and more anxious than ever.

## The family systems perspective

**Emily:**
[I have both positive and negative impressions of this chapter. This perspective is more] difficult to relate to, to understand where she's coming from. [There is] no need to say what all the different theories are: which one does she think is best in my case?

[On the positive side,] it is difficult to disagree with the concept of family therapy. Definitely it was lacking in the two spells of in-patient detoxification which Paul underwent, which concentrated entirely on him and had no place for how it affected me, our relationship and the wider family. I wish family therapy had been offered to me. I was not included in either of Paul's two in-patient episodes and should have been!

*187*

[*As far as my own experience went, it is*] difficult to find references in this chapter to myself and to how family therapy may have helped me. Which family therapy 'system' does this author practise? What help would it have given me? How *could* family therapy have helped me? I get no idea from this piece. How do you include in family therapy people who do not want to be included? For example, Paul didn't want help in this situation except to stop drinking. He hated going to Relate who he thought very biased towards me. Would family therapy have been different? How?

The chapter still does not make a lot of sense to me. It feels very long, and contains far too many academic references. Surely it's not as complicated as this chapter makes it appear?

[*I think that it is*] important for family therapy to be used, but this chapter didn't stress that.

**May:**
I found this quite difficult in places to read with understanding, partly because of the use of language and terminology that I am not familiar with.

[*There is also a split between theory and practice:*] I see myself in this chapter nearly all the time. [*But although*] I can see myself and my family in this perspective in theory, I cannot in reality, not in practice: [*she states*] "Family therapy was developed in the 1950s and 1960s", [*but*] I was not offered any. In theory family therapy is fine, [*but*] I was never able to take advantage of it then – [*it was*] not offered, so my experience is limited.

I can see it as invaluable but my first husband would not have agreed to "drag the children into a marital dispute" that was *my* fault. My second husband had offer after offer, but never kept some appointments, lied when he did – in fact was refused to continue family therapy because of his lies.

Family therapy is cost-effective, yes. But there are problems, because it's all based on [*believing that the therapy has*] truthful, willing participants. [*Do you get at the truth, with two people sitting there?*] Some families might be lucky enough to take advantage of all that expertise. [*But*] to get at the real truths though, it is *very* necessary to talk to the two people involved separately, *then* together. Our children sadly had grave difficulties in knowing fact from fiction, and truth from lies, as a result of his behaviour.

[*There are some excellent ideas here.*] 'The hallmark – *supervision* as well as consultation' – what a brilliant idea, but neither husband would allow that, and if they did 'agree' for appearance sake to appear to be co-operating, I would have had a very severe beating afterwards and verbal abuse enough to make your ears drop off. I think the systems view of background knowledge is vital. [*On the other hand,*] I can't see "how drinking might serve to stabilise the family".

[*Many of the systemic issues and themes resonate with May. She states that her first husband would have*] short periods of abstinence, hours or days at the most, and the brain is so fuddled and withdrawal symptoms are so great that nothing is achieved, except a resentment of me/the children, so off he goes drinking again, and drinks more than before. *[She commented about]* feeling 'trapped into staying', about "learned helplessness", about prevailing 'family and cultural beliefs' – 'public school boys are good boys'. *[Another theme May picked out was that of the]* "dangerous professional": more dangerous than the alcoholic as they give the alcoholic ever more power over the spouse. *[Finally, May commented on]* 'transitions' in the family: parents, step-parents and grandparents died, I coped with everything, all the funerals gave him a real reason for staying in the pub.

*[Would family therapy have helped?]* Yes, of course this would have helped a lot, if it had been offered and accepted. But I don't think that family therapy would have helped motivate *[either of my husbands]* to get treatment.

## The coping perspective

**Emily:**
I liked this perspective best – as you can imagine, as he quotes Liz Howells' work a lot, and she was the person who interviewed me for the biography. *[I found this chapter]* easy to read, despite my irritation at the use of initials. *[This author]* genuinely seems to have read the biographies, to see how people cope – interesting. *[This chapter is]* close to my own view – I certainly felt left to cope with no help from the mental health system, which is the only place for alcoholics and their carers. *[In fact,]* coping with codependence should be the title!

*[On the other hand]* I don't think he's got me quite right. He doesn't talk about rejecting Al-Anon and 'children' (or rather the lack of a 'children' perspective).

*[It is]* interesting that the word 'carer' is absent not just from this, but from all the chapters. Why?

It would have been empowering to know that I was coping, and *[be]* helped to cope if I wanted to. The Al-Anon approach seems *[to be:]* it's me, it's my problem. Well it isn't, it's his problem and he's the only one who can sort it out. I coped despite myself and I wonder how therapy from Jim Orford would have helped change Paul's behaviour? Or would he have just made me feel better about the situation I was in!

**May:**
Yes, this made a great deal of sense, in fact I can relate to this perspective more than any of the others. This chapter has summarised my story – it is all there, in a nutshell. And it's all absolutely true, every word.

The first few pages are all true. The CFM comes into this problem (in my case with no experience), with 'no inkling'. The PDP is so pickled with alcohol that at times they remember they have a problem, and then they forget. The PDP is likely to say that anything else, or anyone else, is the problem, and not the drink (I think that's an inborn fear of the drink being taken away: if you – the PDP – have treatment you won't have alcohol, you will lose control over your supply of it).

I hope that this book will make doctors aware, and patients too, that the CFM can't ever control the PDP. AA say that the PDP has to get to rock bottom to want to stop, to want to stay stopped, and this is absolutely true, an alcoholic who 'slips' is no good to anyone. [So] where is the term 'recovering alcoholic'? Once stopped, they are all recovering alcoholics unless they slip (have one or a few drinks then stop again). My ex (Chris) hasn't drunk for 21 years but he's still a PDP.

There were no professionals to help in the 1950s. I had nowhere to run to, no money, no-one believed me. I was entombed by marriage vows and Quaker beliefs. I was told at one stage that I could have a social worker, and I thought "Thank God, maybe somebody will believe me." But as I was a professional, and lived in a detached house, and as there was a shortage of social workers, I was told that I could cope, and that others had a greater need than I! If I'd lived in a council house with 10 children on family allowance, I'd have got help. Dangerous middle-class thinking and decision making by the so-called 'experts'.

There is so much in this chapter that is true:

- I am thankful that "We are looking at the ordinariness of people's lives, not at abnormality". Thank God, or else I and all other spouses, partners of alcoholics would be lost for ever. Don't ever let the professionals or experts run away with any other ideas. [As this chapter states] CFMs must not be blamed for their predicament: very, very true. This message needs to be loud and clear in the book. Remember some of the 'professionals', some of the 'experts', will be alcoholics!
- Oh, I love the person who wrote this report, "Stress is too mild, torture is a word that springs to mind", torture that scars you and your children for ever.

*On the other hand, May's comments below imply that she feels that the titles given to the types of coping make it sound simpler that it was!*

*[This chapter mentions]*
- "Tolerant ways of coping": I never had a night's sleep in 25 years. I like order and I had chaos. In my professional capacity I am capable; in my domestic life I was so fearful I was a jelly.
- "May . . . got frightened and lonely": every evening for years I got lonely, forever feeling lonely, fearful and unsafe, *forever*.
- The trouble is that keeping quiet during violence suggests to the alcoholic that it is acceptable: "If I'm such a baddy, why do you stay", said Henry.
- [Also,] you get hooked into the PDP, and once fear sets in you are lost. You need to plan to escape, "you do not lend them money", so they will

borrow, steal, put it on the slate, mug, lie, they will always get money for booze. If I'd poured Henry's drink down the sink, he would have killed me for that. So we are trapped and full of fear, I never feel safe, not ever, even now.

- I didn't like Al-Anon, I was the telephone contact for AA, or rather my first husband was, but as he was never in I did it. It made me ill, stress, angina. Don't say I didn't change, I tried to help others, hoping Chris would like this and be proud of me!! [It] gave me angina in the end, or allowed angina to develop as is it genetic. Yes, yes, yes I did stay for my marriage and vows and I did feel guilty discussing him at Al-Anon. I never trusted Al-Anon. Then I never trust anyone even now – I may not say so or give that impression, but that's how it is.
- I wish I'd known "the only person she had control over is herself" in 1959! And yes, I wish I'd left earlier.
- [The extracts from the story of Helen in The Tenant of Wildfell Hall are interesting:] These things are not easy to do if you are cold, hungry and have got hepatitis from him.
- Yes, there is a conspiracy of silence: "hope" numbs you into staying.
- [Some of the other biographees have had] "good stable periods": I had perhaps five days in 25 years. I never gave up wanting or trying to make him stop. I never told anyone until 1984 about his attempted suicides, as it was a criminal offence.
- [This chapter comments on the fact that it took Sylvia some years to make] the 'connection between Bill's violence and his drinking'. Well, I didn't connect behaviour with drink until 1987.

*[What's missing with the coping perspective?]*
- The coping perspective is excellent, but it leaves out the background of the CFM. I went into therapy in 1994. I found a psychotherapist (through my back pain group) and had to pay £25 per hour from my invalidity benefit, but she got me sorted out. But only because she went back in time, right back. The problems were there in childhood and stemmed from there. Maybe not for everyone but certainly for me! Page 145, yes their behaviour is objectionable. What they get up to is unbelievable. But you have, have to go back in the past. My first husband drank at 14. His parents divorced at 15. He always said he'd never ever divorce as it was so awful an experience. His mother told me in 1980 that her divorce "never affected her son". How cruel, how selfish, how unknowing and uncaring for her to say so. That divorce crucified him, starting him drinking to drown his pain. You have to go back in time to uncover the 'why's and wherefore's'. Again on another page this chapter states that "past history is irrelevant". No, no, no! Past history is not irrelevant, may I respectfully jump up and down and say! The section on 'Can we ignore the women's histories prior to meeting their partners': I appreciate his point of view, but no, no, no!

- The coping perspective attaches blame to the drinking, not the drinker. Brilliant, but it could be translated by the alcoholic as another excuse for not blaming him. They do feel guilty at times, frightened too. Alcoholism may be genetic, but has anybody yet proved that?
- There are circumstances as well which restrict choices. I could not work in the 1950s or 60s, no crèches, no help. I had no money for clothes, shoes or bus fares.
- *[At another point, the chapter compares alcoholism with Alzheimer's disease.]* Again no, Alzheimer's disease cannot be equated with alcoholism. Alzheimer's Disease is not self-inflicted (as far as I know), whereas alcoholism is. No-one asked the alcoholic to pick up a drink and go on picking up a drink. He chose to – in the beginning at least.

In commenting on Lisa's story, this chapter talks about her 'being let down by a psychiatrist': I have had that experience. A psychiatrist told my second husband he was OK, even though he'd tried to strangle me 20 minutes earlier outside the psychiatrist's office and the staff had separated us. The psychiatrist interviewed us together. For my safety, I needed interviewing alone. Experts! – that man nearly cost me my life. We waited 18 months for that interview. Afterwards in private I wept, I just didn't know what to do.

Would this have helped me? Yes, yes, yes. And yes, we do need help, current help: this is very true. And with this perspective – at last, a package – good. 'PHCWs often lack grounding', let's hope they read this book, believe it and act upon it.

# The feminist perspective

*[Emily was relatively critical of this perspective.]*
**Emily:**
Her 'feminist' understanding of my situation is quite right but very superficial. It would have been interesting to have more comment on the men in my life and how I was 'conditioned' to respond in the way I did. I do think you have to look at life in a holistic way. Therefore how we are moulded by society is important, but the feminist approach is just part of the picture.

*[I found some of the language in this chapter complex.]* I had no idea what many of the words she used meant. Does she have to be so academic and complicated? I think what she's saying is that society has conditioned us to accept unacceptable behaviour in males because we are female and therefore that is what we do.

This chapter makes sense, once you get away from the psychobabble; but there was nothing here that I didn't know already. There were no solutions offered, except to 'change society' (how?) and to 'empower me' (again, how)? Although it is a good idea to make men aware of their mental health, once again – how?

*[May on the other hand was far more positive about it.]*
**May:**
This perspective was relatively easy to understand. It is a little difficult at times to translate the adjectives used and specialist terminology. Having done a Cert. Ed., meant I could understand more than perhaps some biographees. I've learnt from this perspective; but as with many of the other perspectives, I just wish I could have known all this in 1959 onwards. As with some of the others, I see myself all the way through this perspective, and I agree with almost all of what Jane has to say.

I found I related time and time again to this perspective, in a practical, logistical, realistic way. She *understood*, perhaps because she's a woman! You know, we can suggest and attempt sexual equality but as long as a female/woman produces the offspring, we will never get equality. It isn't meant to be. But we can improve the current situation, which is what Jane suggests.

Much in this chapter is very realistic, very true:

- "The discursive", an interesting background of woman as a "whore" or "Madonna", man as an "invulnerable phallic hero".
- The process of becoming a 'woman' is still the perception that most people have of most women. I trained in 1950–52, very much a woman in a man's world, and the men did not like it. Things haven't changed much yet 40–50 years on!
- Frog to prince, 'ever hopeful' say I, but you die in despair trying. Why doesn't someone tell you/me/us/women/females that it just isn't possible, and that any change has to come from within him, and from him wanting to change. That is the crux of it.
- If Dobash and Dobash (1979) use this as an explanation, then publish it loud and clear in a leaflet and put it in every Al-Anon meeting or doctor's surgery. All the 38 years I lived with drinkers, the drink problem was never discussed, but the behaviour was!
- The factors 'encapsulated' when Jane talks about "the level of material practice" are absolutely spot on. It shows an understanding of the situation. My comment is: It is very easy to say what women should do, but if you've never had a night's sleep, are ill with stress, in debt, hungry, have stressed children all the time, no friends or family to help, no professional help . . . In the 1950s there was no help at all, and remember that my experiences were in the 1950s, 1960s, 1970s. Even in the 1980s and 1990s, many women are still trapped.
- Again, when Jane discussed "exploring the heterosexual matrix", what she says is so very true: the problems are grasped and understood. I feel I'm still learning from reading.

- "Evidence of violence as 'normal'", yes, yes, very true. It is normal, so it feels 'safe', but it is not safe – a crazy mixed-up world of opposites. What she says here is exactly as it is, very well written and explained: so true again, every word true.
- Another example, where she talks about the traditional scripts of femininity and masculinity: "always blackmailing you", for example, "if you don't cook me lunch every day I'll go to the pub" – always waiting, but he never ate that lunch. Every word, every line exactly as it was. I just wish I'd had something to read like this in my misery years ago.

I agree that, yes, yes, we need to make it more acceptable for men to receive help, [and to change the idea that] 'big boys don't cry'. And although I agree that "we now have a vast body of research on social support", we need to use trained experienced people (like me) to counsel people. It's like Relate: much more effective if you've first-hand experience.

I would have needed support to move on. I'd planned to move on in 1963, but I think that my first husband knew it and made sure I got pregnant, and so I stayed – [he took] control again.

Jane's conclusion is true; as it is when she states that the ways forward are not simple: very true. I am delighted Jane has actually been able to put forward suggestions, as this is desperately needed and is sadly lacking in some of these chapters. True, there are "no quick solutions, no unilinear fixes". I say prevention is better than cure, but sadly most people are 'deaf' and don't want to hear. But can I add here one of the most effective ways to get schoolchildren to listen and to think about it. My first husband goes to schools talking about 'alcoholism' and his opening gambit is "I am an alcoholic", but no one believes him [because he looks so well]. The image of an alcoholic is dirty mac or violent young man with knife in hand. The danger is they see him as he is now, not as he was.

"A reconceptualisation of masculinity and femininity", yes, yes, it's emerging slowly – but I was trapped with a belief that:

1. He [Chris] didn't want a divorce as his parents had one. How wrong I was, but we never talked about it.
2. With a Quaker upbringing I could not break my marriage vows.
3. A bad marriage was better than no marriage.
4. The family unit was to be held together at all costs.

Now, in 1997, I am still not sure that my third or fourth point are not true for me. My children have a good relationship with their father, so maybe, for me, my third and fourth point were right, even though I went through hell for it. I can't agree with Jane [in her opinion about] the notion 'women can't exist without a man' – I can't! I don't mean sexually, but I do need a man in my life. It's the image ('she's not on her own', I can still attract and keep a man). He can do the cooking, driving, gardening, is company, gives me a man's perspective, takes me to the pub. You may say I haven't changed (not true). You may say I haven't learnt anything (I have). But *I* am built that way, I feel lost and lonely and inadequate without a man friend (not lover) in my life. I don't think that will ever change. My current friend lives quite a few miles away, I lead my life, he leads his. Some days/weeks we are together, sometimes apart. For me that is the solution and it took me many years to get there (and he doesn't drink).

## The community perspective

**Emily:**
This perspective makes a lot of sense. It is easy to read, I recognise myself, and feel well described, valued and empowered. It fits my view very well. I liked his conclusion and admission that we are the experts.

This approach would certainly have been worthwhile and maybe helped me manage the situation better, because my opinions would have mattered and been taken into account. I love the acknowledgement of the power imbalance. Is there a community psychologist in my area?

I think my negative experience of Al-Anon should have been included to balance the positive experiences. Al-Anon to me concentrates on looking at yourself rather than giving you back-up to deal with the problem drinker. Self-help is a great idea but '12 steps' are not for everyone!

*[However,]* I still do not understand *how* a community psychologist could have helped me more than any 'expert'. It would have been useful to see what intervention he would have recommended to help me. *[I am still unclear as to]* how they fit into community mental health teams, *[and as to]* whose view wins, the psychiatrist or the psychologist?

I would really like to talk to this man and find out more about his approach and how it can be implemented. So: long live community psychology – but what happens, what do they do?

**May:**
Yes, I recognise myself time and time again. The nettle has been grasped, the sting hurts for years. Let us find some dock to reduce the pain and hurt, earlier rather than later. I think this gives another point of view from a community psychologist who is an 'expert': he certainly is wiser now, just a little. Let's hope other community psychologists note David's writings. There is the value, for he has written well *[although]* I had to read this several times as I found some of the terminology unfamiliar. I'd like to meet David.

I am pleased he wrote *[when discussing our contributions]* "the appalling psychological distress so eloquently . . . disclosed". "Psychologically toxic situations . . . cope . . .", yes we are excellent copers: that's why we survived, blamed for what is happening. 'Trivialisation . . . collusive secrecy', an excellent paragraph, the whole situation there, David, yes you do understand and believe – thank God for that, for in your first page, I feared you did not.

"Social dislocation", I agree. "Responsibility . . ." yes it's all there – me. "Chronic helplessness", yes, true, nothing you say or do stops the drinking. "Secrecy", you live a public and private life but others see, but say nothing – all true. "Social support", yes it's all true and makes sense, except both my children have helped me. ". . . from partners" all makes good sense. Yes we give support to our partners, still do. ". . . from health professionals", my doctor is still using us as a family (albeit a split family) as a role model. He's learnt via us! ". . . from non-professionals", AA and Al-Anon are the answers without any doubt. To go hand in hand with doctors who understand. ". . . from the labour market", remember (David probably wasn't born) 1950, 1960 – a different world: no crèches, no income support, nothing but family allowance (for the second child only). No HP worth talking about, no plastic cards, no bank account unless you were recommended, no maternity leave and so on.

*[When David writes about]* treatment, intervention and prevention, *[he provides some]* frightening figures. If one-to-one can't be provided, there is an even greater need for AA and Al-Anon, or the development of something else alongside. *[What he says is]* all very realistic and practical. If "emotional security and nurturing are important" (and I'm sure they are), then this high-lights my suggestion that parenting, not just the sexual angle, needs to be on the national curriculum: the responsibilities involved, the respect needed. If you can't cope, don't parent. What David writes on page 177, especially the paragraph stating "At the organisational and neighbourhood levels . . .", is perhaps one of the most important statements made, and needs putting in big block letters. His final paragraph is very honest, especially "Although the pen . . .".

*[Having stated how useful she thinks community psychology would have been for her, May does go on to take issue with a number of David Fryer's points:]*

- I don't agree that it is difficult to determine or define what community psychology is, nor is "impression" difficult to define. To me it's simple.
- Maybe I'm just a down to earth logical female and David Fryer is on a pink cloud, a non-logical (not illogical) academic. I do not mean to be rude but I get the distinct impression he is of the academic psychology school, and the fact that "a tiny minority of zealots pre-occupied with their own arcane lore surviving under the institutionalised professional and academic protection in sterile environments isolated from the real world" suggests that many academics are hiding away doing 'research' which has little or no bearing on the real world, using questionnaires that are irrelevant, outmoded, unrealistic, not to the point and will bias the result and so on.
- If community psychologists are really involved in "society" etc. then I am relieved to hear it, but if they have gone from grammar or public school to university to be appointed community psychologists, they only

have a limited experience of *real* life and none of the dirty end of life at all – too protected from that.

- The reason I 'go on' at length is because I tried all sorts of ways to get clinical psychology and/or community psychology or psychiatric help and when I did it was so useless it was dangerous. I had to survive almost unbelievable violence as a result of those interviews even when the facts were staring them in the face, the battered bruised proof was sitting in front of them. I could only assume they behaved in the same way, so had no advice to offer.

- So I'm biased, but I'll try not to be too narrow-minded nor too dictatorial for this paper.

- To follow on, the section 'Social causation' – to prove my point from above, why does a Community Psychologist assume that "not every psychological problem has a psychological origin or has a psychological answer". Why on earth not?

- But I'm glad he spurns inter and intradisciplinary demarcation disputes.

- "Personal agency" – good, I agree, and am relieved he feels the "social world affects people largely etc." and that he prefers to deal with persons and realities, but he didn't give that impression to me at first!

- "Agents in context" – yes I agree. "Power . . ." – alcoholics have power. They bully too and threaten. Power corrupts. When I did sociology for my Cert. Ed. I was taught to add 'education' to David's list of themes through which power is structured (and being very obtuse I would add Masons as well, which would upset a lot of apple carts).

- I agree that inadequate social support is a major contributor to many, if not most, mental health problems. About 980 people lived at the local psychiatric unit. Now it is closed, most of them struggle to survive here, as there are just 21 beds at the local hospital. That is another issue for recovering alcoholics, there is no mental hospital 'in' care which is desperately needed.

- So all the community psychologists in the world have to dig deep, unmask the *un*obvious, draw the seventh veil to get at the truth. "Competence and expertise" – his disquiet at "expert" status – yes, yes, yes, how very true. Did you know that some children were taken into care as their parents 'sat in a circle and chanted'. It was nothing more or less than a Quaker meeting – circle yes, chant no.

If I'd known about this [approach] I could have felt less isolated, less alone, believed it wasn't me causing the problem. But I/we never discussed the drinking with Chris. I did with Henry, in fact I frightened him by saying he'd got a drink problem as a bout drinker. What frightens me is the problem is set to escalate.

I am conscious of the need to evaluate these perspectives as coming from different sexes and different schools of thought and presumably various educational basis and academic training systems. I am old fashioned – proud of it – but I am alarmed when I read that the "BPS . . . has neither a section or a division of community psychology". Now is that because Community Psychologist is not acknowledged as worthwhile, or has someone forgotten to tell the powers that be that it exists, or is it that so far no-one has considered it worthy of part of the 'empire building', career wise? Or is it because it is so obviously needed that it is excluded? We seem to be living in an age where often the common sense common need by the common majority is excluded or worse ignored. Hence no or very little help with "living with problem drinkers".

# *General*

*[What Emily and May thought about each of the commentaries in turn (codependency, psychodynamic, family systems, coping, feminist, and community) has been outlined above, with Emily's comments appearing first. Both May and Emily (in May's words)]* "describe in detail how each perspective does or not *[make sense]* or whether I agree with what is said."

*[In general, the participants did recognise themselves and their situations in all six of the perspectives. May was more certain of this, and less critical. She stated generally]:* "Yes, I recognise myself in most, if not all the situations", and "Yes, they all make sense" *[whereas, for her part, Emily was more critical of some perspectives].*

*[Both Emily and May also made some other general comments, and these are summarised below]*

## Emily

The chapters have all, some more successfully than others, explained how their pet theory can fit the biographies. It's a shame some of them are so academic. What happened to practical psychotherapy? Did it ever exist!

*[This was an]* interesting idea. But apparently there are at least 400 models used in psychology – how did you choose the six? And where is cognitive behaviour therapy, transactional analysis and God knows what else.

*[May's comments are more wide-ranging:]*
## May:
*[These perspectives]* are all different but very valuable: they have all grasped the situation, analysed it, researched it – sometimes in great depth – and each has a very worthwhile contribution to make. If one goes for help, it's pot luck which school of thought your professional expert might offer you, so it may be that 'help' could be on a team basis, not on an individual expert basis. Although in retrospect that would be too complicated for the client to cope with mentally.

There is a common thread with all the perspectives. The objective of the perspectives is to listen, dissect, discuss, probe, (sometimes) suggest support – emotional, physical, therapy, not drugs or sedatives, that just masks it – but solutions must be worked out.

Would these have helped me? Yes, yes, yes. Any of these would have been 'manna from heaven'. Anything would have helped. If only someone, anyone, had listened and believed me. An offer of help never came, not once!

- I feel sad there is still so much ghastly suffering, or torture as one writer put it. I feel glad so much effort and care is being put into this book. It should be a bible if read.
- I feel sad that I couldn't get help. I have found all this reporting very sad to do. I wasted so much of my life being unhappy and lonely. I hope I've helped you to get help for others more quickly than I got help.
- I feel angry there are so many professional 'helpers' who do more harm than good.
- I just wish I could do more to help as I really know what goes on. I did counselling for staff and students, both alcohol and non-alcohol related. I enjoyed that, I'd enjoy doing something similar. I think on second thoughts, I'll stay quietly in my corner and watch the world go by. Being disabled by a 'loving' husband means that I can't do too much anyway. I spend hours and hours in bed each day in considerable pain. It's true, it's true, it's true, *please put that in the book.*
- There needs to be a non-AA network of help or work in conjunction with AA, but it's hard work, demoralising at times.
- My current boyfriend drinks about six pints of beer a year, is good, kind company – boring, dim at times, but what Robin Norwood says I need. So I'm lucky.

None of these reports mention the term 'recovering alcoholic'. AA use it and the world needs to. My first husband has not had a drink for 21 years, he is and has been a recovering (not cured, never is) alcoholic for 21 years and unless he has a 'slip' he'll be a 'recovering alcoholic' for the rest of his life. My younger son has had eight years the same. Also, please note, once an alcoholic always an alcoholic and most true alcoholics are never drunk. Some 'upmarket' persons announce they are "allergic to alcohol"; what they mean is they are alcoholic but they are too proud or ashamed to say so. 'Recovering alcoholic' is the correct term.

*[May's concluding thoughts:]*
I feel that as a result of providing this biography, that at last someone is hearing, believing and now in 1997, offering help, offering solutions, offering options. I just hope other sufferers get help and get help sooner than I did, and this is why I write so much now.

We need to use trained experienced people (like me) to counsel people. I've read everything you *[the editors]* have sent very carefully, taken me hours, but out of all this I do hope we can pass the message across in the book that ill-advised or inexperienced counsellors who dabble are lethal. We need to set up a course, a school of advising/counselling for this particular problem. Same principle for sexual abuse, drugs etc., but how this is done is debatable. We need to get something entered in the national curriculum at schools. We need to educate on living, on parenting.

I was trapped for 35 years. I only got free because a psychotherapist I was having counselling with in 1994 (I'd decided if I couldn't free myself by 31 Dec 1994, I'd commit suicide) said "write down what you feel, go home and we'll discuss what you've written next week". I wrote down:

"I feel:
- exhausted;
- ill;
- sad;
- lonely;
- useless;
- depressed;
- frightened;
- can't cope anymore;
- I've coped for years helping everyone else, why can't I be helped, I need help."

As a Quaker I'd always believed, been told, you must always put other people first, never yourself (that theory nearly cost me my life). My therapist said she couldn't believe what she read. In the therapy group I'd been a leading light, confident, attractive, coping, always willing to suggest help or advice for others. I disguised my need because I coped. That's why we women put up with alcoholics, because we have a high level of ability to cope! I still help my first husband, but I have learnt to be top dog with him and withdraw when it suits me!

You know, I found doing the tapes distressing. I'm talking about going back to 1959. I'm talking about a very violent second husband, 1990, and I still don't go shopping on my own in case he finds me. I find writing all this exhausting but I feel I must. The problem is so much bigger and with alcopops it will get enormous. Doctors in their surgeries, middle-class social workers, health visitors, nurses, teachers must address the problem. I taught for 40 years, I was a senior lecturer, I had a career until I went on holiday with Henry. He tried to kill me, he didn't succeed but he crippled me for life. I am now disabled and handicapped. Drink does this.

I'd like to meet all the contributors. I'd like the six participants and the different perspectives to meet. Perhaps when the book is published we could get together over lunch – I'm serious. Many of my friends can't understand why I don't get paid for this. I don't want paying, but I do want the book to be a success.

May I add that the more I read, the more I think this work is *so* important and I'm so pleased to be part of it, albeit a small part!

## *Note*

1. The biographees did not know the identity of all the authors at the time they read and commented in their chapters.

# CHAPTER 16

# Overview and conclusions: Normal people, abnormal circumstances

*Alex Copello, Jenny Maslin and Richard Velleman*

We set out to obtain detailed information about real life experiences of women living with problem drinking men. Some of our original aims are outlined in Chapter 2. The process reflected in this book involved a number of stages and, as stated previously, it could be argued that further exchanges of written materials between biographees and the different contributors could have followed. For the purpose of this book, however, we offer the results obtained so far. This chapter therefore reflects on both the commentaries and the subsequent responses from Emily and May. More specifically, in this chapter we will:

- discuss some contrasts and similarities between approaches on a number of key dimensions;
- examine some common questions that partners may ask of themselves; and
- explore possibilities for change.

A number of key dimensions emerged from our reading of the six perspectives. We discuss some of the similarities and contrasts between the perspectives, particularly in relation to the focus of analysis, notions of illness, the women's responsibility, issues of power, and changes in thinking.

## The focus of analysis: individual versus society at large

To varying degrees, all perspectives make reference to the relative contribution that different factors make to the situation that the women are facing, for example, individual, family, society. The different approaches vary, however, as to where they centre the analysis of the situations, ranging from looking at the problem at the individual level of each particular woman to, at the other end, focusing upon society at large. It follows that strategies for helping the concerned and affected women tend to be broadly located within the area where the approach focuses.

Approaches such as codependence, described by Cutland, place the focus firmly upon each of the individual women and their codependent need. Even though the codependence is enacted in relation to their partner, the basic 'problem' lies in the women's response to their situation. A clear example of the limited extent of influence that the actual drinking (as an external source of stress) can play in the problem is illustrated by the fact that according to Cutland, women could become worse when their partners get better or in her own words (p. 90): "very often the extent of the wife's dependence on her husband needing her does not show until he reaches a period of time in recovery. Many are shocked to find themselves trying to sabotage what they have hoped and prayed for, for years: their husband's sobriety and health". Indeed, according to Cutland, this characteristic may outlive the relationship with the drinker, as she goes on to describe (p. 90): "Some others move on to seek another alcoholic relationship because, at some level, that is what they know, this is what they have become dependent on". Although understandable, and perhaps adequate in explaining some cases, this notion is not always supported by available evidence which suggests that in some cases, the problems and symptoms for the wife are reduced significantly if the alcohol problem resolves itself (e.g. Bailey, 1967), a fact which challenges the notion of both drinker and partner wishing (for whatever reason and either consciously or unconsciously) to continue a destructive pattern of behaviour. Furthermore, it is important to note how close the idea is of the problem being the *wife's* problem (her response to the situation, her dependence on a problem drinking partner), to those early attempts to find personality deficits in spouses of problem drinkers, which were so evident in the 1950s (e.g. Whalen, 1953; Futterman, 1953) and which we examined in Chapter 1. Implicit within these concepts are a tendency both to 'pathologise' spouses, and to blame them for the situation that they are in.

In relation to its focus, the codependence model finds common ground with the psychodynamic approach which chooses as its central point the individual women, and places the women's early experiences in relationships at the core of the psychodynamic way of thinking. Implicit within this notion is the idea that the women are bringing into current relationships previous experiences of past relationships, and their ability to deal successfully with the situation or 'escape' from it is, to a large extent, determined by these experiences.

The focus becomes rather broader both within the family systems perspective described by Vetere and the coping perspective described by Orford.

203

The former is mainly concerned with the family (even though, as acknowledged by the author, systemic ideas could be extended beyond family systems). Within the coping perspective, the focus considers the interactions between the women and their partners as central. These interactions, however, are not specific to women and their partners but could also take place between the drinking partner and any other person concerned enough to take an interest and some action in relation to his predicament. Despite the commonality in focus between these two perspectives, there are some fundamental differences in the way in which interactions are conceptualised. The coping approach sees interactions as resulting from the attempts made by the women to respond to their circumstances, which clearly have arisen as a result of the stress associated with the drinker and his behaviour. The systems perspective, on the other hand, tends to conceptualise the drinking as a 'symptom' of other dysfunctions which at times serves to stabilise the family.

An even broader focus is provided by the community psychology approach of Fryer and the feminist perspective described by Ussher, in that both stress the importance of societal forces in the generation and maintenance of the problem. Albee's incidence formula (Gullotta, 1997) quoted by Fryer illustrates the powerful role of the environment in the causation, and indeed the prevention, of problems such as those described in this book. As Fryer points out, it is impossible to ignore individuals in any attempt to understand their situation but it is precisely the *individual in his or her context* that needs to be looked at. Fryer asserts that not all psychological problems have psychological causes or solutions, a view which is in marked contrast to some of the more individually focused approaches which tend to stress the women's psychological make-up in their analyses of cause, maintenance and potential solutions to the problem. As Fryer later states (p. 163): "most psychological states result from a reciprocal interaction over time of many factors on many levels from micro, psychophysiological processes via individual, family, organisational and neighbourhood to macro, intra, inter and multinational structural factors". He goes on to urge us to conduct analyses at many levels in order to understand psychological processes. In the feminist perspective chapter, Ussher introduces us to the three levels within which she focuses her analysis. This includes the social and linguistic domain (i.e. the 'discursive'), the 'material' and the 'intrapsychic'. In essence, she argues that the women's experience is a result of their situation, which is influenced by the way in which society defines and perpetuates through its language the inequalities between the different genders; the way in which society organises its material resources, which are again gender biased; and the way in which some women internalise concepts associated with their unequal role. Despite its overall focus on society's view of women, there is an implicit interplay between individuals and the environment within which they exist.

# Part of an illness or coping with adversity?

One issue that is evident from reading the six perspectives is the extent to which the problems described in the book are seen on the one hand as manifestations of illness (and the six women as part of a 'disease') with an assumed clear set and pattern of symptoms, or on the other hand as manifestations of extreme stress arising from circumstances which in varying degrees are very common within our society at large and are not 'abnormal'. Perhaps the strongest contrast is evident between the codependency approach and the coping perspective. Cutland states within her codependency perspective (p. 90): "In short, some wives become addicted to their alcoholic. The term that has evolved to describe this condition is codependence. The meaning of this word has grown to describe an addiction to any kind of destructive relationship, although it originated in the alcoholism field". It follows that codependence is an abnormal condition, indeed the term addiction is extended to describe the women, and hence the codependent person becomes part of the problem in his or her own right. A potential problem inherent in the codependence construct, as discussed by Haaken (1990, p. 405) in her critical analysis, is that it "embraces much of humanity in a common psychological net". If the concept of addiction is expanded to include the whole range of conflictive relationships with people, substances, or activities, where there exists a tension manifested in the form of an approach–avoidance conflict which is fuelled by contrasting motivations to engage in versus avoid, it follows that most of human activity would fall within the label of addiction. In such circumstances we would argue that the concept itself and its usefulness would need to be re-examined.

What seems to be crucial here is the extent to which processes are seen as abnormal *because* they happen to occur in the context of relationships where there are drinking problems, while at the same time, the same processes (which are part and parcel of human relationships and hence very common) may not be labelled as abnormal in other relationships. To give an example, a fear of leaving a partner may be seen as a difficult but not abnormal dilemma in a non-drinking relationship, but as a clear sign of codependence within a relationship where there is problematic drinking.

In contrast to the codependence view of women as 'addicted', Orford states (p. 132), "The coping position . . . is that the CFMs, such as the women whose lives are told in this book, are ordinary people caught in unpleasant and difficult family circumstances and struggling, as any of us would, to find ways of managing. Although the women's stories are often dramatic, in considering how they responded we are looking at the ordinariness of people's lives, not at abnormality". These two views reflect an important distinction between seeing women such as those who told us their story in this book as either "*abnormal*" or alternatively as "*normal people in abnormal circumstances*".

Of the remaining four approaches, perhaps unsurprisingly the psycho-dynamic and family therapy perspectives, both developed from therapy traditions, are more concerned with symptoms and dysfunction either within the individual or the slightly wider family network respectively. The feminist and community psychology approaches move away from traditional notions of illness, and stress the role of community and societal factors as important causes. The feminist perspective stresses all the inequalities arising from society's different treatment of male and female roles, leaving males unable to acknowledge their problem and ask for help and women trapped in unsatisfactory relationships. The community psychology perspective conceptualises the problem as arising from the way in which communities are affected and organised and describes the experiences of women in terms of psychological distress, perhaps a concept more akin to that used in the coping perspective, rather than as addiction-specific patterns of interactions or diseases.

## Responsible or innocent victims?

The biographies provide ample illustration of the women's worries in relation to the part that they themselves may have played in the problem. Questions such as: "Am I to blame?" "Is it my fault?" are repeatedly postulated. Messages about this issue can often be subtle, yet are often implicit in some of the central concepts of each perspective.

For example, codependence sees the women (or indeed anyone who is codependent, whether male or female, as Cutland points out) as *part of the problem,* in that they are addicted themselves (albeit to their partners) which gives rise to a significant amount of their suffering.

Yet Fryer, in exploring the issue of responsibility, contrasts the way in which the women are seen by others as responsible, whereas their partners are conceptualised as innocent victims of an 'illness'. He illustrates this point with reference to Ruth, whose partner and son blamed her for what had happened, while Ruth's partner, who himself had a problem with drinking, excused himself from blame for his behaviour. This raises interesting questions about the role of illness labels in allowing people to free themselves from responsibility (and related guilt), and may offer an explanation for the fact that some diagnostic labels may be readily accepted by women who are actively wondering whether they *are* responsible for their partner's drinking. Furthermore, as a society we tend to accept 'illnesses' as worthy of services perhaps more readily than problems which are not labelled in this way, and hence the acceptance of the 'illness' label may allow services to become more accessible.

We will return to the issue of services towards the end of this chapter. However, although there can be positive elements to the acceptance of an 'illness' label, as outlined above, such labels also carry with them a negative dimension. Concepts such as 'illness' are derived essentially from the medical tradition. As such they carry implicit assumptions about the need for 'treatment', usually delivered by outside agents; and hence acceptance of an 'illness' label tends to minimise the amount of control that individuals (in this case the female partners) feel they have over their situation.

Orford's approach in relation to the issue of responsibility is clear: the position of the coping approach is illustrated by the following quote (p. 128) ". . . CFMs come to this experience as 'innocents', perhaps with some general experience of alcohol problems and possibly some specific knowledge based on experience of family and friends, but essentially unprepared for the task of coping with living with a PDP and all the stresses that may involve". Hence, what is implicit within this perspective is the relatives' position as innocent victims faced with a situation that gives rise to stress in the context of the family. In further exploring the question of blame, Orford suggests, "blame attaches to the drinking but not to the drinker" (p. 131).

The psychodynamic model is interested in mental processes and the women's own history and their contribution to the situation in which they find themselves. The issue of responsibility is not openly discussed but is perhaps implicit in the assumption that traumatic circumstances or conflictive relationships earlier in life are determinants of the women's position at the point of living with someone with a drink problem. The family systems perspective once again stresses the notion of the alcohol use being a symptom of family dysfunction, perhaps with implicit assumptions of responsibility in that the wives are a part of the system. As such, the role of the women is partly causal as they are a component of such a system. Finally, the feminist perspective is clear on the notion that women are in an unequal position to their drinking partners and hence victims as opposed to responsible for the problem.

## Powerful or powerless?

To some extent, all perspectives agree that to varying degrees the six women were powerless at the time of experiencing the severe drinking problems at home. Fryer, for example, describes the women as "being normally invisible, voiceless and powerless" (p. 179). The difference between perspectives appear to lie in the different factors which influence the women's power over their reality.

Two important aspects appear to be related to the issue of power. First, the extent to which the women are powerful in being able to generate change in the drinking partner. Both the coping and family systems perspective describe the powerful influence that the women can have, particularly in bringing their partner into contact with treatment. Recent research in the area of alcohol treatment, some of which has been described in Chapter 1 (e.g. Meyers et al., 1996; O'Farrell, 1993; Barber and Crisp, 1995) has lent support to this assertion.

The codependence approach perhaps offers the clearest contrast by stating that the women are indeed powerless over the drinking of their partners and the work that needs to be done involves becoming detached, yet maintaining love for their partners. There are two potential problems here. First, although – as Cutland points out – not everyone living with a problem drinker is codependent, we do not know how to distinguish those who are from those who are not. Second, the concept of detaching with love implies a clear-cut distinction between distancing and rejecting, which in our research experience is difficult for relatives to understand, let alone carry out.

The second issue related to power is the extent to which the women are powerful in being able to generate change in themselves. The community psychology perspective views this power as being shared both at the individual and societal level, and this is similar within the feminist perspective. Both the coping and codependency models share the view that the possibility for change is firmly within the power of the women. The systemic perspective partly places power within the individual women, although at the same time it restricts this power by suggesting that change needs to happen within the whole system. Finally the psychodynamic perspective suggests that power to change can emerge from surveying our past and present experience and clarifying what can and cannot be changed.

## Changes in thinking

A powerful issue to emerge from reading the commentaries (and the responses by Emily and May) is how useful it is for people to have a menu of possible ways of understanding the problem and hence, associated with that, a menu of possible solutions. This also suggests the dangers inherent in being too narrow in the way in which the situation is conceptualised, as this may restrict possible options for change. A further implication is that changes in thinking about and/or understanding the problem are important in relieving some of the suffering endured by the women who 'live with drink'. The changes in thinking, however, are not restricted to the women; they are also important to those around them such as neighbours, other professionals, society at large. The coping approach talks about replacing confusion with a clearer way of thinking about the problem, having fresh ideas, seeing things differently and moving away from taking responsibility. Within the codependency approach, the change involves an acceptance and understanding of codependent needs, self-recognition as a codependent and a move towards being detached, all of which could be helped by increased knowledge. Second order change, within systemic thinking, involves searching for different meanings and different ways of looking at the problem which might free the system from previous 'dysfunctional' patterns of interaction. The psychodynamic approach tells us about the recognition of pain and suffering and the acceptance of things that we cannot change. Ussher talks about the need to increase our understanding of male and female roles, leading to more egalitarianism, and thus freeing men to seek and receive treatment (and hence think differently about the problem), and women to tell their stories and meet their need to be heard.

In reviewing contrasts and similarities it becomes evident that there are at least two important dimensions on which some of the perspectives differ: first, the extent of the emphasis on the individual as opposed to the individual's social context; and second, the view of these problems as diseases or not. It is interesting to note, on the other hand, that there is some common ground, including for example the need to empower women in positions such as those described in the biographies and to facilitate a change in thinking so that independence can be facilitated. How precisely this is achieved varies between perspectives, as already discussed.

## Some of the common questions women ask themselves

It seems clear that there are a number of questions that women in the situations which are the theme of this book repeatedly ask themselves and to which answers are not forthcoming, or at best confused and contradictory. This confusion can be highly disempowering and can compound the problem. Some of the most common questions are briefly discussed below.

### How did I get here?

On the basis of the material included in this book, we can conclude that the reasons why women find themselves in situations such as the ones described in the six biographies are wide-ranging and multiple. How each of the female partners got to the position described appears to have been influenced by a range of factors, and it is not easy to see how any one factor could explain the common scenario for all six cases. Even though there are numerous common themes between the biographies, these tend to reflect the *consequences* of excessive alcohol consumption as opposed to the causes. It follows that perhaps looking for an answer to this question may be important for each individual partner in order to make sense of her own history, yet it seems unlikely that a common universal path will be found.

### Am I abnormal?

Based on our discussion so far, it is our view that what we are looking at is a range of psychological processes, most of which result from the complex interaction between stressful circumstances, the female partner's ways of responding to these circumstances and the way in which other people's attitudes and those of society as a whole support, ignore or even complicate this process. It is our view that what is abnormal is the situation, as opposed to the people within it.

### Am I to blame?

On the basis of the discussion in this chapter so far, we would assert that partners need not blame themselves for the drinking of their respective spouses. There may be ways in which responses compound the difficulties, there may be fears about taking extremely painful decisions, and there may be a tremendous ambivalence arising from the love for the partner and the hate for their behaviour; but what appears to be clear is that the concept of 'self-blame' has little to offer and can reduce power and self-esteem.

### Am I mad?

As is so clearly illustrated by some of the biographies, the experience can sometimes feel akin to madness. What is more likely is that the feelings and behaviours result from exposure to extreme and long-standing stressful circumstances and have little to do with 'going crazy'. Perhaps the less the experience is shared and the less people know about how common these feelings are, the more likely it is for a woman 'living with drink' to perceive herself as unique, abnormal and possibly crazy.

## The participant's perspective on the commentaries

Emily and May's comments, although critical of some aspects, seem to be positive overall: all six approaches make sense, and Emily and May recognised themselves in most situations. However, one of the most striking points emerging from this dialogue in print between the real-life experts (i.e. the six women) and the professional experts, is the fact that even though all six approaches have merit and value in increasing our understanding of the predicament of Dawn, Emily, Lisa, May, Ruth and Sylvia, a clear lack of accessible help is evident from the biographical accounts, particularly:

- at the time of most need,
- when the problems were at their worst,
- when on some occasions the 'stress' from living with a problem drinker came closer to an experience of 'torture',
- and when some of the female partners wondered if they were mad.

In May's own words (p. 199): "If only someone had listened and believed me. An offer of help never came, not once." Meeting this need, when it matters, remains our most important and significant challenge.

# Meeting the challenge

To meet the challenge we need to recognise the extent of the problem and the severe disruption associated with these type of experiences, and articulate a response at a number of levels.

At an individual level we need to make sure that support is available and accessible for partners in situations such as those described in this book. As we have learnt, support can come from a variety of sources including personal, self-help and professional, yet the most common experience described by these women is one of isolation. The need to talk to someone who will believe the stories has already been highlighted. In order to meet this need, however, support has to be accessible, that is, help needs to be close to those needing it. In addition to self-help groups such as Al-Anon, the primary care setting offers an opportunity to reach people 'living with drink', given that most people are in some form of contact with their general practitioner or other members of the primary health care team. Primary care workers, however, need to have available to them strategies to respond to this need, based on a sound knowledge of the problems faced and information about possible ways in which partners could respond to the situation. In our current work, we are developing and evaluating a package of materials and support so that primary care workers can engage and help people such as Dawn, Emily, Lisa, May, Ruth and Sylvia. Our work to date has clearly confirmed the women's need to feel able to tell their stories to someone who can listen non-judgementally.

Specialist services for alcohol problems have also to recognise this need, and take into account those closely related to the clients with the alcohol problems. We have seen in this book that these relatives can have significant needs, and are often left out of the drinker's treatment. Furthermore, services must see this group as having need for a service in their own right, irrespective of whether the person with the drinking problem comes forward for help.

At a community level, we need to tackle some of the causal factors including sexism, poverty and lack of community support. As Fryer reminds us at the end of his chapter (p. 179) "the real task is to tackle these structural factors to prevent and reduce distress and injustice". In addition, we need to minimise the secrecy and shame associated with these highly prevalent problems which at times result in people suffering in silence for fear of a negative response or of being criticised.

In different ways, all approaches suggest some critical conditions that can facilitate change for women in these situations. These include: better understanding, alternative perspectives which allow the women to think differently about themselves and the problem, freedom from notions of guilt and responsibility, acknowledgement of the dilemmas and ambivalence arising from the relationship, and for the women to be able to feel powerful enough to act on their needs for independence and freedom based on a solid experience of self-respect.

We also need to educate those in a position to help, to avoid what has emerged in both accounts and commentaries as the 'dangerous professional': judgemental professionals who, based on poor knowledge, may at best ignore the women's needs, and at worst blame them for the situation that they are in or fail to address issues of serious violence.

## *Concluding remarks*

This chapter has attempted to highlight some of the issues that have emerged from the process of writing this book. We have discussed only a small number of themes, partly due to lack of space but also because we would like the material to speak for itself. Readers have been given the material in the form of biographies and commentaries and can therefore continue to analyse and dissect it in order to increase their understanding. We believe that this book can make an important contribution to understanding and debate.

Finally, we hope that in offering this information we can reach not only those experiencing the problem but those in a position to help. In doing so, we believe that we are going some way towards meeting the needs of the large number of people 'living with drink'.

# References

Al-Anon Family Groups (1967) *The Dilemma of the Alcoholic Marriage*. Cornwall, New York: Cornwall Press.

Al-Anon Family Groups (1972) *Alcoholism: The Family Disease*. Cornwall, New York: Cornwall Press.

Al-Anon Family Groups (1975) *Al-Anon Faces Alcoholism*. Cornwall, New York: Cornwall Press.

Albee, G. (1984) Reply to Lantz. *American Psychologist*, **39**, 82–84.

Albee, G. and Gullotta, T. (1997) *Primary Prevention Works*. London: Sage.

Alcohol Research Group (1995) *National Alcohol Survey*. Berkeley, CA: ARG.

Alcoholics Anonymous (1967) *Alcoholics Anonymous*. New York: AA World Services Inc.

Anderson, H., Goolishian, H. and Winderman, L. (1986) Problem determined systems: towards transformation in family therapy. *Journal of Strategic and Systemic Therapy*, **5**, 1–14.

Bahrick, H., Bahrick, P. and Wittlinger, R. (1975) Fifty years of memory for names and faces: a cross-sectional approach. *Journal of Experimental Psychology: General*, **104**, 54–75.

Bailey, M. (1967) Psychophysiological impairment in wives of alcoholics as related to their husbands' drinking and sobriety. In: R. Fox (Ed.) *Alcoholism: Behavioural Research: Therapeutic Approaches*. New York: Springer, 134–44.

Bandura, M.M. and Goldman, C. (1995) Expanding the contextual analysis of clinical problems. *Cognitive and Behavioral Practice*, **2**, 119–41.

Bannister, D. (1975) Biographies as a Source in Psychology. Paper given at the Psychology and Psychotherapy Association Conference on "Alternatives in Psychology", January 1975.

Barber, J. and Crisp, B. (1995) The "pressures to change" approach to working with the partners of heavy drinkers. *Addiction*, **90**, 269–76.

Bateson, G. (1973) *Steps to an Ecology of Mind*. New York: Granada.

Beattie, M. (1987) *Co-dependent No More*. Center City, Minnesota: Hazelden.

Bertaux, D. (1981) (Ed.) *Biography and Society: The Life History Approach in the Social Sciences*. Newbury Park, California: Sage.

Birchwood, M. and Smith, J. (1987) Schizophrenia and the family. In J. Orford (Ed.) *Coping with Disorder in the Family*. Beckenham: Croom Helm, 7–39.

Black, B. (1982) *It Will Never Happen To Me*. Denver, Colorado: M.A.C.

Blum, K. (1991) *Alcohol and The Addictive Brain*. New York: Free Press.

Brontë, A. (1848/1996) *The Tenant of Wildfell Hall*. London: Penguin.

Brown, G. and Harris, T. (1978) *Social Origins of Depression*. London: Tavistock.

Busfield, J. (1996) *Men, Women and Madness: Understanding Gender and Mental Disorder*. London: Macmillan.

Butler, J. (1990) *Gender Trouble: Feminism and the Subversion of Identity*. London: Routledge.

Caplan, G. (1964) *Principles of Preventative Psychiatry*. New York: Basic Books.

Carpenter, J. and Treacher, A. (1989) *Problems and Solutions in Marital and Family Therapy*. Oxford: Blackwell.

Carter, B. and McGoldrick, M. (1989) *The Changing Family Lifecycle* (2nd edn). New York: Allyn and Bacon.

Copello, A., Orford, J. and Velleman, R. (1996) *Responding to Alcohol and Drug Problems in the Family. A Guide for Primary Health Care Professionals*. Available from authors, University of Birmingham and University of Bath.

Copello, A., Templeton, L., Krishnan, M., Orford, J., Velleman, R. and Merriman, C. (1998) Recruiting primary care professionals to develop and pilot a package to improve effectiveness in working with family members of problem alcohol and drug users. *New Directions in the Study of Alcohol*, **22**, 41–50.

Cowen, E. (1982) Help is where you find it. *American Psychologist*, **37**, 385–95.

Cronen, V.E. and Pearce, W.B. (1985) Towards an explanation of how the "Milan method" works: an invitation to systemic epistemology and evolution of family systems. In D. Campbell and R. Draper (Eds) *Applications of Systemic Family Therapy*. New York: Grune and Stratton, 69–84.

Cutland, L. (1990) *Freedom from the Bottle*. Bath: Gateway Books.

David, H., Dytrych, Z., Matejcek, Z. and Roth, Z. (1992) Partner choice among young adults born from unwanted and accepted pregnancies in Czechoslovakia. In M. Kessler, S. Goldston and J. Joffe (Eds) *The Present and Future of Prevention*. London: Sage, 169–81.

Davies, S. (1996) Information and notes to: *The Tenant of Wildfell Hall* by Anne Brontë. London: Penguin.

de Zulueta, Felicity (1993) *From Pain to Violence: The Traumatic Roots of Destructiveness*. London: Whurr.

Denzin, N. (1989) *Interpretive Biography*. Qualitative Research Methods Series, 17. London: Sage.

Ditzler J. and Ditzler, J. (1989) *If You Really Loved Me*. London: Papermac.

Dobash, R. & Dobash, R. (1979) *Violence Against Wives. A Case Against the Patriarchy*. London: Open Books.

Dobash, R. and Dobash, R. (1987) Violence towards wives. In J. Orford (Ed.) *Coping with Disorder in the Family*. Beckenham: Croom Helm, 169–93.

Dooley, D., Catalano, R. & Hough, R. (1992) Unemployment and alcohol disorder in 1910 and 1990: drift versus social causation. *Journal of Occupational and Organisational Psychology*, **65**, 277–90.

Durlak, J. (1979) Comparative effectiveness of para-professional and professional helpers. *Psychological Bulletin*, **86**, 80–92.

Dusenbury, L. and Botvin, G. (1992) Applying the competency enhancement model to substance abuse prevention. In M. Kessler, S. Goldston and J. Joffe (Eds) *The Present and Future of Prevention*. London: Sage, 182–95.

Edwards, M.E. and Steinglass, P. (1995) Family therapy treatment outcomes for alcoholism. *Journal of Marital and Family Therapy*, **21**, 475–509.

Elms, A. (1994) *Uncovered Lives: The Uneasy Alliance of Biography and Psychology*. Oxford: Oxford University Press.

Fisher, S. and Reason, J. (1988) *Handbook of Life Stress, Cognition and Health*. Chichester: Wiley.

Fitzgerald, K. (1996) *Alcoholism: The Genetic Inheritance*. Illinois: Whales Tale Press.

Fonagy, P. and Target, M. (1997) Memories are irrelevant to Psychotherapy: Discuss. Paper given to "Dilemmas in Psychotherapy": Royal College of Psychiatrists, Psychotherapy Section, Annual Residential Conference, April 1997, Bristol.

Freedman, J. and Combs, G. (1996) *Narrative Therapy: The Social Construction of Preferred Realities*. New York: Norton.

Freud, S. (1933) *New Introductory Lectures on Psychoanalysis*. London: Hogarth.

Fryer, D. (1985) The positive functions of unemployment. *Radical Community Medicine*, **21**, 3–10.

Fryer, D. (1986) Employment deprivation and personal agency during unemployment. *Social Behaviour*, **1**, 3–23.

Fryer, D. (1995a) Benefit agency? Labour market disadvantage, deprivation and mental health. *The Psychologist*, **8**, 265–72.

Fryer, D. (1995b) Agency restriction theory. In N. Nicholson (Ed.) *The Blackwell Dictionary of Organisational Behaviour*. Oxford: Blackwell, 12.

Fryer, D. and Fagan, R. (1993) Coping with unemployment: a community psychological perspective. *International Journal of Political Economy*, Fall, 96–121.

Fryer, D. and Fagan, R. (1994) The role of social psychological aspects of income in the mental health costs of unemployment. *The Community Psychologist*, **27**, 16–17.

Futterman, S. (1953) Personality trends in wives of alcoholics. *Journal of Psychiatric Social Work*, **23** (1), 37–41.

Goldberg, D. and Huxley, P. (1980) *Mental Illness in the Community: The Pathway to Psychiatric Care*. London: Tavistock.

Goldner, V. (1988) Generation and gender: normative and covert hierarchies. *Family Process*, **27**, 17–31.

Gullotta, T. (1997) Operationalizing Albee's incidence formula. In G. Albee and T. Gullotta (Eds) *Primary Prevention Works*. London: Sage, 23–37.

Gurman, A.S., Kniskern, D.P. and Pinsof, W. (1986) Research on the process and outcome of marital and family therapy. In S. Garfield and A. Bergin (Eds) *Handbook of Psychotherapy and Behavior Change* (3rd edn). New York: Wiley, 565–626.

Haaken, J. (1990) A critical analysis of the co-dependence construct. *Psychiatry*, **53**, 396–406.

Hall, A. and Wellman, B. (1985) Social networks and social support. In S. Cohen and S. Syme (Eds) *Social Support and Health*. New York: Academic Press, 23–42.

Hamel, J., Dufour, S. and Fortin, D. (1993) *Case Study Methods*. Qualitative Research Methods Series, 32. London: Sage.

Hands, M. and Dear, G. (1994) Co-dependency: a critical review. *Drug and Alcohol Review, Special Issue Alcohol Drugs and the Family*, **13**, 437–45.

Harré, R. (1976) (Ed.) *Life Sentences*. New York: Wiley.

Hatch, J. and Wisniewski, R. (1995) Life history and narrative: questions, issues, and exemplary works. In J. Hatch and R. Wisniewski (Eds) *Life history and narrative: Qualitative Studies Series 1*. London: Falmer Press, 113–35.

Hattie, J., Sharpley, C. and Rogers, H. (1984) Comparative effectiveness of professional and non-professional helpers. *Psychological Bulletin*, **95**, 534–41.

Helling, I. (1976) Autobiography as self-presentation: the carpenters of Konstanz. In R. Harré (Ed.) *Life Sentences*. New York: Wiley, pp. 42–8.

Herbert, M. (1995) Paper presented at the Annual Conference of the British Psychological Society, University of Warwick.

Holland, S. (1988) Defining and experimenting with prevention. In S. Ramon (Ed.) *Psychiatry in Transition*. London: Pluto, 125–37.

Hollway, W. (1989) *Subjectivity and Method in Psychology*. London: Sage.

Holman, R. (1988) Research from the underside. *Community Care*, 18 February, 24–6.

Holmes, Jeremy (1996) *Attachment, Intimacy, Autonomy*: Using Attachment Theory in Adult Psychotherapy. Northvale, NJ: Jason Aronson.

Holmila, M. (1988) Wives, husbands and alcohol. A study of informal drinking control within the family. The Finnish Foundation for Alcohol Studies, Helsinki, Monograph No. 36.

Hooper, C. (1992) *Mothers Surviving Child Sexual Abuse*. London: Routledge.

Horney, K. (1935/1967) *Feminine Psychology*. London: Norton.

Howe, M. (1982) Biographical evidence and the development of outstanding individuals. *American Psychologist*, **37**, 1071–81.

Howells, E. (1997) Coping with a problem drinker: The development and evaluation of a therapeutic intervention for the partners of problem drinkers in their own right. Unpublished PhD thesis. University of Exeter.

Humm, M. (1993) *Feminisms: A Reader*. Hemel Hempstead: Harvester Wheatsheaf.

Jackson, J. (1954) The adjustment of the family to the crisis of alcoholism. *Quarterly Journal of Studies on Alcohol*, **15**, 562–86.

Janlert, U. and Hammarstrom, A. (1992) Alcohol consumption among unemployed youths: results from a prospective study. *British Journal of Addiction*, **87**, 703–14.

Jellinek, E. (1960) *The Disease Concept of Alcoholism*. New Haven: Yale College & University Press.

Jenkins, C., Hurst, M. and Rose, R. (1979) Life changes: do people remember? *Archives of General Psychiatry*, **36**, 379–84.

Job, E. (1983) Retrospective life span analysis: a method for studying extreme old age. *Journal of Gerontology*, **38**, 369–74.

Johnson, R., McLennan, G., Schwarz, B. and Sutton, D. (1982) (Eds) *Making History: Studies in History Writing and Politics*. London: Hutchinson.

Kahn, R. and Antonucci, T. (1980) Convoys over the life course: attachments, roles, and social support. In P. Baltes and O. Brim (Eds) *Life-Span Development and Behaviour*, vol. 3. New York: Academic Press, 253–86.

Kaplan, L. (1991) *Female Perversions*. London: Penguin.

Kessler, M., Goldston, S. and Joffe, J. (Eds) (1992) *The Present and Future of Prevention*. London: Sage.

Kratochwill, T. and Levin, J. (1992) *Single-Case Research Design and Analysis: New Directions for Psychology and Education*. Hillsdale, NJ: Lawrence Erlbaum.

Kuipers, E. (1987) Depression and the family. In J. Orford (Ed.) *Coping with Disorder in the Family*. Beckenham: Croom Helm, 194–216.

Lau, A. (1987) Family therapy and ethnic minorities. In E. Street and W. Dryden (Eds) *Family Therapy in Britain*. Milton Keynes: Open University Press, 270–90.

Lederer, W. and Jackson, D.D. (1968) *The Mirages of Marriage*. New York: Norton.

Lees, S. (1996) *Carnal Knowledge: Rape on Trial*. London: Penguin.

Levinson, D. (1981) Explorations in biography: evolution of the individual life structure in adulthood. In I. Rabin, J. Aronoff, A. Barclay and R. Zucker (Eds) *Further Explorations in Personality*. New York: Wiley, 44–79.

Lieberman, S. (1979) *Transgenerational Family Therapy*. London: Croom Helm.

Liepman, M.R., Nirenberg, T.D., Doolittle, R.H., Begin, A.M., Broffman, T.E. and Babich, M.A. (1989) Family functioning of male alcoholics and their female partners during periods of drinking and abstinence. *Family Process*, **28**, 239–49.

Lindzey, G. (1980) (Ed.) *A History of Psychology in Autobiography, Vol 7*. San Fransisco: Freeman.

Love, C., Longabaugh, R., Clifford, P., Beattie, M. and Peaslee, C. (1993) The significant-other behaviour questionnaire (SBQ): an instrument for measuring the behaviour of significant others towards a person's drinking and abstinence. *Addiction*, **88**, 1267–79.

Marcus, L. (1994) *Auto/Biographical Discources: Theory, Criticism, Practice*. Manchester: Manchester University Press.

Maslin, J., Dalton, S., Ferrins-Brown, M., Hartney, E., Kerr, C. and Orford, J. (1998) The "ups and downs" of drinking: The drinking careers of untreated heavy drinkers living in the West Midlands, UK. Paper presented at the 2nd International Conference on Drinking Patterns and their Consequences, Perth, Western Australia, 1–5 February.

Matson, N. (1995) Coping in context: strategic and tactical coping in carers of stroke survivors and carers of older confused people. *Journal of Community and Applied Social Psychology*, **2**, 89–104.

McCormack, C. (1988) Letter from a housing scheme: a mother's thoughts. *Scottish Child*, November, 18–19.

McCrady, B. and Hay, W. (1987) Coping with problem drinking in the family. In J. Orford (Ed.) *Coping with Disorder in the Family*. Beckenham: Croom Helm, 86–116.

Meltzer, H., Gill, B., Pettigrew, M. and Hinds, K. (1995) *The Prevalence of Psychiatric Morbidity Among Adults Living in Private Households*. London: HMSO.

Messé, L. Buldain, R. and Watts, B. (1981) Recall of social events with the passage of time. *Personality and Social Psychology Bulletin*, **7**, 33–38.

Meyers, R., Dominguez, T. and Smith, J. (1996) Community reinforcement training with concerned others. In V. Van Hasselt and M. Hersen (Eds) *Source Book of Psychological Treatment Manuals for Adult Disorders*. New York: Plenum Press, 257–94.

Miller, D. and Jang, M. (1977) Children of alcoholics: a 20-year longitudinal study. *Social Work Research and Abstracts*, **13**, 23–29.

Miller, S. and Berg, I. (1995) *The Miracle Method: A Radically New Approach to Problem Drinking*. New York: Norton.

Minuchin, S. (1974) *Families and Family Therapy*. London: Tavistock.

Moos, R., Finney, J. and Cronkite, R. (1990) *Alcoholism Treatment: Context, Process and Outcome*. Oxford University Press: New York.

Murray, H. (1938) *Explorations in Personality*. New York; Oxford University Press.

Nace, E. (1987) *The Treatment of Alcoholism*. New York: Brunner/Mazel.

Norwood, R. (1986) *Women Who Love Too Much*. London: Arrow.

O'Farrell, T. (1993) (Ed.) *Treating Alcohol Problems: Marital and Family Interventions*. New York: Guilford Press.

Orbach, S. and Eichenbaum, L. (1985) *Bittersweet: Relationships Between Women*. London: Fontana.

Orford, J. (1985) *Excessive Appetites: A Psychological View of Addiction.* Chichester: Wiley.

Orford, J. (1987) The need for a community response to alcohol-related problems. In T. Stockwell and S. Clement (Eds) *Helping the Problem Drinker: New Initiatives in Community Care.* London: Croom Helm, 4–32.

Orford, J. (1992) *Community Psychology: Theory and Practice.* Chichester: Wiley.

Orford, J., Guthrie, S., Nicholls, P., Oppenheimer, E., Egert, S. and Hensman, C. (1975) Self-reported coping behaviour of wives of alcoholics and its associations with drinking outcome. *Journal of Studies on Alcohol,* **36**, 1254–67.

Orford, J., Natera, G., Davies, J., Nava, A., Mora, J., Rigby, K., Bradbury, C., Bowie, N., Copello, A. and Velleman, R. (1998a) Tolerate, engage or withdraw: a study of the structure of family coping in England and Mexico. *Addiction,* in press.

Orford, J., Natera, G., Davies, J., Nava, A., Mora, J., Rigby, K., Bradbury, C., Bowie, N., Copello, A. and Velleman, R. (1998b) Stresses and strains for family members living with drinking or drug problems in England and Mexico. *Salud Mental,* in press.

Orford, J., Natera, G., Davies, J., Nava, A., Mora, J., Rigby, K., Bradbury, C., Bowie, N., Copello, A. and Velleman, R. (1998c) Social support in coping with alcohol and drug problems at home: findings from Mexican and English families. *Addiction Research,* in press.

Orford, J., Natera, G., Davies, J., Nava, A., Mora, J., Rigby, K., Bradbury, C., Bowie, N., Copello, A. and Velleman, R. (1998d). How families cope: A quantitative and qualitative study using data from two countries. Submitted for publication.

Orford, J., Rigby, K., Miller, T., Tod, A., Bennett, G. and Velleman, R. (1992) Ways of coping with excessive drug use in the family: a provisional typology based on the accounts of fifty close relatives. *Journal of Community and Applied Social Psychology,* **2**, 163–83.

Pam, A. (1993) Family systems theory: a critical view. *New Ideas in Psychology,* **11**, 77–94.

Potter, J. and Edwards, D. (1992) *Discursive Psychology.* London: Sage.

Reason, P. and Rowan, J. (1983) (Eds) *Human Inquiry: A Sourcebook of New Paradigm Research.* Chichester: Wiley.

Reiss, D. (1981) *The Family Construction of Reality.* Cambridge, MA.: Harvard University Press.

Ridley, J., Bachrach, C. and Dawson, D. (1979) Recall and reliability of interview data from older women. *Journal of Gerontology,* **34**, 99–105.

Robbins, L. (1963) The accuracy of parental recall of aspects of child development and of child rearing practices. *Journal of Abnormal and Social Psychology,* **66**, 261–70.

Robins, L., Schoenberg, S., Holmes, S., Ratcliff, K. Benham, A. and Works, J. (1985) Early home environment and retrospective recall: a test for concordance between siblings with and without psychiatric disorder. *American Journal of Orthopsychiatry,* **55**, 27–41.

Robinson, J. (1980) Affect and retrieval of personal memories. *Motivation and Emotion,* **4**, 149–74.

Rosenberg, M.S. and Rossman, B.B.R. (1990). The child witness to marital violence. In R. Ammerman and M. Hersen (Eds) *Treatment of Family Violence.* New York: Wiley, 183–210.

Ross, M. and Sicoly, F. (1979) Egocentric biases in availability and attribution. *Journal of Personality and Social Psychology,* **37**, 322–36.

Runyan, W. (1988) (Ed.) *Psychology and Historical Interpretation*. New York: Oxford University Press.

Ryan, W. (1971) *Blaming the Victim*, New York: Random House.

Rychtarik, R., Carstensen, L., Alford, G., Schlundt, D. and Scott, W. (1988) Situational assessment of alcohol-related coping skills in wives of alcoholics. *Psychology of Addictive Behaviour*, **2**, 66–73.

Ryle, Anthony, Poynton, A. and Brockman, B. (1990) *Cognitive Analytic Therapy: Active Participation in Change: a New Integration in Brief Psychotherapy*. Chichester: Wiley.

Schaffer, J. and Tyler, J. (1979) Degree of sobriety in male alcoholics and coping styles used by their wives. *British Journal of Psychiatry*, **135**, 431–37.

Seligman, M.E.P. (1975) *Helplessness: On Depression, Development and Death*. San Francisco: Freeman.

Selvini-Palazolli, M., Boscolo, L., Cecchin, G. and Prata, G. (1978) *Paradox and Counterparadox*. New York: Aronson.

Selvini-Palazolli, M., Boscolo, L., Cecchin, G. and Prata, G. (1980) Hypothesizing – circularity – neutrality: three guidelines for the conductor of the session. *Family Process*, **19**, 3–12.

Smail, D. (1993) *The Origins of Unhappiness: A New Understanding of Personal Distress*. London: HarperCollins.

Smith, L. (1994) Biographical method. In N. Denzin and Y. Lincoln (Eds) *Handbook of Qualitative Methods*. Newbury Park, California: Sage, 286–305.

Spicer, J. (1994) *The Minnesota Model*. Center City, Minnesota: Hazelden.

Stanley, L. (1992) *The Auto/Biographical I: the Theory and Practice of Feminist Auto/Biography*. Manchester: Manchester University Press.

Steinglass, P. (1981) The alcoholic family at home: patterns of interaction in dry, wet and transitional stages of alcoholism. *Archives of General Psychiatry*, **38**, 578–84.

Steinglass, P., Bennett, L., Wolin, S. and Reiss, D. (1987) *The Alcoholic Family. Drinking Problems in a Family Context*. New York: Basic Books.

Stern, Daniel (1985) *The Interpersonal World of the Infant*. New York: Basic Books.

Templeton, L., Copello, A., Velleman, R., Krishnan, M., Orford, J. and Merriman, C. (1998) Responding to alcohol and drug problems in the family: working with primary health care professionals. *Drug News*, Spring, 7–10.

Thomas, D. and Veno, A. (1996) *Community Psychology and Social Change: Australian and New Zealand Perspectives*. Palmerston North: Dunmore Press.

Thomas, E. and Ager, R. (1993) Unilateral family therapy with spouses of uncooperative alcohol abusers. In T. O'Farrell (Ed.) *Treating Alcohol Problems: Marital and Family Interventions*. New York: Guildford Press, 3–33.

Thompson, P. (1978) *The Voice of the Past: Oral History*. Oxford: Oxford University Press.

Turner, R. and Barlow, J. (1951) Memory for pleasant and unpleasant experiences: some methodological considerations. *Journal of Experimental Psychology*, **42**, 189–96.

Ussher, J. (1991) *Women's Madness: Misogyny or Mental Illness*. Hemel Hempstead: Harvester Wheatsheaf.

Ussher, J. (1994) Theorising female sexuality. In P. Nicolson and P. Choi (Eds) *The Psychology and Biology of Female Sexuality*. Hemel Hempstead: Harvester Wheatsheaf, 32–49.

Ussher, J. (1997a) *Fantasies of Femininity: Reframing the Boundaries of Sex*. London: Penguin.

Ussher, J. (1997b) (Ed.) *Body Talk: The Material-Discursive Construction of Sexuality, Madness and Reproduction.* London: Routledge.

Vansina, J. (1961) *Oral Tradition: A Study in Historical Methodology.* London: R & KP.

Velleman, R. (1993) *Alcohol and the Family.* London: Institute of Alcohol Studies.

Velleman, R. and Orford, J. (1990) Young adult offspring of parents with drinking problems: recollections of parents' drinking and its immediate effects. *British Journal of Clinical Psychology,* **29,** 297–317.

Velleman, R. and Orford, J. (1993a) The importance of family discord in explaining childhood problems in the children of problem drinkers. *Addiction Research,* **1,** 39–57.

Velleman, R. and Orford, J. (1993b) The adult adjustment of offspring of parents with drinking problems. *British Journal of Psychiatry,* **162,** 503–16.

Velleman, R. and Orford, J. (1998) *Risk or Resilience: The Children of Problem Drinking Parents Grown Up.* Reading: Harwood.

Velleman, R., Bennett, G., Miller, T., Orford, J., Rigby, K. and Tod, A. (1993) The families of problem drug users: a study of 50 close relatives. *Addiction,* **88,** 1281–89.

Vetere, A.L. (1987) General system theory and the family: a critical evaluation. In A. Vetere and A. Gale (Eds) *Ecological Studies of Family Life.* Chichester: Wiley, 18–33.

von Bertalanffy, L. (1968) *General System Theory.* Harmondsworth: Penguin.

Wachtel, E.F. and Wachtel, P.L. (1986) *Family Dynamics in Individual Psychotherapy: A Guide to Clinical Strategies.* New York: Guilford Press.

Waldfogel, S. (1948) The frequency and effective character of childhood memories. *Psychological Monographs,* **64,** whole issue.

Watzlawick, P., Beavin, J. and Jackson, D.D. (1967) *Pragmatics of Human Communication.* New York: Norton.

Whalen, T. (1953) Wives of alcoholics: four types observed in a family service agency. *Quarterly Journal of Studies on Alcohol,* **14,** 632–41.

Whiffen, R. and Byng-Hall, J. (Eds) (1982) *Family Therapy Supervision.* London: Academic Press.

White, R. (1952) *Lives in Progress: A Study of the Natural Growth of Personality.* New York: Holt, Rinehart and Winston.

White, R. (1966) *Lives in Progress: A Study of the Natural Growth of Personality,* 2nd edn. New York: Holt, Rinehart and Winston.

White, R. (1975) *Lives in Progress: A Study of the Natural Growth of Personality,* 3rd edn. New York: Holt, Rinehart and Winston.

White, R. (1981) Exploring personality the long way: the study of lives. In A. Rabin, J. Aronoff, A. Barclay and R. Zucker (Eds) *Further Explorations in Personality.* New York: Wiley, 3–19.

Wight, D. (1993) *Workers Not Wasters: Masculine Respectability, Consumption and Employment in Central Scotland.* Edinburgh: Edinburgh University Press.

Wilkinson, R.G. (1996) *Unhealthy Societies: The Afflictions of Inequalities.* London: Routledge.

Williams, T. (1995) *Brave New Families.* Center City, Minnesota: Hazelden.

Winefield, A. and Fryer, D. (1996) Some emerging threats to the validity of research on unemployment and mental health. *The Australian Journal of Social Research,* **12** (1), 115–34.

Winnicott, D. (1960) Ego distortion in terms of time and false self, Anthologised in *The Maturational Processes and the Facilitating Environment.* International Psychoanalytic Library, 64. London: Hogarth and Institute of Psychoanalysis, 1965.

Wiseman, J. (1980) The home treatment: The first steps in trying to cope with an alcoholic husband. *Family Relations*, **29**, 541–49.

Yardley, L. (1997) *Material-Discourses of Health and Illness*. London: Routledge.

Yarrow, M., Campbell, J. and Burton, R. (1964) Reliability of maternal retrospection: a preliminary report. *Family Process*, **3**, 207–18.

Yarrow, M., Campbell, J. and Burton, R. (1970) *Recollection of Childhood: A Study of the Retrospective Method*. Monographs of the Society for Research in Child Development, 33, Chicago.

Yates, F. (1988) The evaluation of a "co-operative counselling" alcohol service which uses family and affected others to reach and influence problem drinkers. *British Journal of Addiction*, **83**, 1309–19.

# Index